The Tet Effect

When democracies decide war, intelligence provides crucial justification. In 1967 intelligence was called upon to bolster support for the war in Vietnam. By the year's end, with revised intelligence, America's leaders portrayed a 'bankrupt' enemy ready to quit the battlefield. The audacious communist Tet Offensive of 1968 shattered this image and shocked an unprepared American public. The credibility of America's leadership was questioned as the public demanded to know how such a 'bankrupt' enemy had been able to launch such a massive, all-out offensive.

This phenomenon is known as the Tet Effect – the loss of credibility when leaders portray a situation based upon intelligence that is shown to be disingenuous.

This book examines intelligence's role in shaping America's perception of the war and looks closely at the intelligence leadership and decision process in Vietnam. From this examination and an understanding of how the enemy viewed itself, the conclusion is made that four severe breaches of intelligence etiquette occurred during the period leading up to Tet. The breaches include the loss of objectivity, shaping the enemy in its own image, becoming overly reliant on technology, and finally, mistaking numbers as the measure of victory, forgetting the enemy's will.

As today's headlines disturb the memories of Vietnam, with leaders again being questioned about their use of intelligence to justify war, this book will provide crucial information to undergraduate and postgraduate students of strategic studies, military history and international relations.

Jake Blood is a retired career intelligence officer with the United States Air Force. His last two assignments on active duty included Chief of Intelligence (J2) for Special Operations Command Korea and Professor of Strategy and Intelligence at the Joint Military Intelligence College in Washington DC.

Cass Military Studies

The Tet Effect

Intelligence and the Public Perception of War

Jake Blood

Routledge
Taylor & Francis Group

LONDON AND NEW YORK

First published 2005
by Routledge
2 Park Square, Milton Park, Abingdon, Oxon OX14 4RN

Simultaneously published in the USA and Canada
by Routledge
711 Third Avenue, New York, NY 10017

Routledge is an imprint of the Taylor & Francis Group

© 2005 Jake Blood

Typeset in Sabon by BC Typesetting Ltd, Bristol

First issued in paperback 2012

British Library Cataloguing in Publication Data
A catalogue record for this book is available from the British Library

Library of Congress Cataloging in Publication Data
A catalog record for this book has been requested

ISBN13: 978-0-415-64226-1 (PBK)

ISBN13: 978-0-415-34997-0 (HBK)

To My Mother

Contents

Figures

Preface

This work has been many years in the making. As a teenager in the late 1960s and early 1970s, I witnessed war both at home and abroad as depicted on the television screen. I was confused and never really felt that anybody truly understood what was going on. Later, in the early 1990s, as a masters student attending a military intelligence college, I took a course on intelligence and Vietnam taught by Mr. George Allen, who had worked as an intelligence analyst for the Army and both the Defense Intelligence Agency and the Central Intelligence Agency and whose area of expertise was Vietnam. It was a fascinating course and was well taught, but the thing I remember most was the haunted look that would enter Mr. Allen's eyes as he tried to explain the performance of intelligence in that war.

Influenced by Mr. Allen, I determined to write my masters thesis on Vietnam. My original purpose was to look at how intelligence had supported the 'operational-level' of war. I was aware of the 'numbers controversy,' but was determined to avoid any discussion of it. I just wanted to look objectively at intelligence and how it had supported the warfighter. I decided to concentrate just on the early years, perhaps hoping to find where intelligence had failed to assess the enemy accurately. I was fortunate in locating and interviewing the first 'real' intelligence officer to serve as the Chief of Intelligence at the Military Assistance Command, Vietnam, retired Major General Joseph A. McChristian. In my interview with him, I persisted in focussing on intelligence support to the 'operational-level' of war and he kindly and patiently answered my questions. But at times, just like with Mr. Allen, there appeared a haunted look in his eyes as he tried to explain the performance of intelligence in Vietnam. This haunted look, both for General McChristian and Mr. Allen, appeared when the order of battle was mentioned.

As I sat down to write my thesis, the order of battle could not be avoided, it was central to the strategy of the key warfighter, US Commander General William C. Westmoreland and his strategy of attrition. To discuss intelligence support to the warfighter at the operational-level meant I had to talk about the order of battle. To discuss the order of battle meant I had to look at the 'numbers controversy.'

The 'numbers controversy' was not the best episode in the annals of intelligence. It was an acrimonious and bitter saga within the intelligence community and closely revolved around those who used intelligence. The resulting thesis was entitled *The Tet Effect: Military Intelligence and the American Will in Vietnam.* While a good thesis, like most graduate theses, it never really answered the questions I had raised, nor even explained exactly what the Tet Effect was. The answers were not to come until years later, after I had retired from 29 years in military intelligence. It was actually the 2003 war in Iraq that brought my thoughts and research into the light of understanding.

While this work started as my masters thesis, it has been greatly revised and expanded with my better understanding of what had gone wrong with intelligence in Vietnam and exactly what the Tet Effect was. The Tet Effect is the loss of credibility that results when the public is given 'skewed,' or just plain bad, intelligence to explain the reasoning for war. It happened in Vietnam during the Tet Offensive when an enemy that had been described as 'bankrupt' ferociously attacked with huge human capital, casting into doubt the credibility of the intelligence community, the military leadership, and even that of President Lyndon B. Johnson. And it happened again in the Iraq war of 2003, as the credibility of the intelligence community and the Bush administration were questioned when weapons of mass destruction, the basis for pre-emptive military action against Iraq, could not be found.

This work has been many, many years in the making and many, many people deserve recognition. I wish I could personally thank every single one and I know I will unintentionally neglect far too many. Thank you first to my family. Thank you to my wife Cynthia, your love and enthusiasm for all we do feeds my creative soul. Thank you to my eldest, Shaunna, whose trials and tribulations delayed this work, but proved that love is more important than any degree. And to my young one, Andrea, who since the day she was born has always made me smile. Thank you also to my former wife, Yonoke, for your patience and faith that I would eventually complete this project. Thank you mother, for your encouragement, inspiration, and editing.

I would also like to give my heartfelt thanks to Colonel Perry Karraker for lighting the flame, to Dr. Max Gross for giving me another opportunity, to Colonel Doug Cook for encouragement, to Lieutenant Colonel Mark Hoffman for taking me in, then shepherding my words and laboring tirelessly for my benefit, to Lieutenant Colonel Carlos Arvizu for understanding as I juggled work, family, and school, to Lieutenant Colonel (Retired) George Jolley for his advice, to Major Otis Campbell, Major John Gentry, and Captain Richard Boltz for their support, and to Captain Jim Borders for acting as a goodwill ambassador on my behalf.

I would also like to thank all those intelligence professionals who shaped military intelligence in the Vietnam War, in particular Major General Joseph

A. McChristian, who understood the enemy's will; Lieutenant General Phillip B. Davidson, who discovered the *Secrets of the Vietnam War*; and Sam Adams, whose persistence brought enlightenment. These three had widely divergent views, but all three were dedicated intelligence professionals who fought their wars with honor and a sense of duty to their country. May we learn from their experiences.

The influences have been many, but the responsibility for these words, be they accurate or inadvertently askew, is mine alone.

Introduction
Disturbing Vietnam memories

> War is a matter of vital importance to the State; the province of life or death;
> the road to survival or ruin. It is mandatory that it be thoroughly studied.
>
> Sun Tzu[1]

The year 1968 seems so distant. Fading memories of war, of protest, of
discord, of distrust. Vietnam and America burned. An all-out communist
offensive set ablaze the cities of South Vietnam. American bombers and artillery responded, setting the jungles aflame in North and South Vietnam. In
American cities, riots erupted in fiery protest, questioning the very credibility
of their President and the military. But it was so long ago; those fires have
long since subsided, smoldered and died, their ashes slowly grown cold.

Vietnam flashback

Yet, like a bad dream, never fully understood nor forgotten, Vietnam remains
a disturbing memory. A memory lying just below the surface, revealing itself
whenever that surface is disturbed. Disturbed by questions of credibility. In
1968 credibility was the question on America's mind. Was the government
being truthful about the war in Vietnam? As 1967 drew to a close, so too
did the war in Vietnam appear to be nearing an end. The American commander in Vietnam, General William C. Westmoreland, had told the country
that the end of the war was in sight. For the first time ever, the always-
cautious Westmoreland hinted before Congress that American troops could
begin phasing down in two years.[2] In a speech to the National Press Club in
November 1967, he described a 'bankrupt' enemy and proclaimed, 'I have
never been more encouraged in my four years in Viet Nam.'[3]

The US was indeed coming off a highly successful year against the enemy;
all outward indications were that the enemy was struggling, beaten by
superior American firepower, and withdrawing to the sanctuary of the
North. But had the will of the enemy truly been broken? What was the intelligence community estimate? Did intelligence foresee an enemy capable of

continuing the war or did it too view the enemy as 'bankrupt' as characterized by General Westmoreland?

As America's involvement in Vietnam increased, so too did the resources available to intelligence. By 1967, intelligence had the infrastructure, resources, and capabilities to examine in detail the enemy the US faced in Vietnam. With this better understanding came a dilemma – the intelligence community realized that they had undercounted the total number of enemy, in particular the militia and guerrilla forces, but to now increase these numbers would seem to contradict the US victories on the battlefield. To correct the imbalance created by the higher numbers and to continue to portray an image of success which was a reality on the battlefield, intelligence arrived at a 'political' decision to drop an entire category of the enemy, the militia forces. By dropping the militia forces, the numbers appeared to show the same downward trend suggested by the battlefield victories; intelligence could now support the image of progress without any convoluted explanations for higher militia numbers based on better intelligence.[4] Thus it was intelligence that allowed General Westmoreland to assess the enemy as 'bankrupt,' and to state, 'We have reached an important point when the end begins to come into view.'[5]

The end of the war as envisioned by General Westmoreland never materialized. On 21 January 1968, less than two months after his confident prediction of an end to the war, at least two North Vietnamese divisions began a siege against US Marines encamped at Khe Sanh, an isolated outpost in the north of South Vietnam. The ensuing battle riveted American public attention, as comparisons were made between Khe Sahn and the isolated outpost of Dien Bien Phu. It was at Dien Bien Phu over a decade earlier where the French had been decisively defeated by the communists, the harbinger of the end of French colonial rule in Vietnam. US forces, unlike the French, held and bloodied the enemy even more. The public wavered, but maintained confidence in the military and their leaders. Warning came that a diversionary enemy attack in the countryside would be coming around the Vietnamese New Year holiday of Tet.

The surprise, shock, and savagery of the enemy's main attack (not diversionary) on Tet (not around) against the cities (not in the countryside) were immediate and devastating. How had this 'bankrupt,' bloodied, and weakened foe managed to mass such a coordinated, extensive attack against every city of major and minor import in South Vietnam, while at the same time having massed such a large army outside of Khe Sanh? The US military appeared off-balance as it reacted to this offensive, having lost all sense of initiative, running helter-skelter to blunt attacks everywhere. Scenes of General Westmoreland on the television standing amongst the confusion and stating that everything was under control seemed contrary to the images.[6]

Something did not ring true, the enemy did not appear to be 'bankrupt,' but instead flush with seemingly inexhaustible human assets, carrying the battle to the city streets of South Vietnam, to the capital city of Saigon, where the sovereign territory of the United States itself was assaulted when the US Embassy came under attack. General Westmoreland, the tall, straight-backed, broad-shouldered, square-jawed epitome of an American general, was openly mocked and compared to a confident Custer riding into Little Big Horn.[7] He was also compared to the French General Henri Navarre who had confidently proclaimed the French had 'seen the light at the end of the tunnel,' just prior to their decisive defeat at Dien Bien Phu.[8]

So, too, was intelligence ridiculed. How could intelligence, which had not foreseen the enemy crawling in the streets of South Vietnam, possibly count an unseen enemy that controlled the impenetrable jungles of Vietnam? An investigation by the President's Foreign Intelligence Advisory Board was conducted to determine the culpability of intelligence.[9] Who could be believed? It was not the enemy that was 'bankrupt,' but the credibility of intelligence, of the military, and even that of the President.

The Tet Effect

The Tet Effect, then, is the loss of credibility suffered by leaders when they attempt to use intelligence to sway the public and are subsequently shown to be disingenuous. There were two important aspects which allowed the Tet Effect to occur. First, the intelligence became skewed with the loss of its objectivity, becoming a mere reflection of the commander's views and not an accurate reflection of the enemy. Second, this skewed intelligence was then portrayed to the American public by military and civilian leaders in an attempt to bolster support for the war. This use of skewed intelligence to sway the public's perception of the war backfired when the enemy's true form took substance in the Tet Offensive. Intelligence set up the American public for a fall with overly optimist reports which military and civilian leaders then used to bolster support for the war. When the Vietnamese communists launched their Tet Offensive, America was shocked and no longer believed intelligence, the military, or their President. The Tet Effect is an important lesson that intelligence must never forget.

Vietnam déjà vu

Unpleasant memories, but best left undisturbed? America is now involved in another war and the American public is again questioning the credibility of their President and whether the intelligence he used was skewed. The United States conducted a pre-emptive attack against Iraq in March of 2003. The battle was quick; decisive American firepower, maneuver, and technology overwhelmed the enemy and the United States was victorious. The United States had pre-empted Iraq, the public was told, to keep them from further developing and using weapons of mass destruction.

The United States has always proclaimed the right to self-preservation, but the threat of pre-emption, as laid out by President George W. Bush in his

2002 National Security Policy, was a new concept for American national security. No longer was the United States going to await the enemy's blow before striking, there would be no more Pearl Harbors, no more September 11ths. If the United States saw a threat to its national security it would act pre-emptively to eliminate that threat. Iraq, with a history of developing weapons of mass destruction, and a leader in Saddam Hussein with a history of using such weapons (against his enemies, both foreign and domestic), was identified as a threat and targeted for pre-emption.

To prepare the American public and the world for pre-emptive US military action against Iraq, the Bush administration released unprecedented amounts of sensitive, classified material. A 'White Paper' was publicly released which was basically an unclassified version of a secret National Intelligence Estimate on Iraq. Even more intelligence was released when the most credible of the Bush administration's cabinet, Secretary of State Colin Powell, briefed the United Nations Security Council in February of 2003.

With American public support, the United States acted and Saddam's Iraq was attacked in March 2003 and defeated in less than two months. Iraq's weapons could now be destroyed; but after over a year of searching, no arsenal of weapons of mass destruction was found. The leading US inspector, David McKay, then a special assistant at the Central Intelligence Agency, appeared before Congress in January 2004 and told the nation that there were no weapons of mass destruction in Iraq. 'It turns out we were all wrong,' he testified.[10] The basis for the pre-emptive attack, to secure America and its allies from Iraqi weapons of mass destruction, was unfounded. Had the President and his administration been honest, credible? What of intelligence, was it just bad or had it been skewed? Unpleasant questions, disturbing the surface, reviving memories of Vietnam.

The morals of intelligence in Vietnam

Vietnam and the use and misuse of intelligence are still relevant issues today. Intelligence was misused in Vietnam, and its misuse led to a major crisis in credibility. The fires of war flamed in Vietnam, yet it was this crisis in credibility that set the streets of America on fire. The public did not believe their own government, their military, or their intelligence community. How did intelligence reach such a state? An examination of intelligence in Vietnam reveals a story of high drama. A story with several important and relevant morals that should stand as precepts for the intelligence community.

The first precept: intelligence must be objective. Have no doubt about it, intelligence is there to support those leaders who need information to make sound decisions. Intelligence will always play liege to the wielder of the sword. However, never can intelligence allow the sword to dictate conclusions. Intelligence must be objective or it risks losing credibility. In Vietnam, intelligence allowed policy concerns to skew its analysis, leading to a politically motivated intelligence estimate instead of an objective conclusion. The result was a loss of credibility of not only intelligence, but also of the military and even the President it served.

The second precept: never portray the enemy in your own image. One of the primary tasks of intelligence is to know the enemy. A difficult task, to think like someone else, someone with a different value system, a different motivation, a different political philosophy, a different religion, a different psyche, a different culture. It is difficult to portray an enemy without being 'ethnocentric,' drawing on one's own value system, motivation, political philosophy, religion, psyche, one's own culture. In Vietnam, intelligence portrayed the enemy in the US image, with divisions, battalions, companies, platoons. Such thinking allowed for an easy decision to drop the militia from the enemy order of battle. The result was skewed intelligence which supported what the commander and the President wanted to hear, the enemy's numbers were decreasing. Violating this second precept made it easier to compromise the first, objectivity.

The third precept: technology does not render the spy useless. Technology is the forte of America, and the forte of US intelligence. Through technology, the US intelligence community has the best imagery and signals collection capability, bar none. Technology, however, could not provide the answers sought in Vietnam; for technology was rendered deaf and blind by a primitive enemy that did not extensively use radios, especially at the guerrilla level, and that hid under a triple-canopied jungle. Technology alone could not accurately portray the enemy. Long before there were satellites or airplanes, the world of intelligence revolved around espionage, the human spy. Unfortunately, intelligence derived from spies, from captured enemy, from deserters, etc. was discounted in Vietnam as useless because it was 'non-technical.'[11] The result was further justification to drop the enemy's militia forces as it was based entirely on 'non-technical' intelligence. As with the second precept, violating the third precept made it easier to violate the first, objectivity.

The fourth and final precept: never forget the enemy's will. In war, neither numbers nor technology ensure victory. War is a contest of wills, and until one side's will has been broken, the fighting will continue. In Vietnam, numbers were the measure of success, the indicator of victory; decreasing enemy numbers assured victory. With an estimate, based on an 'ethnocentric' and 'technocentric' view of the enemy, intelligence gave General Westmoreland and President Johnson exactly what they wanted to hear. The enemy's numbers were decreasing; victory was assured. What the intelligence community, General Westmoreland, and President Johnson forgot was that although the enemy was bloodied and losing thousands of men, the war was not over. The enemy's will to continue the fight was unbroken and America was in for a shock to its own will when the Tet Offensive was unleashed.

Finding the morals

The morals gleaned from the intelligence drama in Vietnam are not to be found in any single book. There were many dramas played out in Vietnam and there are a prodigious number of books detailing the many different aspects and views of the war. On the Tet Offensive alone, there are a large number of books detailing that 'turning point.' Dan Oberdorfer's *Tet! The Turning Point in the Vietnam War* probably remains the best at conveying both the story and the effect on America. Specifically addressing the intelligence aspect, two books stand out, *The Tet Offensive* by James J. Wirtz and *Tet 1968: Understanding the Surprise* by Ronnie E. Ford. While Wirtz's work looks closely at how intelligence misread the Tet Offensive, Ford looks specifically at what the enemy hoped to accomplish. Both books are outstanding and effectively meet their purpose in detailing intelligence on Tet. However, there was more to the story than just Tet.

In *CIA and the Vietnam Policymakers: Three Episodes 1962–1968*, Harold P. Ford looks at intelligence and how it was used by America's leaders. In his study, published by the CIA's Center for the Study of Intelligence, Ford looks at three key decisions made by policymakers regarding Vietnam and the intelligence used to support those choices. The last episode involves the misreading of the Tet Offensive and the disagreements within the intelligence community on the enemy's numbers. While closely related to this book, Ford is concerned primarily with the use of intelligence by the policymakers and does not look at the consequences or lessons to be learned in the aftermath of Tet.

Tet was the defining moment in the Vietnam War, but as highlighted by Ford in *CIA and the Vietnam Policymakers*, it was not the only intelligence controversy. The fracas within the intelligence community on how to count the enemy produced hard feelings amongst those involved and generated several accusations and rejoinders. In January 1982, CBS broadcast a documentary called the 'Uncounted Enemy: A Vietnam Deception.' The broadcast was based upon allegations by a former CIA employee, Sam Adams, that intelligence and the military had intentionally lied and deceived the American public regarding the enemy's numbers.

The result of this broadcast was a lawsuit filed by General William Westmoreland against CBS. The ensuing trial (which ended when CBS apologized and stated they never intended to question General Westmoreland's patriotism and the General then dropped the case) generated a number of books. While revealing a detailed picture of the workings of intelligence in Vietnam, these books focus on the trial itself and make no attempt to draw lessons for intelligence. Two books which are representative are *Vietnam on Trial* by Bob Brewin and Sydney Shaw and *The Juror and the General* as told by M. Patricia Roth.

There are also several important books written by the participants themselves, but which also tell only a part of the drama. Key among these are

Sam Adams's account and memoir, *War of Numbers*, and *Secrets of the Vietnam War* by Lieutenant General Phillip B. Davidson who served as the Chief of Military Intelligence in Vietnam from 1967 to 1969. Another excellent intelligence memoir is *None So Blind* by George W. Allen who followed Vietnam as an Army intelligence analyst, a Defense Intelligence Agency analyst, and a Central Intelligence Agency analyst. The head of the CIA at the time, Richard Helms, also wrote a memoir, *A Look Over My Shoulder: A Life in the Central Intelligence Agency*, which includes his thoughts on Vietnam and the intelligence controversies. These books are outstanding in providing their view of the drama, but tend towards an emotional representation and, at times, reveal the authors' personal bias.

What is lacking in the literature is an unbiased look at intelligence in Vietnam, a retelling, drawing upon all the major actors, of the drama which unfolded in Vietnam and led to a tragic loss of confidence by the public in its leadership. Further, no attempt has been made to learn from this tragedy, to educe a moral from this drama, to ascertain precepts to guide future intelligence efforts. This book, *The Tet Effect: Intelligence and the Public Perception of War* intends to tell this tale and elicit its moral and precepts.

Disturbing Vietnam memories

To tell this tale, this book is divided into three parts. Part I, *The Tet Effect*, concentrates on Tet, both the events leading up to Tet and the consequences afterward. Part II, *On intelligence and Vietnam*, takes a closer look at the role of intelligence and the lessons to be learned, while Part III, *The Tet Effect and intelligence principles in the twenty-first century*, looks at the role of intelligence and credibility in the pre-emptive war against Iraq in 2003 and reaffirms the continued importance into the twenty-first century of the intelligence principles learned in Vietnam.

Part I, *The Tet Effect* consists of five chapters. Chapter 1, *Tet: The surprise*, briefly looks at the 1968 Tet Offensive and the military situation leading up to the communist surprise. This provides the background against which the rest of the book revolves. Chapter 2, *After Tet: The reality*, reveals the stark aftermath of the Tet Offensive. While a tactical defeat for the communists, the political ramifications in the United States were devastating. Within two months of the offensive, public opinion was decidedly against the war, and the top three American war leaders were effectively removed – the President announced his decision not to seek re-election, the Secretary of Defense left office, and the military commander in Vietnam was reassigned. Chapter 3, *Before Tet: The delusion*, attempts to account for the dramatic changes that occurred after Tet by looking at the critical events leading up to the offensive. From these events, the elements comprising the Tet Effect can be identified. These events include General Westmoreland's adoption of a strategy of attrition and its delusional measure of success, the crossover point, that point when more enemy are killed than can be replaced; the intelligence community's buy-in to the delusion of the crossover point and its assessment that the crossover point had been reached; and the public relations campaign to sell the American public a message that the enemy was 'bankrupt' and therefore the end of the war was near. Tet revealed that the crossover point as a measure of success was a delusion; the true measure of success in war, as taught by the ancient eastern master of war, Sun Tzu, and the western warrior-philosopher, Carl von Clausewitz, is will.

Chapter 4, *The effect of Tet: A loss of trust*, looks more closely at the aftermath of Tet in light of the delusion propagated by the military, intelligence, and the Johnson administration, with the primary effect being the American public's loss of trust in their civilian and military leadership. Chapter 5, *The Tet Effect: Intelligence and the public perception of war*, then specifically identifies and discusses the Tet Effect phenomena – the loss of credibility suffered by leaders when the image they have projected of a situation, based upon intelligence they themselves shaped, is shown to be disingenuous.

Having examined the Tet Effect, Part II, *On intelligence and Vietnam* takes a closer look at the drama played out in Vietnam in 1967 and the role intelligence played. The drama reveals several morals, or lessons, to guide future intelligence endeavors. The first two chapters set the stage, while the middle two retell the drama, and the final chapter in this section details the morals of the drama.

Chapter 6, *Setting the stage: The enemy's war*, looks closely at the enemy and how they viewed themselves and what motivated them. These are important details as the drama revolves around how US intelligence perceived the enemy. Chapter 7, *Setting the stage: Vietnam intelligence in 1967*, then looks at how intelligence operated in Vietnam in late 1967. Intelligence was a team player on the MACV staff, supporting the 'American Way of War' with the latest technology to count the enemy as the measure of success.

Having set the stage, the next two chapters look at the intelligence drama played out as intelligence lost its objectivity. In Chapter 8, *An intelligence drama: The protagonists*, the primary players in shaping US intelligence on Vietnam are introduced and examined – Sam Adams of the Central Intelligence Agency, Brigadier General Joseph A. McChristian, Chief of Intelligence for General Westmoreland from 1965 to mid-1967, and Brigadier General Phillip B. Davidson, who replaced McChristian in May 1967. Chapter 9, *An intelligence drama: A three-act tragedy* recounts the three conferences which the intelligence community held to try to resolve the issue of how many enemy there were and how to count them, the critical component in assessing whether the crossover point had been reached. In the end, intelligence abdicated its objectivity and became the standard bearer for the leadership perspective.

In the final chapter of this section, Chapter 10, *From tragedy, four morals: Intelligence principles*, the lessons from intelligence in Vietnam are learned. First, intelligence must remain objective or it compromises its ability to assess and evaluate the enemy and fulfill its duty to America's leaders and the public. Second, intelligence must overcome ethnocentrism and accurately portray the enemy without bias and preconceptions. Third, technology is wonderful, but not a be-all and end-all. Intelligence began as a human endeavor and remains a human endeavor, the human element must never be overlooked or belittled. And finally, the measure of success in war is not numbers, but the willingness of the enemy to continue the fight.

The final portion of this book looks at the present day and the future in Part III, *The Tet Effect and intelligence principles in the twenty-first century*. Chapter 11, *The Tet Effect in Iraq: Pre-empting credibility*, looks at how the world changed after September 11, 2001 and the ensuing war with Iraq in 2003. Intelligence to prepare the public and the world for the pre-emptive attack based upon the claim that Iraq had weapons of mass destruction is examined, as is the resultant loss of credibility when no such weapons were found; the Tet Effect has been invoked.

The final chapter, Chapter 12, *Intelligence principles in the twenty-first century: Still valid after all these years*, looks at the intelligence principles learned from the Tet Effect in Vietnam and reaffirms their importance in light of the intelligence performance preceding the Iraq war. Objectivity, guarding against ethnocentrism and technocentrism, and remembering that war is a contest of wills are precepts that can still guide intelligence in this new century.

Unpleasant memories from Vietnam, disingenuous images from today. Vietnam was a harsh period in American history, with harsh lessons. This book attempts to learn, explore, and illustrate those lessons and to provide guidance for present and future intelligence endeavors.

Part I
The Tet Effect

1 Tet

The surprise

This spring far outshines the previous Springs,
Of victories throughout the land
come happy tidings.
Let South and North emulate each other
in fighting the US aggressors!
Forward!
Total victory shall be ours.
   Ho Chi Minh, Poem signaling Tet Offensive[1]

No other event of the Vietnam War evokes more memories or emotions. It was the battle which defined the war more than any other. It was the 'turning point,' the event that broke America's will to continue the war. Before Tet, America was prepared to stop the encroachment of communism into South Vietnam. After Tet, America planned its withdrawal and gave notice to South Vietnam that the war was theirs to win or lose. America had reached the limits of its intervention.[2]

Tet struck like a monsoon from the east, when all forecasts had predicted a small storm from the north. America had been lulled into a sense of hope by the optimistic reports from the field presented by General William C. Westmoreland on his visit back to the United States in November 1967. The enemy, he had told Americans, was in no condition to undertake a major offensive. December was a lull, with only a series of small showers. In January, there were signs of a gathering storm and even ominous indicators that something big was just over the horizon, but the forecasters were focused in the wrong direction, looking outward to an isolated Marine camp, Khe Sanh. And there a storm did erupt on January 21 and all eyes turned to that battle – but it was only a storm, not a monsoon.

On 31 January 1968, during the Vietnamese New Year holiday of Tet, the monsoon struck. The communists hit with a force and intensity that magnified the surprise induced by the timing of the attacks. Further amplifying the effect were the size and scope of the attacks which attested to a co-ordinated effort far beyond the meager capability attributed to the primitive communist forces. Most disconcerting was that the intensity, scope, coordination, and timing of the attacks were targeted against the cities of South Vietnam, not against US military forces as had been forecast.

The US reacted quickly to the attacks as did the Army of the Republic of Vietnam (ARVN). Together, US and ARVN forces blunted, then turned back the communist attacks, badly mauling them in the process. The communists had planned as part of the Tet attacks to incite the South Vietnamese populace to rise up against their government. The communists counted on this revolt to reinforce their attacks and disable and disorientate the government of South Vietnam. The revolt never occurred and the communists, who had gained the initial impetus, quickly lost the initiative and were forced to flee or die in the cities. In the end, the communists held no cities and were shattered by the US and ARVN counter-attacks, with the enemy losing over half of their attacking force. It was a disastrous defeat for the communists.

North Vietnamese General Vo Nguyen Giap was fond of reciting a Maoist principle – what seems a victory may not be a victory, and what seems a defeat may not be a defeat. No better illustration of this ironic axiom could be found than that of the Tet Offensive of 1968. For while the US and South Vietnamese military forces were busy turning the tide to their overwhelming favor, in the United States turmoil ensued. The American public accepted the optimistic view of General Westmoreland, a view based upon the intelligence coming out of the Military Assistance Command-Vietnam (MACV) and the Central Intelligence Agency (CIA). The public was unprepared for the intense and disturbing scenes it witnessed on television and the accounts it read in the press.

What the American public saw and read about the enemy was incongruous with the message imparted by General Westmoreland and the intelligence community. The size and intensity of the attacks were not indicative of an enemy so worn down by attrition that they could not replace their own forces in the field. The coordination and scope of the attack was not compatible with the image of a primitive force unable to withstand the onslaught of American technical know-how. This was not an enemy who appeared willing to concede the battlefield in two years as predicted by General Westmoreland just over two months earlier. The credibility of intelligence, of General Westmoreland, and of the Johnson administration, for all intents and purposes, was gone.

The calm before the monsoon

The US military had been highly successful against the enemy in 1967. But the victories were not reflected in the public opinion polls. Despite the military successes, the American public was already growing weary of the war and support was on the decline. Concerned about flagging support for the war, President Johnson called upon his military commander in Vietnam to rally support at home. Ostensibly called back to America for consultations with the President in November of 1967, Westmoreland returned to the States to speak before Congress, the press, and the American public to predict an end to the war. Describing the enemy as 'bankrupt,' Westmoreland told the nation that US troops could begin withdrawing in two years. General Westmoreland was successful in his efforts as support for the war rebounded.

When General Westmoreland returned to Vietnam after his public relations campaign in the United States, the outward signs throughout Vietnam were that the enemy was indeed badly beaten and forced to seek refuge in the periphery of the country. The South Vietnamese were also buoyed by the optimism from General Westmoreland's trip.[3]

Building upon the successes earlier in the year, in December General Westmoreland launched a new phase in his strategy, an attempt to keep the enemy on the periphery of South Vietnam. He deployed the newly arrived 101st Airborne Division to positions that would block the main body of North Vietnamese forces from penetrating into South Vietnam.[4] He hoped that by holding the enemy at bay on the periphery of the country and using the tried tactics of locating, fixing, then destroying the enemy, the communist forces would continue to decrease. However, there were ominous clouds gathering on the horizon. While holding the enemy at bay on the periphery, the US left itself and its allies vulnerable to attacks from within the country.

The gathering monsoon clouds

Beginning in the fall of 1967, a series of engagements known as the 'border battles' erupted along the periphery of South Vietnam. On 27 October 1967 a North Vietnamese Army (NVA) regiment attacked an ARVN battalion in the village of Song Be in Phuoc Long province which bordered Cambodia. Two days later, an indigenous South Vietnamese Communist, or as they were more commonly referred to, Viet Cong (VC), regiment attacked the village of Loc Ninh in Binh Long province which also bordered Cambodia. In November, intelligence reports indicated increased enemy activity around the Dak To base camp near the city of Pleiku in Kontum province, also adjacent to the Cambodian border. Dak To was in a valley surrounded by peaks and ridges up to 6,000 feet in altitude; to ensure security the high ground needed to be controlled. Fierce fighting erupted as US and ARVN forces moved to secure the high ground, some of the bloodiest occurring between 17 and 21 November as US forces steadily crept up Hill 875, or Hamburger Hill as it became known.[5] As with the other engagements, the enemy was beaten back with heavy losses.

During the same time-frame, intelligence began picking up increased NVA activity across the border from Khe Sanh, a base camp for a reinforced Marine regiment. Khe Sanh was located in the northwest corner of South Vietnam and bordered both North Vietnam and Laos. By January 1968, three NVA divisions had been identified poised around Khe Sanh. On 21 January the NVA forces launched a mortar attack which destroyed several helicopters and scored a direct hit on the main ammunition dump, setting off 16,000 artillery shells, a sizable amount of C-4 plastic explosives, and numerous other munitions.[6] Khe Sanh became the focus of General Westmoreland in Saigon and President Johnson in Washington, DC. In their minds, the enemy offensive, which more and more intelligence data indicated was forthcoming, was to be centered on Khe Sanh. As General Westmoreland explained in his book *A Soldier Reports*:

> Much of the attention of the press, my own command, and Washington officials understandably focused on Khe Sanh. It was an obvious objective, essential to the enemy if he were to get behind the defensive posts facing the DMZ and move deep into Quan Tri province. Khe Sanh was isolated enough and bore enough similarities to Dien Bien Phu to excite armchair strategists. President Johnson, I learned later, had begun to develop a fixation about it.[7]

The attack on Khe Sanh seemed to be the culmination of the periphery border battles. *Time* magazine had noted earlier in the 22 December 1967 issue that military strategists were puzzled by the enemy's border attacks and questioned how long the enemy would be able to sustain them. By the 19 January 1968 issue, *Time* reported that Hanoi had ordered a savage increase in the war's tempo.[8] General Westmoreland noted to reporters that the fighting had been 'the most intense of the entire war.'[9] 'The most intense of the entire war,' Westmoreland said, and the month of January was only half over; Khe Sanh had yet to be attacked and the enemy's main offensive which was to engulf the entire country was still weeks away. With Khe Sanh now surrounded by 15,000 to 20,000 NVA in two divisions and with another division nearby, just how many more troops did this foe retain?

The Tet monsoon unleashed

On 30 January 1968 Viet Cong forces launched attacks on six cities and towns in the central section of South Vietnam which were quickly repulsed.[10] The MACV Chief of Staff for Intelligence, Brigadier General Phillip Davidson, reported the attacks to General Westmoreland and his staff the next morning and assessed that the attacks had probably been premature and that the main attacks would probably come that night.[11] That evening, he returned to his billet, as did General Westmoreland and the rest of his staff. They were armed with their sidearms and rifles, normally not seen on senior officers in Saigon. The coming offensive was of concern, but evidently was not something to lose sleep over or cause them to remain closer to the command center. The Headquarters was in Saigon and the enemy was unlikely to attack the capital.

True to the assessment given by Davidson, the enemy launched its offensive early on the morning of 31 January. As described by author Dan Oberdorfer in his book *Tet!*, the 'attacks erupted in the night like a string of firecrackers.'

> 1:35 a.m. – Ban Me Thout in the central highlands
> 2:00 a.m. – Kontum, another mountain city
> 2:55 a.m. – Hoi An, a province capital on the coast
> 3:30 a.m. – Da Nang, the country's second largest city, on the coast
> 4:10 a.m. – Qui Nhon, a major coastal city
> 4:40 a.m. – Pleiku, a mountain city[12]

In a single surge, over 100 cities and towns were attacked, including the capital city of Saigon, 39 of the 44 provincial capitals and 71 of the district capitals. Besides the cities and towns, specific political and military targets were also attacked, including the US Embassy, the Presidential Palace, the South Vietnamese Joint General Staff Headquarters, and all four military region headquarters.[13]

When the offensive came the MACV staff was unprepared. Davidson later recalled in an interview given in 1982, 'Why the VC didn't attack some of those houses – they could have captured Westmoreland and Abrams and any of the rest of us with a couple of squads.'[14]

The enemy committed an estimated 84,000 troops to the Tet Offensive.[15] While the onslaught was intense and broad in scope, the purpose of the offensive was more political in nature than military. The Tet Offensive was planned to be an uprising, the final push of the Maoist guerrilla warfare strategy, where the people rise up to overthrow the government while the guerrilla forces attack and defeat the government troops. The Viet Cong, who had their roots in the villages and countryside of Vietnam, were out of place and unfamiliar with the locale and populace of the cities. There was no popular uprising to follow up the shock of the initial attacks. In most areas, the fighting was over in a matter of days. In Saigon, heavy fighting continued for several weeks and in the historic city of Hue, the communists held on for nearly a month. In the end, the enemy was dealt a horrific blow. Of the estimated attacking force of 84,000, approximately 45,000, mostly Viet Cong, were killed.[16] This was attrition in the fullest sense of the strategy.

Whatever the communist objective of the Tet Offensive, the costs were severe. The intended outcome of a general uprising never materialized. No cities or towns were held, even in areas considered sympathetic to the Viet Cong. If anything, the attack served to unite and stiffen the resolve of the South Vietnamese army. In Vietnam, the enemy was in a dire condition. The Viet Cong, according to most analysts, were never again to be a factor in the war.[17]

Yet in the United States, the images of Tet seemed to mock the words of General Westmoreland; the enemy, though far from rich, was clearly not 'bankrupt,' willing to sacrifice over 45,000 soldiers. Even though the enemy had been soundly defeated and had suffered tremendous losses, the images of the enemy continuing to fight laid low the notion that simply reaching the crossover point was going to stop the war. To the American public, the enemy appeared determined to fight to the last man.

2 After Tet
The reality

Was the word of a professional military man who bore over-all military responsibility for the war in South Vietnam . . . to have no precedence over rumor?

General William C. Westmoreland[1]

The enemy never planned, nor could have hoped, for a more desirable outcome. Even though the Tet Offensive was a devastating tactical defeat for the enemy, the strategic consequences in America were far more damning. The American public no longer supported the war, its will effectively broken. The highest echelons of America's war effort were eliminated; the commanding general in Vietnam was removed from command, the Secretary of Defense left his post, and the President announced his intention not to seek re-election.

Tet marked 'The Turning Point' of US involvement in Vietnam. Before Tet, the American public was behind the war; after Tet, it was not. On March 31, two months after Tet, the American president, Lyndon Baines Johnson, announced to the nation he would not seek re-election. He would instead seek peace in Vietnam; peace he would not find. On February 29, less than a month after Tet, the president's Secretary of Defense, Robert Strange McNamara, stepped down from his position, a position he had held since 1961 (McNamara had announced in November 1967 that he would be leaving at an unspecified date). Secretary McNamara had been the longest serving Secretary of Defense; his conviction that the war could not be won would not allow him to serve any longer, even in the hour of President Johnson's greatest need. On March 22, less than two months after Tet, President Johnson announced that the American commander in Vietnam, General William Childs Westmoreland, was coming back to the United States to become the Army's Chief of Staff. General Westmoreland had been promoted out of command; he would command no more soldiers in battle. Johnson, McNamara, Westmoreland – all affected by Tet.

Tet had an effect on the full spectrum of American life, from the President, his Cabinet, and military leadership, to the American public. It was the

American public, however, that proved most shaken by the Tet Offensive and it was this disturbance that shook the foundations of a presidency.

The American will: gone

American public opinion on the war in Vietnam had never been overwhelming, one way or the other[2] (see Figure 1). Early on, in late 1965, a clear majority of Americans, just over 60 percent, supported the war. However, as the American effort increased, support began to decrease, and by the middle of 1966, less than 50 percent supported the war. US military successes in early 1967 inched support back over the 50 percent mark, but by middle of the year, support had again slipped below 50.

At the same time, those who opposed the war followed the same curves, but in the opposite direction. Whereas in mid-1966, less than 25 percent opposed the war, by mid-1966 over 35 percent were against the war. The military successes in early 1967 sent opposition lower, down to nearly 30 percent, but by the middle of the year it had recovered to over the 35 percent mark, and kept on increasing. Up to this point, opposition and support for the war basically mirrored each other, as one increased, the other decreased and vice versa; there was a symmetry. But in late 1967, this symmetry broke; those who opposed the war continued to increase at a rate greater than those who supported the war. The deciding factor was those who had previously held no opinion.

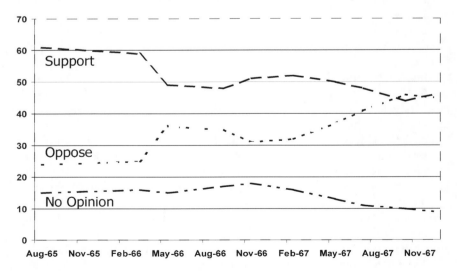

Figure 1 Public opinion 1965–1967.

Source: Data compiled from John E. Mueller, *War, Presidents and Public Opinion* (New York: John Wiley & Sons, Inc., 1973), 54–55.

Those who had been undecided, who neither supported nor opposed the war in Vietnam, remained fairly constant in 1965 and 1966, from just over 15 percent in 1965 to just under 20 percent by the beginning of 1967. In 1967, however, those who declared themselves as having 'no opinion' on the war, began a steady decrease, from just under 20 percent at the start of the year, to just under 10 percent by the end of the year. This 10 percent who had gained an 'opinion' went predominantly against the war.

In late 1967, for the first time more Americans opposed the war than supported it. In October 1967, 46 percent opposed and 44 percent supported the war, with just 10 percent undecided. President Johnson's concerns increased and in November he had General Westmoreland return to the United States in a coordinated public relations campaign to bolster support. With pronouncements by General Westmoreland of a 'bankrupt' enemy and the end of the war coming into view, the trend against the war was halted and support for the war revised, barely. At the end of 1967, 46 percent supported the war, 45 percent were opposed and 9 percent had no opinion. American public opinion on the war stood in the balance.

Tet unequivocally shifted the balance, and public opinion never swung back in favor of the war. After Tet, in February 1968, public support for the war fell to 42 percent and opposition increased to 46 percent. By the end of March, nearly half, 49 percent, now opposed the war with 41 percent supporting it. By August, a majority of 53 percent were against the war while support had dropped to 35 percent, marking a near reversal of opinion from February 1967 when 52 percent had supported and 32 percent had opposed the war. Opinion had changed and support for the war would never recover.

The American President: gone

Support for the war was a constant concern for President Johnson. He had called in his top-gun, General Westmoreland in November of 1967 to stem the tide of public dissatisfaction with the war, and now, just two months later, Tet had irreversibly set public opinion against the war. Within President Johnson's administration, many who had supported the war before Tet, began to question it. One of the most ardent supporters of the war, Clark Clifford, who was to replace McNamara as Secretary of Defense, was called upon to evaluate the war and the President's options. In early March, Clifford presented to President Johnson a memorandum which, for the first time, called for a limit to be determined on just how far American support in Vietnam would extend. The limits of American will were extending to the Presidency.

Amazed at the failing American support for the war, and shaken by the increasing pessimism within his own administration, President Johnson pondered his own future and on 31 March 1968, announced that he would not seek, nor accept, his party's nomination for another term as president. The President of the United States, haunted by increasing opposition to the war, yet dedicated to the ending of the division of the nation, sacrificed his position in an effort to find peace. The effects of Tet had reached the highest office of the land.

The American Secretary of Defense: gone

The key architect of President Johnson's efforts in Vietnam had been Robert S. McNamara. Even before Tet, McNamara had begun to express his own doubts about just how far America would be willing to go in order to win the war in Vietnam. In November of 1967, when President Johnson was attempting to bolster support for the war, McNamara announced his departure as Secretary of Defense at a future date to be determined. The Tet Offensive determined his departure date. Just one month after Tet, when America was equally divided on the war, just when President Johnson and his administration were finally coming closer to McNamara's own view of the war, this was the time McNamara chose to leave. In his book *In Retrospect*, McNamara details his experience with Vietnam; he mentions Tet only once. His silence speaks volumes.

McNamara had seen the writing on the wall. He was not involved in the November 1967 public relations bid to bolster support for the war. He had already made up his mind that 'we could not achieve our objective in Vietnam through any reasonable military means, and we therefore should seek a lesser political objective through negotiations.'[3] This opinion, of course, did not reflect the message President Johnson wanted the American public to hear.

While General Westmoreland was trying to rally American support for the war, President Johnson was suggesting to the World Bank that McNamara would make a good candidate to fill the vacancy as president of the bank.[4] Once McNamara decided to leave as Secretary of Defense and become the president of the World Bank, he devotes only one paragraph in his book to cover the intervening three months. Three months in which, as he describes it, 'crisis piled upon crisis ... Khe Sahn ... Pueblo ... the bloody Tet Offensive.'[5] Crisis upon crisis, and McNamara leaves, convinced that 'the American public, frustrated by the slow rate of progress, fearing continued escalation, and doubting that all approaches to peace have been sincerely probed, does not have the appearance of having the will to persist.'[6]

The American Commanding General: gone

The conviction of General William C. Westmoreland was never shaken. He was an American soldier, dedicated to serving his nation. He answered the call in World War II, in Korea, and in Vietnam. In Vietnam he was the commander of all military forces fighting in South Vietnam and the one charged with protecting that nation from being overun by communism. He answered the call of his President in November 1967 and led the public relations campaign to boost American support for the war. He told the US Congress that American troops would begin returning in just two years. Now his credibility was on the line. Having given such an optimistic report in November he was now openly mocked in February as he tried in vain to explain that the enemy was on the verge of a monumental defeat. Many did not believe and instead placed higher confidence in rumor than in the word of an American general.[7]

He had overseen the US build-up in Vietnam, had developed the US strategy of attrition to defeat the enemy, and was now just two years away from US victory. But it was not to be. Without even consulting him, on 22 March 1968, President Johnson announced that General Westmoreland was to become the US Army Chief of Staff – a promotion.

A promotion to non-command. As the Chief of Staff, Westmoreland was to ensure the Army was ready to fight, overseeing logistics, training, and readiness. Readying the Army to fight for some other general. The Army Chief of Staff never commands troops in combat. Despite being the titular pinnacle of the Army, the position is for those closing out their career. Having been the commander in Vietnam, commanding the military forces of his nation in combat, to be called home before tasting victory was not a reward. No general wants to leave command before completing the mission he was assigned, to attain victory. Westmoreland was no exception, 'I received the news of the appointment (as Chief of Staff) with mixed emotions. I had hoped to remain in Vietnam until the fighting ended, yet I was honored by the selection.'[8] Westmoreland was not elated, not happy, not excited, not jubilant, but honored.

Within months of the Tet Offensive, the three top Americans responsible for the war effort in Vietnam were effectively removed from their positions of leadership. President Johnson became a lame duck President when he announced on 31 March 1968, his intention not to run for the Presidency. He would be out of office within a year. Secretary of Defense Robert McNamara accepted another job before Tet struck and he stood by that choice, leaving the President in the midst of a crisis on 29 February 1968. And General William Westmoreland was promoted out of his command when President Johnson announced him as the next Army Chief of Staff on 22 March 1968.

On the battlefield, the Tet Offensive was a decisive communist tactical defeat. Yet in the political realm, to have the top three men responsible for the war removed, had to be considered a strategic victory for the enemy. Of course, the enemy could never have intended such an effect as a result of the attacks, nor could they have predicted the downward spiral in American public support for the war. How did such far-reaching consequences arise? The answer lies not with the enemy, but as the result of our own design. We had set up ourselves through our own delusion; in effect, deceiving ourselves.

3 Before Tet

The delusion

Although I estimate the troops of Yueh as many, of what benefit is this superiority in respect to the outcome?

Sun Tzu[1]

Deception often plays a decisive role in military battles. Tet was no exception. However, the deception came not from the enemy, but was self-induced, a delusion. While the enemy did conduct a deception campaign before Tet, lulling the US into false hopes for new peace talks, a far greater deception, or delusional, campaign was being conducted by the US military and the Johnson administration. An all-out public relations campaign was conducted in November 1967 in which the American public was told for the first time that the enemy was on the run and that the end was in sight. The public relations campaign was founded on a fallacy; a fallacy based upon numbers and statistics, not upon an understanding of the enemy and their motivation. When the Tet Offensive was launched, with a ferocity and intensity that belied the predictions made in November, the American public lost faith in their leaders, their military, and the intelligence community. The 'turning point' had been reached in the Vietnam War.

The Americanization of a war

Vietnam was a strange war in a strange land against a strange enemy. There were no battlefronts nor strategic objectives to be seized. The enemy was constantly defeated, yet constantly reappeared. It was not even America's war; US troops had originally been sent to Vietnam to act only as advisors. Yet even as an ever-increasing number of Americans were killed, the headquarters for US forces there remained till the end Military *Assistance* Command, Vietnam (MACV).

MACV was originally set up in 1954 under the Eisenhower administration as the Military Assistance Advisory Group (MAAG), with a strictly advisory mission. In 1955, the MAAG mission was expanded to organize, train, and equip the military forces of South Vietnam. US military personnel were to train, organize, and equip, but not fight for the South Vietnamese, and were not even permitted to accompany them on operational missions. This changed in 1961 under President Kennedy when he authorized US personnel to accompany South Vietnamese military units into the field, but still only to act as advisors. He also dispatched two US Army helicopter units to Vietnam to provide operational support to the South Vietnamese military. Even so, by the end of the year, US military personnel in Vietnam numbered under 3,000.

The numbers increased to nearly 11,000 by the end of 1962, a year which also saw the MAAG renamed to the more familiar moniker, MACV. More turbulent was the year 1963, when both South Vietnam and America lost their presidents. President Ngo Dinh Diem was overthrown and assassinated by a military coup on November 1. Nearly three weeks later, on November 22, President John F. Kennedy was assassinated in Dallas, Texas. A shared loss now increasingly became a shared war. On 2 August 1964, a North Vietnamese gunboat attacked the USS Destroyer Maddox and on 7 August Congress passed the Gulf of Tonkin resolution, authorizing President Johnson to take military action in Vietnam. Earlier that same year, General William C. Westmoreland had arrived in Vietnam and in June had assumed command of MACV.

General Westmoreland was to oversee the 'Americanization' of the war, which saw the US presence increase from 23,000 at the end of 1964, to 148,300 by October 1965, and to over 385,000 by the end of 1966. In December 1967, on the eve of the Tet Offensive, US forces in Vietnam totaled over 486,000.[2]

An American strategy of attrition

General Westmoreland was also responsible for developing and executing the strategy by which the United States conducted the war, a strategy of attrition. As General Westmoreland explained in his Vietnam memoirs, 'The U.S. military strategy employed in Vietnam, dictated by political decisions, was essentially that of a war of attrition . . . the war in Vietnam was not against Asian hordes but against an enemy with relatively limited manpower.'[3] In a war of attrition, numbers were the measure of progress. In a war without fronts, the numbers took on an even greater value, as they provided the only graphic representation of success. In Vietnam, numbers reigned supreme.

Vietnam was a war full of numbers – body counts, US troops deployed in country, the enemy order of battle, infiltration rates, aircraft losses, killed in action (KIA), missing in action (MIA), etc. The numbers allowed for a wealth of statistics in a war barren of traditional measures of military success. The wealth of numbers and statistics and the dearth of any other viable measures of military progress allowed any and all viewpoints to twist and manipulate the data to paint a picture of the war conforming to their own views. In the words of Benjamin Disraeli (often attributed to Mark Twain, who in his autobiography attributes the quote to Disraeli), 'There are three kinds of lies: lies, damned lies and statistics.'[4]

In the war of attrition fought by the United States and by the nature of the guerrilla warfare used by the enemy, there were few measures of progress. The military needed numbers to explain how the war was progressing to the US leadership and the media. The US leadership and media then used the numbers to advance their own viewpoint of the war in explaining it to the American public. The conflicting views, using the same data, naturally left the public feeling one side or the other was not being totally forthcoming, leading to much discussion of credibility.

Former President Dwight D. Eisenhower felt he had a much easier time as the Supreme Allied Commander during World War II than did General Westmoreland in Vietnam. Eisenhower explained, 'I always knew where the enemy was.'[5] In Vietnam, the enemy was everywhere, even in government controlled areas. A map of Vietnam showing government and enemy controlled areas looked like a checkerboard, and even government controlled areas were a misnomer, as the enemy could move virtually anywhere uncontested at night. Even after major military operations, the enemy would be back in their old positions, sometimes in only a matter of days.[6] Snipers and booby traps could spring up anywhere and soldiers had to be constantly on guard. General Bruce Palmer, Jr., in his book *The 25-Year War*, described the consternation, 'for the fighting troops it was frustrating to destroy the same enemy units every few months in battles that took place in the same general locations.'[7]

The enemy recognized the tactical mobility of the US forces, but emphasized that they too had mobility, in the strategic sense. They controlled when and where the battles would occur and could shift and mass their forces at the time and location of their choice. General Giap used the seemingly contradictory phrase to explain, 'battlefronts exist everywhere, yet they do not exist anywhere.'[8] While the US had helicopters and a dominant Air Force, the enemy used mortars and sapper attacks on US air bases which they viewed as being 'as effective as if we had an Air Force.'[9]

Without fronts, without large areas of uncontested territory, with an enemy capable of striking anywhere in the country, it was difficult to demonstrate and explain to the troops, to the US leadership, to the American people, that the United States military was making any progress in this war halfway around the world. It was even more difficult to predict when the conflict would eventually end. Compounding this was the lack of clear guidance from the US leadership on just what the mission and objectives of the military were in Vietnam.

Following a summit between the leaders of South Vietnam and the United States held in Honolulu, Hawaii in February of 1966, Secretary of Defense Robert McNamara and Secretary of State Dean Rusk remained in Hawaii and met with General Westmoreland to establish goals and objectives for the military in Vietnam and a means to measure their progress. Percentages were set for securing and pacifying areas, for opening roads and railroads, and for denying enemy access to base areas. The most prominent and telling goal, which was to shape the strategy and set the tone for the war, was 'to destroy the enemy forces at a rate at least as high as the enemy's capability to put more men in the field.'[10]

General Westmoreland accepted these goals unhesitatingly and without question as they reinforced the strategy of attrition he had developed. 'Nothing about those goals conflicted with the broad outline of how the war was to be fought as I had worked it out over months of consultation with South Vietnamese officials, Admiral Sharp (Commander in Chief of the Pacific Command which included Vietnam in its Area of Responsibility), and the Joint Chiefs of Staff.'[11]

The goal to destroy the enemy faster than they could reconstitute was the entire focus of General Westmoreland's strategy of attrition. The objective of attrition is to locate and destroy as many of the enemy as possible, until the losses become unbearable. The US leadership had blessed Westmoreland's plan for the conduct of the war and endorsed the key measurement of success in conducting such a strategy, the crossover point.

The crossover point

The crossover point was the goal of Westmoreland's attrition strategy. With attrition, the purpose is to kill as many enemy as possible, to make their losses so unbearable that they cannot replace those killed or lost in action. When the enemy's numbers begin to decrease, the crossover point has been reached. This was the goal, blessed by the Johnson administration and embraced by the military.

Having adopted an attrition strategy with the key measure being the crossover point, the importance of numbers grew several magnitudes. The most important number was the enemy order of battle. Monitored on a month-by-month basis, the US leadership, military leadership, media, and public digested the enemy strength statistics looking for the trends that would signal success and ultimately victory. They were all searching for the crossover point.

General Westmoreland was extremely cautious whenever he was asked how long the war in Vietnam would last. He knew a war of attrition would take time and counted on the patience of the American people to persevere.[12] Yet, he also recognized that Americans were impatient and expected results once the flow of troops began.[13] However, he felt that the war was not against the entire hordes of Asia, only one small and backward country with a limited manpower pool. Each encounter ate away at the enemy's numbers, and even if the enemy could rebuild, it took time and it was with personnel who had less training and less experience than the troops they replaced.[14] He believed that eventually the enemy would reach a point when they could no longer maintain the replacement rates and their numbers would begin to decline; the crossover point was his sign that the end of the war was coming into view.

The April crossover

At a short conference held in Guam on 20 and 21 March 1967, General Westmoreland told both President Johnson and South Vietnamese President Nguyen Van Thieu that the enemy's losses would soon exceed his gains. As recounted in the Pentagon Papers,

> Recent American successes reinforced the belief that we had hit upon the key to winning – despite continued large scale infiltration, Westmoreland and others on his staff believed we were again flirting with the illusive 'crossover point' when the enemy total strength would begin to decline, battle, disease and desertion losses would exceed gains.[15]

General Westmoreland was more emphatic in April 1967, the crossover point had been reached. On his first of three trips back to the United States in 1967, General Westmoreland told President Johnson on April 27, 'The VC (Viet Cong, communist forces from within South Vietnam) and DRV (Democratic Republic of Vietnam, communist forces from North Vietnam) strength in SVN (South Vietnam) now totals 285,000 men. It appears that last month we reached the crossover point in areas excluding the two northern provinces. Attritions will be greater than additions to the force.'[16]

Communist forces in South Vietnam were indeed declining (see Figure 2). Intelligence showed that communist forces, as listed in the MACV Order of Battle Summary, had peaked in August of 1966 at 301,100 men. By February 1967, the latest figures General Westmoreland probably would have had available to him, the numbers had dropped to 288,900.[17] The numbers backed General Westmoreland in his assessment that the enemy's forces had peaked and were on the decline.

In retrospect and based upon the last Order of Battle Summary published by MACV in November of 1972, General Westmoreland's assessment that a crossover point had been reached was basically correct, although the enemy's numbers would reach another crossover point with higher numbers during the Tet Offensive. With a better understanding and refinement over the following years, the final order of battle listing carried higher numbers, but essentially followed the same increase and decrease rates (see Figure 3). The later figures show the communist forces reached their first peak in October 1966 (instead of August) with a substantially higher number of 371,358 (the increase was an additional 40,000 in the number of political infrastructure personnel and another additional 28,000 administrative and

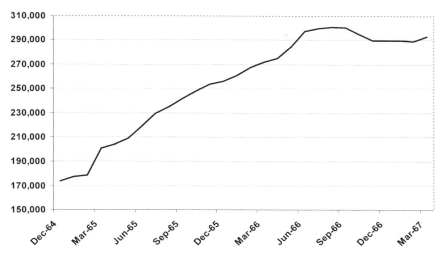

Figure 2 Communist strength totals through April 1967.

Source: Military Assistance Command, Vietnam (MACV) monthly order of battle for April 1967.

services troops). The numbers then steadily decreased throughout 1967, which supported Westmoreland's assessment given to the President in April.

However, as the enemy prepared for the Tet Offensive, their numbers spiked to a new high of 372,165 in January 1968. After Tet, the numbers sharply decreased (the Viet Cong guerrillas were essentially destroyed as a combat force) and continued a general downward decline until 1972, when American ground forces were departing. In retrospect, there were two cross-over points, one in October 1966 and another in January 1968. General Westmoreland was not wrong in assessing that a crossover point had been reached in late 1966.

The delusion

From General Westmoreland's vantage point in April 1967, the numbers had peaked and were in a general decline. However correct General West-moreland was in his assessment that a crossover point had been reached, he was incorrect in assuming this meant that the end of the war was in sight. The crossover point was a delusion; a delusion he was to propagate to the President and to the American public. The crossover point is just a straightforward statistic gauging the enemy's numbers; the enemy was far more complex than a simple set of figures.

The crossover point does not foretell the impending defeat of the enemy. One of the first dictums of war deals not with numbers, but with will. The

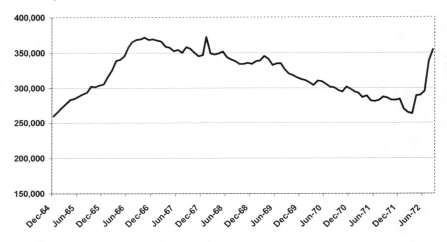

Figure 3 Communist strength totals through August 1972.

Source: Military Assistance Command, Vietnam (MACV) monthly order of battle for August 1972.

two grandmasters of military strategy, Sun Tzu and Carl von Clausewitz, both agree that war is not a matter of numbers, but is instead a contest of wills, where moral influence can negate numerical advantage. When assessing the enemy, Sun Tzu offered five fundamental factors which must be considered, the first being moral influence, the willingness to die for the cause.[18] He further admonished, 'In war, numbers alone confer no advantage.'[19]

Clausewitz defined war as 'an act of force to compel our enemy to do our will.'[20] Clausewitz offered two primary factors that must be considered when looking at the enemy, 'The total means at his disposal and the strength of his will.'[21] Clausewitz went further and stressed that the most important judgment that the statesman and military commander must make is to determine the nature of the war they are embarking upon. When looking at the nature of war, the strength of the motivation is a primary consideration. 'The more powerful and inspiring the motives for war, the more they affect the belligerent nations . . .'[22]

General Westmoreland did pay lip service to this important precept. After telling the President that the crossover point had been reached, he cautioned that 'unless the will of the enemy is broken or unless there is an unraveling of the VC infrastructure the war could go on for 5 years.' But in his very next sentence, the caution was revealed for what it was, a hedge to get more troops. He continued, 'If our forces were increased that period could be reduced . . .' He concluded his brief by forecasting that with 665,000 men, the war could be concluded in two years.[23]

In Westmoreland's view, victory in Vietnam was dependent upon numbers. More US troops and an enemy whose numbers had reached the crossover point insured victory in two years. General Westmoreland had read Sun Tzu,[24] but was at heart a student of what has been coined by Russell F. Weigley as the 'American Way of War;' superior numbers can pound anything into submission.[25] More US troops could more quickly eliminate more enemy troops.

Intelligence crosses over

In April of 1967 when General Westmoreland had determined the crossover point had been reached, his intelligence chief, or J2 in military parlance, was thinking more along the lines of Sun Tzu and Clausewitz. Joseph A. McChristian, then a Brigadier General, had arrived in Vietnam in May of 1965 and had overseen the 'Americanization' of the war's intelligence efforts. But in April of 1967, his tour of duty was drawing to a close. One aspect of his tour remained constant throughout, every intelligence briefing on the enemy he gave ended with 'The North Vietnamese and Viet Cong have *the will and capability* to conduct a protracted war of attrition at current levels of activity *indefinitely*.'[26] General Westmoreland's assessment that the crossover point had been reached did not come from his J2, who did not see manpower as one of the enemy's vulnerabilities.[27]

McChristian, however, was nearing the end of his two-year tour in Vietnam, and on 1 June 1967 he was replaced by Phillip B. Davidson, then a Brigadier General. The first thing Davidson did was to drop what he called McChristian's 'pat' assessment that the enemy had the will and capability to continue indefinitely.[28] He believed the enemy's numbers were hurting and he also subscribed to the viewpoint that the crossover point was important and that it had been reached. In a briefing to Secretary of Defense McNamara in July 1967, he said:

> Overall, the enemy must be having personnel problems. His losses have been heavy, and his in-country recruiting efforts unsatisfactory. He is probably attempting to make good his losses by heavy infiltration, but we cannot conclusively prove this, nor do we know how successful he has been. We hear frequently of the so-called 'Crossover point' – that is, when we put out of action more enemy per month than we estimate he brought into country and recruited for that month. This is a nebulous figure, composed as you have seen of several tenuous variables. We may have reached the 'crossover point' in March and May of this year, but we will not know for some months.[29]

Intelligence at MACV had crossed over to the simplistic calculation that decreasing enemy numbers equals success.

Graphing the crossover

The numbers gauging the enemy's strength were closely analyzed and monitored. These numbers were published monthly by MACV in their Order of Battle Summary. The summary was first published in December of 1964 and continued until November of 1972. The MACV Monthly Order of Battle Summary was used to track the enemy strength and thus gauge the progress of the war. The summary was used by intelligence, the military leadership, the national leadership, the media, and ultimately, the American people, to measure the success of General Westmoreland's strategy of attrition.

Compiled on a monthly basis, the Order of Battle Summary was an evolving document, which took in all available non-sensitive information, often weeks or months old, to refine and recalculate the enemy's strength. Sanitized technical intelligence was used, as were more abundant and less reliable sources such as prisoner interrogations, defector interrogations, informants, and captured documents.

Timeliness was not an attainable goal in producing the summary. As the information became available it was used, but interrogation reports, for example, were typically months old and it took considerable time to translate enemy documents. An accurate count was only possible after this information was belatedly factored in and the numbers retroactively adjusted. Thus, an accurate picture of the enemy's strength only became clear after several months had passed. By then, MACV was already several months behind the 'new' current picture, and so the cycle continued.

When General McChristian first arrived in Vietnam in 1965, intelligence had little understanding of, or capability to count, the enemy. The enemy America faced in Vietnam took many forms. There were enemy units composed of just North Vietnamese; these units were organized in a way similar to US forces into brigades and divisions. There were also the Viet Cong (VC), who were indigenous South Vietnamese communists; their organizational structure was varied, with main forces that were similar to the brigades of the North Vietnamese, and local forces which were closely tied to a limited geographic area and sometimes operated as brigades, but just as often took on less stringently defined structures. Then there were the VC guerrillas who were closely tied to a particular geographic area and were loosely organized in a manner that did not mirror any US force structure. There were also the militia, or self-defense forces, composed of mostly youngsters and the elderly who never left their villages and seldom even had rifles. All of these forces were also supported by administrative and services troops. Overseeing every aspect of the military and the war effort were the members of what became known as the political infrastructure.

McChristian built an organization and obtained the resources necessary to conduct viable intelligence in Vietnam. He first concentrated his new organization and resources on the task of determining the number, capability, and intent of the main and local forces. Once he felt confident he had reliable figures for these forces, he turned his attention to the guerrillas, the self-defense forces, and the political infrastructure. At about the same time as General Westmoreland told President Johnson that the crossover point had been reached, McChristian's intelligence organization had reached a more accurate total for the enemy's overall numbers. The greatest change was in the self-defense forces, which had been undercounted by at least 50,000.[30]

The more accurate intelligence presented a dilemma for General West-moreland. The numbers were going down, the intelligence data showed this, but now the numbers had to be corrected upward, not because the enemy had increased his numbers, but because they had been originally undercounted. The enemy had in fact peaked and his numbers were decreas-ing, but if someone just looked at the order of battle numbers with the new, more accurate self-defense figures, it would appear that the enemy's forces were increasing.

Serendipitously for General Westmoreland, McChristian was nearing the end of his tour, and his replacement, Brigadier General Phillip Davidson, had a solution for this dilemma. For McChristian, anything that could affect the mission of the US military in Vietnam should be counted in the order of battle; this included the self-defense forces.[31] However, his replace-ment did not hold the same point of view. For Davidson, the self-defense forces were not combat troops, being composed of the elderly and the young with few weapons, and therefore, should not be included in enemy strength figures.[32] Under Davidson, the self-defense forces were officially dropped from the order of battle in September 1967. Thus, the more accurate numbers (minus the self-defense forces) depicted the continued decline (see Figure 4). General Westmoreland's dilemma was solved and the crossover delusion preserved without complicated explanations.

MACV was the primary purveyor of the enemy strength figures. However, in April of 1967, Secretary of Defense McNamara tasked the CIA to double check the MACV numbers.[33] The CIA now became a potential rival source for the enemy strength figures, and a potential detractor of the crossover delusion.

Crossing the Agency

The Central Intelligence Agency is the nation's foremost intelligence organi-zation. The community of intelligence organizations is not large, but is far from a single voice. Both the State and Defense Departments maintain a robust intelligence capability as do the individual military services and the combatant military commands. But only one works for the President. The Director of Central Intelligence (DCI), while the nominal head of the entire intelligence community, is first and foremost, the head of the CIA, and he works for the President.

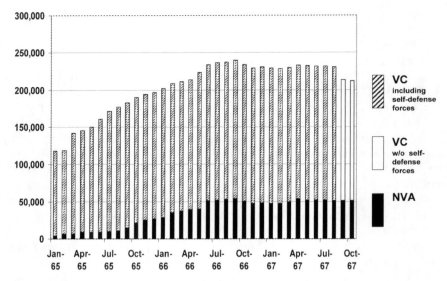

Figure 4 Communist combat strength through October 1967.

Source: Military Assistance Command, Vietnam (MACV) monthly order of battle for October 1967.

The CIA had been following the situation in Vietnam for some time, and under President Kennedy, the CIA had established the Special Assistant for Vietnamese Affairs (SAVA) to provide exclusive expertise on Vietnam. Richard Helms, the DCI from June 1966 to February 1973, found Vietnam to be a vexing problem throughout his tenure; 'Vietnam was my nightmare for a good ten years.'[34] A nightmare on many levels, including the bureaucratic. When it came to Vietnam, CIA and MACV seldom agreed, particularly with regard to the enemy's numbers and the enemy's willingness to continue fighting.

Both MACV and CIA followed the enemy's numbers and had varied opinions as to who should be counted and just how many there were. The intelligence community, and particularly the DCI, wanted to speak with one authoritative voice. Having two sets of varying numbers and different categories for counting the enemy did not benefit any decision maker using the intelligence, nor did it help the President's administration in attempting to explain to the American public how the war was progressing. The seeds for a bureaucratic fight were germinated and ready to sprout as unwanted weeds.

As described by DCI Richard Helms in his memoirs, *A Look Over My Shoulder*,

> The discrepancy between the Agency's O/B [order of battle] estimates of the enemy military and guerrilla forces in South Vietnam and the more

optimistic figures prepared by the MACV intelligence staff was one of the most persistent of the various intelligence bones of contention between the Agency and the Department of Defense. It had existed from the early days of our military involvement in Vietnam, and by 1966 had developed into a mean and nasty conflict.[35]

Just who should have the responsibility to count the enemy? Should it be the nation's foremost intelligence agency with their talented analysts sitting in Washington, DC, or should it be the soldiers on the ground fighting the enemy? In CIA's defense, they did have a large contingent of personnel in Vietnam and their analysts tended to work Vietnam issues even before they arrived in country and continued their involvement with Vietnam after they left. The intelligence personnel at MACV, while fighting the enemy and getting at the truth on the ground, had little understanding of Vietnam or the enemy before their arrival and tended to work the issue only during their one- or two-year tour in Vietnam. But, and this is a big but, it was the MACV commander, General Westmoreland who had to fight the enemy, not the DCI. It was his soldiers who fought and died against the enemy and it was his responsibility to the President and the country to know and defeat the enemy.

As the crossover point took on greater significance to General Westmoreland and the military, the importance of speaking with one voice became not only the DCI's concern, but the military's as well. In January 1967, voicing concerns over 'contradictory order of battle and infiltration statistics,' the Chairman of the Joint Chiefs of Staff, General Earle Wheeler, directed the military to meet with their civilian counterparts to 'standardize methods for developing and presenting statistics on order of battle and infiltration trends; and insure that this system is used as the single formal source for this information by all agencies involved.'[36]

Intelligence representatives from MACV, CIA, the National Security Agency (NSA), and the Defense Intelligence Agency (DIA) gathered for a conference to resolve once and for all who had the responsibility in accounting for the enemy, MACV on the ground in Vietnam, or CIA with all their analysts in Washington, DC. From the beginning of the conference, held in Hawaii from 6 to 11 February, there was no doubt who counted the enemy. General McChristian, MACV/J2, told the conferees in his opening remarks, 'The Viet Cong order of battle is MACV's business, which is to say, my business.'[37]

By the end of the conference, MACV's definitions, methods, and numbers were accepted by all attendees and published in the *Report of the Conference to Standardize Methods for Developing and Presenting Statistics on Order of Battle, Infiltration Trends and Estimates*. In the cover letter signed by the Commander of the US Forces in the Pacific, Admiral U.S. Grant Sharp, all participants 'agreed to implement as soon as possible all specific recommendations which are within their purview.'[38] One of the specific recommendations stated that MACV was to be 'the primary source for statistical computation on enemy order of battle, infiltration and base areas in South Vietnam.' Further, all attendees agreed that statistical data from MACV 'should be utilized by all agencies which prepare reports, estimates, briefings, etc.'[39]

The conference ended amicably, with the participants in basic agreement and a bit surprised that no major conflicts had erupted; a truce of sorts had been achieved. Both MACV and CIA were in agreement on the numbers and who should be counted. CIA representatives were pleased when McChristian informed the conference that he had new intelligence which revealed the need to revise the enemy's numbers upward.[40] They were also in agreement with the definitions, which included self-defense forces.[41]

The Agency crosses over

The truce, however, was short-lived. General McChristian left Vietnam four months later, and his replacement, General Davidson, did not see the enemy in the same manner as did McChristian nor as described in the *Report of the Conference to Standardize Methods for Developing and Presenting Statistics on Order of Battle, Infiltration Trends and Estimates*. When the CIA convened its own conference at its headquarters in Langley, Virginia, to formulate the National Intelligence Estimate (NIE) for Vietnam in August of 1967, MACV did not agree with CIA's numbers and the categories for the enemy order of battle. The numbers and categories were not at variance with the agreed guidelines established at the February Order of Battle conference, but they were at odds with General Davidson's solution to General Westmoreland's crossover dilemma. In order to show a continued decline in the enemy's numbers without any convoluted explanations, MACV insisted that the self-defense forces be dropped from the order of battle numbers.

General Westmoreland himself weighed in on the issue in a message sent from the Philippines where he was on vacation with his family.

> I do not concur with the inclusion of SD [self-defense] and SSD [secret self-defense] strength figures in the overall enemy strength. It distorts the situation and makes no sense. No possible explanations could prevent the erroneous conclusions that would result.[42]

The NIE conference ended in an impasse, leaving CIA director Richard Helms with his own dilemma, to go with his own analyst's view of the order of battle using the agreed-upon categories arrived at during the Hawaii Order of Battle Conference in February 1967, or to go with the new view of the enemy order of battle as now envisioned by MACV. In Hawaii, CIA had agreed that MACV would be the final word regarding the order of battle, but now MACV was disregarding the definitions and methods agreed upon at that same conference.

Not wishing to highlight disagreements within the intelligence community and to speak as a single voice, Richard Helms sent a delegation to Saigon in September of 1967 to settle the order of battle contention once and for all. He made it known to MACV that he alone signed the NIE, but he was also very much aware that it was the military on the ground who faced the enemy of which they debated. After six days of acrimonious, caustic, and at times very personal debate, the MACV position was accepted; no figures on the self-defense forces would be included in the NIE. As a compromise, MACV relented in allowing the self-defense forces to be mentioned, but not in any figures or graphs, only textually and with no numbers assigned.

Richard Helms explains his reasoning for the compromise in his memoirs:

> The responsibility for estimating the strength of the forces it faces in the field is traditionally, and properly, the responsibility of the military. Even in static positions with opposing forces in uniform, O/B estimates are a far cry from laboratory science. In paramilitary/guerrilla situations, O/B estimates are of necessity often based on extrapolations from shaky evidence, a process not to be confused with a test-tube DNA analysis. It was never my intention to insist that the Agency estimate – prepared by civilian staffs in Washington – override those of the military who were face-to-face with the enemy in the field.[43]

At the same time, however, Helms does not agree with the MACV reasoning.

> There was also a significant political problem. The MACV staff had long claimed that the enemy was suffering such significant losses in South Vietnam that by mid-1967 the casualties might be expected to exceed the replacement capability. In view of the continuing increase in U.S. personnel and armaments in South Vietnam, any admission that the Viet Cong were actually gaining strength would obviously have stirred a severe public reaction on the home front.[44]

Helms holds General Westmoreland responsible. 'In effect, the general commanding MACV had taken a 'Command Decision' as to the facts bearing on the O/B problem, and his subordinates had no choice but to fall in line.'[45]

Special National Intelligence Estimate (SNIE) Number 14.3–67, *Capabilities of the Vietnamese Communists for Fighting in South Vietnam* was issued on 13 November 1967 and contained no figures disputing the crossover delusion. In fact, the estimate endorsed General Westmoreland's assessment that the enemy had reached the crossover point and its forces were in decline.

Manpower is a major problem confronting the Communists. Losses have been increasing and recruitment in South Vietnam is becoming more difficult. Despite heavy infiltration from North Vietnam, the strength of the Communist military forces and political organizations in South Vietnam declined in the last year. . . . we believe there is a fairly good chance that the overall strength and effectiveness of the military forces and the political infrastructure will continue to decline.[46]

Helms and the CIA too had fallen into line and accepted the crossover delusion.

Deluding the Johnson administration

With intelligence now speaking with one voice and endorsing the measure of success as being the crossover point, the Johnson administration sought to unify support for the war within its own ranks. Inside the White House there were two camps: a small contingent questioned the US involvement in Vietnam, and a much larger camp that supported the war. There were some, including Secretary of Defense Robert McNamara, who outwardly carried on the war against the communists in Vietnam, but who harbored increasing doubts as to its efficacy. To shore up support within his administration, President Johnson summoned a group of elder statesmen known as the 'Wise Men' for advice in early November 1967.

As he had at the time of escalation in 1965, the President turned to his Senior Advisory Group, the Wise Old Men (or WOMS, as they were called by White House staffers). There were eleven who responded to Johnson's summons in early November: Dean Acheson, the chief elder; Clark Clifford, LBJ's closest private adviser and a resolute backer of the war; Supreme Court Justice Abe Fortas, another LBJ crony and Clifford's fellow hawk; McGeorge Bundy, the former National Security Adviser who had graduated to Wise Men status; Maxwell Taylor, the Kennedys' favorite general and former ambassador to Saigon; Omar Bradley, the chairman of the JCS during the Korean War; Robert Murphy, General Lucius Clay's political adviser in Berlin and a high State Department official under Dulles; Henry Cabot Lodge, former ambassador to Vietnam; Arthur Dean, Dulles's law partner and US armistice negotiator in Korea; Douglas Dillon, Kennedy's Treasury secretary and leader of the New York Establishment; and George Ball, the in-house dove who had resigned as Under Secretary of State the year before. One elder statesman who had never left government was also included: Averell Harriman.

It was a formidable assemblage, a rich blend of Wall Street and Washington, soldiers and diplomats, men who had shaped and preserved a bipartisan foreign policy consensus for two decades. . . . But all shared a familiarity with power and a conviction that the US must fulfill its rightful role as world leader.[47]

This 'formidable assemblage' gathered for cocktails and briefings on 1 November 1967. Chairman of the Joint Chiefs of Staff, General Earle Wheeler presented the latest figures, numbers, and statistics from General Westmoreland in Vietnam, all of which clearly showed that the US military was making progress and winning the war in Vietnam. The Wise Men were also told by Secretary of State Dean Rusk that while there was nothing but good news coming from Vietnam, the American public was unaware of the progress.[48]

The next morning the Wise Men gathered in the Cabinet Room and met with President Johnson. Dean Acheson led off, stating that he was very encouraged by the briefing from General Wheeler. 'I got the impression that this is a matter we can and will win,' he told the President. 'We certainly should not get out of Vietnam.' Acheson recalled for President Johnson how he had organized the Citizen's Committee for the Marshall Plan to mobilize public support for European revitalization. He suggested to the President that such a committee was needed for Vietnam.[49] McGeorge Bundy seconded Acheson, stating, 'Getting out of Vietnam is as impossible as it is undesirable.' He felt that what was needed was more public support and concluded that the Administration should emphasize 'the light at the end of the tunnel.'[50] General Omar Bradley built on this theme and said that more patriotic slogans were needed.

The Johnson Administration embraced the recommendations of the Wise Men and immediately set about implementing a public relations campaign. General Westmoreland was recalled home and led the campaign tour that evoked 'the light at the end of the tunnel.'[51]

The crossover delusion was now accepted by the Johnson administration, the next step was to convince the American public to jump on the bandwagon. As recommended by the Wise Men, General Westmoreland was called upon to lead the campaign. As General Westmoreland relates, 'President Johnson summoned me home again, along with Ambassador Bunker, in November 1967, ostensibly for further consultations, but in reality for public relations purposes. Dissent in the press and the Congress was growing.'[52]

Deluding the American public

With figures from his own intelligence at MACV that clearly illustrated that the enemy had reached the crossover point, and with the endorsement from the CIA and the rest of the intelligence community in SNIE 14.3-67 that the enemy was suffering manpower problems and its numbers were on the decline, General Westmoreland was prepared to tell the public in November 1967 what he had told the President in private in April: the end was in sight.

Up until November 1967, General Westmoreland had proven very difficult to pin down on just how long he thought the war effort would last in Vietnam. Although he had been back to the United States three times in 1967 (April, July, November), it was not until the last trip that he felt confident enough to make any predictions on how long the war in Vietnam would continue. In his April 1967 trip, General Westmoreland had expressed to President Johnson that he felt the crossover point had been reached, but could not answer all of President Johnson's questions. General Westmoreland was reluctant to give the President any forecast of when the US could begin drawing down, but under persistent questioning from Secretary of Defense McNamara, General Westmoreland begrudgingly replied, 'With the optimum force, about three years; with the minimum force, at least five.'[53] This was a gloomy prospect after what had already been two years of involvement, especially so when the President had approved the minimum force General Westmoreland had requested. No such forecast was given to the press or public.

General Westmoreland made another trip in July 1967, this time to attend the funeral of his mother in South Carolina. He visited Washington, DC before returning to Vietnam and at a press conference there he talked of 'tremendous progress,' but when asked to forecast how much longer the US would remain in Vietnam he replied, 'I am in no position to speculate on that.'[54] In November 1967, however, with intelligence to back him up, he was in a position to answer authoritatively.

The confidence to look into the future and proclaim the enemy 'bankrupt' was bolstered by the new intelligence coming out of MACV/J2 with new and improved numbers and by the intelligence community's guarded optimism in SNIE 14.3–67. With numbers that could graphically illustrate the enemy's downward slide, and the intelligence community's assessment that the enemy was hurting, with the guerrillas suffering 'substantial reduction' and that the 'overall strength and effectiveness of the military forces and the political infrastructure will continue to decline,'[55] General Westmoreland had the evidence and backing he needed to show that the US had been effective in his war of attrition. He now felt confident and optimistic enough to announce, 'It is conceivable to me that within two years or less, it will be possible for us to phase down our level of commitment and turn more of the burden of the war over to the Vietnamese Armed Forces who are improving and who, I believe, will be prepared to assume this greater burden.'[56]

General Westmoreland's optimism was carried over into the press which printed his enthusiastic statements, such as the 27 November 1967 issue of *Time*, in which he said, 'I have never been more encouraged in my four years in Vietnam.'[57] To his staff back in MACV, General Westmoreland sent a cable explaining his public optimism. He told them he felt his confidence was in line with the progress of the war and that he wanted to portray to the American public that there was 'some light at the end of the tunnel.'[58]

In the words of Don Oberdorfer, author of *Tet!*, General Westmoreland 'uttered fourteen words which the public was longing to hear,' at the National Press Club on 21 November 1967. 'We have reached an important point when the end begins to come into view.'[59]

With a definite end of the war in sight, the American public caught some of the optimism General Westmoreland brought with him to the United States in November 1967. Even the popularity of President Johnson, which had been on a long downward spiral, recovered 10 points in one month to reach almost 50 percent after General Westmoreland's optimistic trip.[60] The number of people responding that they supported the war also halted a downward trend after General Westmoreland's predictions. The number of people opposing the war also stopped increasing. The overall public trends, which had been increasingly anti-war, were halted in November 1967. The public seemed willing to await a verdict on the validity of General Westmoreland's words.

In August 1965, when asked 'In view of the developments since we entered the fighting in Vietnam, do you think the US made a mistake sending troops to fight in Vietnam?' 61 percent responded that they supported the war effort in Vietnam, with 24 percent opposing, leaving 15 percent voicing no opinion. By September of 1966, the percent approving of the war had slipped 13 points to 48 percent, while those opposed to the war had increased 11 points to 35 percent. By October of 1967, one month before General Westmoreland's public relations tour, a crossover point had been reached in the American public, with more people opposing the war than support-ing it. In answer to the same question above, 44 percent supported the war while 46 percent now opposed the war.[61]

After General Westmoreland's November 1967 visit, the trend was halted, with a slight reversal countering the October crossover, with those support-ing the war, at 46 percent, now slightly outnumbering those who opposed the war, at 45 percent. American public opinion was delicately balanced, awaiting a sign that what General Westmoreland had said was true, that America had mauled the enemy into bankruptcy, and its 'overall strength and effectiveness . . . will continue to decline'[62] (see Figure 5).

Walter W. Rostow, in his book *The Diffusion of Power*, described the public mood as follows:

> In November 1967 there was a pause in the erosion of support for Johnson's policy in Vietnam. There were temperately optimistic reports from General William Westmoreland and Ambassador Ellsworth Bunker, home from Saigon. Westmoreland's suggestion that American troops might begin safely to withdraw in two years was noted with some skep-ticism in the press; but it represented in the worst case – of neither a negotiated settlement nor a clear military victory – a significant element of hope.[63]

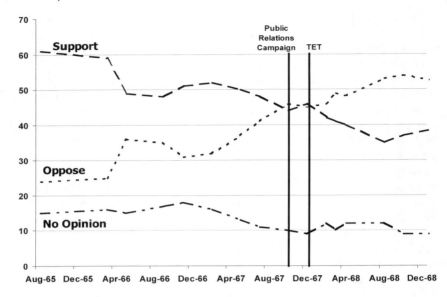

Figure 5 Public opinion 1965–1968.

Source: Data compiled from John E. Mueller, *War, Presidents and Public Opinion* (New York: John Wiley & Sons, Inc., 1973), 54–55.

Rostow then noted that at the end of 1967, with the 'pause in the erosion' of support for the war in effect, 50 percent of Americans thought the US was making progress in the war in Vietnam. Only 33 percent thought the US was standing still, while a scant 8 percent thought the US was losing ground.[64] The crossover point delusion was complete, but even as November ended there were ominous clouds on the horizon; the Tet monsoon would soon bring home reality with a vengeance. Although the enemy's numbers had declined in 1967, the enemy's will was far from broken.

Delusion meets reality

The crossover point, which was the measure of success used by General Westmoreland and MACV, was a delusion. As Sun Tzu warned, numbers alone confer no advantage in war; it is the determination and conviction for the cause, the will to fight, which is the true measure of victory. Clausewitz characterized war as a contest of wills, and the will of the communists in South Vietnam was far from broken. But General Westmoreland, deprived of more traditional methods to measure victory, fought the war as he had learned to fight, attack and attack again, until the enemy can no longer muster.

The enemy, however, did not subscribe to this point of view and mustered over 84,000 on 31 January 1968. Just two months after the rousing public relations campaign of General Westmoreland, the communists attacked with a ferocity and intensity that challenged the November forecast of a 'bankrupt' enemy. The reality of the enemy's will quickly smashed the delusion of their depleted numbers. But beyond the enemy's will, the reality called into question the credibility of those who had propagated the delusion. The credibility of General Westmoreland, the intelligence community, and the Johnson administration was shattered. The real loss, however, befell the American public. Feeling a growing sense of frustration – seeing more and more troops going to Vietnam and more and more troops dying, seeing their military, intelligence and President portray a defeated enemy only to then see that same enemy rise up en masse and mount a massive, coordinated, country-wide attack – the American public lost its faith in its leaders and its will to continue the fight.

4 The effect of Tet

A loss of trust

As a consequence, the offensive seemed to many in direct contradiction to President Johnson's campaign to demonstrate progress in the war, a refutation of my remarks at the Press Club two months earlier.

General William C. Westmoreland[1]

The effects of Tet were far-ranging, affecting the will of the American public, the credibility of intelligence, and the credibility of the leadership of both the military and the nation. Tet, in and of itself, was not the sole cause of these effects, but was the culmination point for a series of actions. In light of General Westmoreland's prognostications to the public in November 1967 and the tainted intelligence used to propagate the 'bankruptcy' of the enemy, the effects of Tet must be re-examined. Tet would not have had the effect it did had the military focused on the enemy's will and not the delusional crossover point. Tet would not have had the effect it did had intelligence understood the enemy's will and not become fixated on declining enemy numbers, perpetuating the crossover delusion. Tet would not have had the effect it did had intelligence not manipulated the enemy's numbers to avoid scrutiny of the crossover delusion. Tet would not have had the effect it did had the public not been told just over two months previously that the enemy was 'bankrupt,' in a public relations campaign to bolster support for the war based upon the crossover delusion.

Tet was a tremendous shock that amplified the fallacy of the crossover point. Tet was also a military surprise in several aspects – intensity, target, scope, coordination, and timing – which further diluted the already shaken credibility of intelligence and the military and national leadership. Tet was the turning point of the Vietnam War, and its effects were far-reaching.

The effects of the 1968 Tet Offensive spread throughout the spectrum of American society. For the American public, Tet marked the crossover point in support for the Vietnam War; whereas in 1967 the American public supported the war, by February of 1968 it did not. This effect on the American public was felt and brought home to President Johnson by the Wise Men; whereas in November 1967 the Wise Men had counseled the President to stay the course in Vietnam, in March 1968 they urged a change of course. President Johnson, seeing support ebbing ever lower, sought to convince the North Vietnamese he was sincere and not politically motivated in his aims for peace in Vietnam. To prove his sincerity, he gave up a chance for another term as President and dedicated the remainder of his term to finding peace. General Westmoreland, the square-jawed, broad shouldered epitome of an American general, who was viewed by President Johnson as a man who had credibility in the eyes of the American public, was mocked. Whereas General Westmoreland was a hero in November 1967, he was surely the scapegoat for many in 1968. And military intelligence, which had wasted so much energy and effort fighting over how to count the enemy in 1967 faced credibility questions of its own. How had 84,000 enemy troops obtained supplies, assembled, and attacked over 100 cities and towns simultaneously under their very noses? The effects of Tet were indeed far-reaching.

On the people: a loss of trust

> 'If this is a failure,' stated Senator George Aiken of Vermont, 'I hope the Viet Cong never have a major success.' The senator's incredulity was shared by millions of Americans watching the carnage nightly on the news, seeing US Marines torch huts with Zippo lighters and hearing one commander calmly explain, 'It became necessary to destroy the town in order to save it.' The press turned on the war: 'What is the end that justifies this slaughter?' asked James Reston. 'How will we save Vietnam if we destroy it in battle?' Once reliable backers of the war effort suddenly began to doubt.
>
> Walter Cronkite, *The Wall Street Journal*, *Time*, and *Life*[2]

The American public had been lulled into a sense of hope and security by the November public relations campaign of General Westmoreland. They grew uneasy with the gathering storm clouds as the US engaged in the 'border battles' in Vietnam. They felt apprehensive when General Westmoreland stated the fighting thus far in January had been the worst he had seen during the war, but surely things could not get any worse. When the Tet Offensive struck it left an indelible image in the minds of the public; the enemy was not cowed and beaten, but instead displayed 'a force, a fury, and a battlefield presence that gave the lie to all that Americans had been told for months.'[3] America's great army, armed with the latest devices of military superiority, seemed incapable of defeating the determined and tenacious enemy as evidenced every morning in the newspapers and witnessed every evening in living color on the television news.

The news analysis became more biased against the war, and even the stalwart of American credibility, the man America trusted more than any other, Walter Cronkite, questioned the viability of continued US fighting in Vietnam. He told his television audience on a CBS News special, *Report from Vietnam by Walter Cronkite*, broadcast on 27 February 1968 and viewed by a reported nine million Americans:

> It seems now more certain than ever that the bloody experience of Vietnam is to end in a stalemate. . . . To say that we are closer to victory today is to believe, in the face of the evidence, the optimists who have been wrong in the past. To suggest we are on the edge of defeat is to yield to unreasonable pessimism. To say that we are mired in stalemate seems the only realistic, yet unsatisfactory conclusion. On the off chance that military and political analysts are right, in the next months we must test the enemy's intentions in case this is indeed his last big gasp before negotiations. But it is increasingly clear to this reporter that the only rational way out then will be to negotiate, not as victors but as an honorable people who lived up to their pledge to defend democracy, and did the best they could. This is Walter Cronkite. Good night.[4]

Opinion, which had briefly been put on 'pause' by the November 1967 public relations tour, now fast forwarded to opposition. Walter W. Rostow, President Johnson's National Security Advisor, later noted, 'In November 1967 there was a pause in the erosion of support for Johnson's policy in Vietnam.'[5] After the Tet Offensive, there was a definite shift in public opinion, Rostow writes:

> But the fact was that Tet, the timing and nature of Johnson's response to it, and the popular interpretation of what had happened and why he had made the decisions he did, altered radically the structure of American public opinion toward the war.[6]

The American public, which had momentarily stopped its slide toward further opposition to the war and had reversed itself slightly after the November 1967 public relations campaign, again began its slide toward opposition of the war after the Tet Offensive. A crossover point was reached in this same time period when more people opposed the war than supported it. This point had been reached before in October 1967, but had been reversed by General Westmoreland's optimistic words. The enemy's actions spoke louder during Tet, and the crossover in public opinion against the war grew only larger as the months progressed. Those who felt the US was mired in stalemate steadily increased in numbers. In November 1967, 50 percent of Americans believed the US was making progress in Vietnam, by June 1968, only 18 percent held that view.[7]

On the Wise Men: a change of course

On 27 February 1968 President Johnson summoned the aging Cold War warrior Dean Acheson to the White House. When he arrived, Johnson began a tirade over the situation at Khe Sanh and never sought or asked any advice from Acheson. When the chance presented itself, Acheson left and returned to work. Shortly thereafter, he received a call from Johnson's National Security Advisor, Walter W. Rostow, asking where he had gone, the President wanted to talk to him. 'You tell the President – and you tell him in precisely these words,' Acheson told Rostow, 'that he can take Vietnam and stick it up his ass.' When President Johnson himself came on the line, Acheson acquiesced. He returned and told Johnson he was in no position to make any judgments on Vietnam. If Johnson wanted his opinion and advice, Acheson didn't want to be spoon-fed briefings as he and the other Wise Men had been in November 1967; he wanted complete access to the military and intelligence data on Vietnam. Johnson agreed.[8]

What Acheson wanted and received was unfiltered access 'to the engine room people.' Acheson was soon meeting with Philip Habib, a diplomat just back from two years in Vietnam, George Carver, the Special Assistant for Vietnam Affairs (SAVA) to the director of the CIA, and Major General William DuPuy, the former MACV/J3 (Chief of Staff for Operations) for General Westmoreland and a former field commander in Vietnam. From these he elicited the facts and figures, reports, background, and assumptions.[9] Acheson was most struck by the reports from the field which gave him the image of an enemy with suicidal determination and a confused American soldier suffering from low morale. One thing he had learned from his experience as Secretary of State for President Truman during the Korean War was not to believe the rosy predictions of generals; the same, he felt, was true for Vietnam. He searched in vain for light at the end of the tunnel, but the end was not coming into view.[10]

Another of the Wise Men was receiving a similar education. Clark Clifford, viewed by the other Wise Men as the most ardent of the hawks, was to take over from Robert McNamara as the Secretary of Defense on 1 March 1968. As part of the transition, he received a full 'A to Z' review of the war. After his swearing in he summoned the Joint Chiefs and began asking questions, hard questions; how many troops will it take, how many more years, what was the plan, were there any signs the enemy was being worn down? The answers he received he found unsatisfactory.[11]

Two of the original eleven Wise Men had arrived at similar conclusions: the war was not as it had been presented to them in November 1967. Acheson was called by the President to present his conclusions on 14 March. 'Mr. President,' Acheson told him, 'you are being led down the garden path.' Acheson said he was skeptical of General Westmoreland's claims, and felt the more important issue was whether South Vietnam could be made strong enough to fight the war on its own. He did not make any recommendation on US disengagement, but was hoping President Johnson would come to that conclusion on his own after ascertaining the true status of the war.[12]

At the same time, President Johnson was witnessing a transformation of Clark Clifford from a 'stout warrior to brooding doubter.'[13] As Clifford's doubts about the war grew, he sought a way to bring President Johnson to the same conclusions. On March 19, Clifford suggested to the President that he might want to reassemble the Wise Men whose counsel he had found so comforting last November; Johnson immediately agreed.[14]

Once again the Wise Men were summoned by their President. They gathered for briefings on 25 March 1968. The group retained the original eleven – Acheson, Clifford, Fortas, Bundy, General Taylor, General Bradley, Murphy, Lodge, Dean, Dillon, and Ball – and picked up two additions; Cyrus Vance, a former Deputy Secretary of Defense and Johnson trouble-shooter, and General Matthew Ridgway, who had stepped in during the Korean War to turn the Chinese tide.[15] That evening they discussed Vietnam and the future course of America's commitment overseas. Walter Isaacson and Evan Thompson described the historic supper in their book *The Wise Men*:

> Though they perhaps did not realize it, the Wise Men were meeting at the high-water mark of US hegemony. Never again would America's global commitments extend so far. After this evening, the US would begin to slowly and painfully pull back, to recognize the limits of its power. These men were about to play a critical role in reversing the momentum that they had done so much to generate over the last two decades. Though few were conscious of it, they were at one of history's turning points.[16]

After dinner the Wise Men received further briefings, this time from Acheson's instructors; Habib from State, General DuPuy from Defense, and Carver from the CIA. The briefings and questioning went on until 11 p.m. and it was a somber group that adjourned, except for one, George Ball. Ball had been the lone voice of dissension back in November, and now he could hardly believe the transformation that had occurred in the last three months.

The Wise Men reconvened the next morning for private discussions. General Ridgway read to the group his views which he had written out the night before. He opposed further troop increases, except those necessary for training the South Vietnamese who should be given two years to develop their own capability to defend their own government. After two years, General Ridgway felt the US could begin to phase down. General Bradley, former Ambassador Lodge and Cyrus Vance agreed that more was required of the South Vietnamese and less of the United States.[17]

After a morning of discussion, they joined President Johnson and his staff for an upbeat briefing from JCS Chairman General Wheeler who said that

General Westmoreland had turned the Tet Offensive around and proclaimed that the US was once again on the offensive. At lunch, President Johnson dismissed everyone except for the Wise Men. McGeorge Bundy, the youngest of the Wise Men, then reported on the group's earlier deliberations and summarized its views. There had been a 'significant shift' since the last meeting of the Wise Men in November, he told the President. He said Acheson had best stated the new majority view at their meeting that morning when he had remarked, 'We can no longer do the job we set out to do in the time we have left, and we must take steps to disengage.'[18]

Johnson scrawled on his note pad, 'Can no longer do job we set out to do. Adjust our course. Move to disengage.'[19] President Johnson, in his memoirs *The Vantage Point*, also recalled Bundy describing the change in attitude since November when they had hoped for slow and steady progress. 'That hope had been shaken by Tet.' Johnson also recalled that the Wise Men had a 'deep concern about the divisions in our country.'[20]

Not all the Wise Men were of such an opinion, but those who did not hold this view were in the minority. General Maxwell Taylor was amazed and at a loss to explain the change of heart, as were Justice Abe Fortas and Robert Murphy.[21] President Johnson was also taken aback and demanded to receive the same briefings the Wise Men had been given. Even after the briefings, Johnson remained baffled as to the near wholesale defection by this hardened group of foreign relations specialists. He could only lament, 'I don't know why they've drawn that conclusion.'[22]

On the President: the end of a presidency

With the press, the American public, many inside his administration, and now his own Wise Men recommending a change of course in American policy in Vietnam, President Lyndon Baines Johnson was at the crossroads of several intersecting political, military, and personal paths. Should he change the military course in Vietnam and seek a diplomatic end, or should he push forward and increase the troop levels that the military wanted? The primary elections for the upcoming 1968 presidential campaign were already underway, and although he was the Democratic incumbent, he had received an unexpectedly strong challenge from the peace candidate George McGovern. More troubling to the President, his nemesis Robert Kennedy, who had said that he would not challenge the President barring 'unforeseen circumstances,' was now viewing Tet as that 'unforeseen' circumstance. Vietnam was the issue dividing not only the Democratic party, but the entire nation. How was Johnson to heal this division? Physically, Johnson was tired. Vietnam had not only siphoned the resources he had hoped to use to create the Great Society he so wanted as his legacy as President, but had also drained him physically as the nation grew more and more divided. His personal goals of saving democracy abroad in Vietnam and ensuring democracy and equality at home were in jeopardy. Which path to choose?

President Johnson was scheduled to address the nation on March 31. This then was the deadline for his decision as to the course he would take in determining the future direction of America.

> My biggest worry was not Vietnam itself; it was the divisiveness and pessimism at home. I knew the American people were deeply worried. I had seen the effects of Tet on some of the Wise Men. I looked on my approaching speech as an opportunity to help right the balance and provide better perspective. For the collapse of the home front, I knew well, was just what Hanoi was counting on. The enemy had failed in Vietnam; would Hanoi succeed in the United States? I did not think so, but I was deeply concerned.[23]

With public opinion having crossed over from support to opposition to the war, with his Wise Men now recommending a change in course, with his Secretary of Defense transformed before his eyes from a hawk to a dove, President Johnson was at a loss to understand. He received the same briefings the Wise Men had, but he could not see what had changed their minds. He admitted in his memoirs he was surprised at the effect Tet had had on the country.

> I did not expect the enemy effort to have the impact on American thinking that it achieved. I was not surprised that elements of the press, the academic community, and the Congress reacted as they did. I was surprised and disappointed that the enemy's efforts produced such a dismal effect on various people inside government and others outside whom I had always regarded as staunch and unflappable.[24]

President Johnson in late March was still unsure what direction to take. He appeared ready to continue his own course in Vietnam, despite the polls, the advice from his Wise Men, and the counsel of his Secretary of Defense. His closest advisor in his Cabinet, however, had not yet spoken. Secretary of State Dean Rusk was stoic and held his thoughts closely guarded, except in private with the President. As the drafts of his upcoming speech were revised and updated, President Johnson's intention was to talk to the American people about the 'war' in Vietnam. In late March, after notes and discussions with Rusk, President Johnson changed the tone of his speech; he would now talk of 'peace' in Vietnam. The last straw stirred up in the monsoon winds of Tet had landed.

> Johnson trusted Rusk more than anyone. The Secretary was so slow, deliberate and cautious that Johnson could count on him to give careful, thoughtful advice. He accepted Rusk's argument that it was time to give diplomacy a chance with a partial bombing halt, as LBJ reasoned in his folksy way, 'Even a blind hog sometimes finds the chestnut.'[25]

A new course on Vietnam was now ready to be set. He would seek earnestly to negotiate with the North Vietnamese, but how to convince them he was sincere? He decided to merge his political and personal goals with those of Vietnam; to convince all that his quest for peace in Vietnam was not politically motivated, he would in essence abdicate the Presidency and not seek another term as President, devoting himself entirely to the search for peace in Vietnam.

> Good evening, my fellow Americans. Tonight I want to speak to you of peace in Vietnam and Southeast Asia. No other question so preoccupies our people.
>
> . . . There is no need to delay the talks that could bring an end to this long and this bloody war.
>
> . . . So, tonight, in the hope that this action will lead to early talks, I am taking the first step to de-escalate the conflict. We are reducing – substantially reducing – the present level of hostilities. And we are doing so unilaterally, and at once.
>
> . . . With America's sons in the fields far away, with America's future under challenge right here at home, with our hopes and the world's hopes for peace in the balance every day, I do not believe that I should devote an hour or a day of my time to any personal partisan causes or to any duties other than the awesome duties of this office – the Presidency of your country.
>
> Accordingly, I shall not seek, and I will not accept, the nomination of my party for another term as your President.
>
> . . . Thank you for listening. Good night and God bless all of you.[26]

The full effect of Tet had reached to the highest level of American government. Just as the French government of Joseph Laniel had collapsed in June of 1954 as a result of the Vietnam communist attacks on Dien Bien Phu, so too had the Johnson administration succumbed to the Viet Cong and North Vietnamese offensive at Tet. President Johnson, for all the briefings and advice and opinions he had received over the long years of the Vietnam War, still did not comprehend the objective or will of the enemy in their efforts to bring Vietnam under communism. For all the sacrifice, determination and intensity of purpose displayed by the enemy during the Tet Offensive, President Johnson still viewed Hanoi as a political foe haggling over a piece of legislation who could be turned if offered the right incentive. He just did not comprehend the motivation of the enemy. His almost naïve grasp of the enemy and their motivation is illustrated by his thoughts that they would be convinced of his sincerity, as if this was the enemy's motivation.

> By renouncing my candidacy, I expressed a fervent wish that problems that had resisted solution would now yield to resolution. I wanted

Hanoi to know that Lyndon Johnson was not using this new move toward peace as a bid for personal gain. Maybe now, with this clearest possible evidence of our sincerity thrown into the balance, North Vietnam would come forward and agree to a dialogue – genuine communication dedicated to peace.

. . . Just before I drifted off to sleep that night [31 March 1968], I prayed that Hanoi had listened and would respond. The chance for peace, the opportunity to stop death and destruction, and opening toward a new decade of hope – all these were enfolded in the words I had spoken. There was nothing more I could do that day. All that I could do I had done.[27]

The communists were uncompromising in their goal and recognized a lame duck when they saw one; they would, however, use his lack of understanding to further their goals. On the strategic level, President Johnson's decision not to seek re-election could be considered a political victory. A military goal was also to be achieved with the removal of General William C. Westmoreland as the Commander in Chief in Vietnam.

On the Commanding General: a loss of credibility

The reporters could hardly believe their ears. Westmoreland was standing in the ruins and saying everything was great.[28]

President Johnson had viewed his selection of General William C. Westmoreland to be the Commander of US forces in Vietnam as the perfect choice; the general invoked credibility. When he spoke, people listened and believed. He was the inevitable general,[29] whose very looks evoked confidence, whose voice spoke with authority; he was America's hope in Vietnam. As Don Oberdorfer described him in his book *Tet!*, 'He was the answer to Lyndon Johnson's prayers. He had credibility. He would be believed.'

The Tet Offensive of 1968 shattered this image. The sources of his downfall were intelligence and his efforts to manage the press through intelligence. General Westmoreland's predilection not to give the press a chance to question the enemy's numbers and to portray an attrited foe allowed him to proceed without distraction on his public relations campaign in November of 1967. He had manipulated the press to his own advantage, avoiding questions which would have detracted and diverted attention from the message he sought to deliver, that the US was winning. His words that the end was in sight were what Americans were longing to hear from their leader on the ground in Vietnam. That he had refused to speculate on such issues before November lent even more credence to his words. The figures and the intelligence supported his claims and were key to his making such a forecast.

The intensity and scope of the enemy's Tet Offensive immediately called into question the validity of General Westmoreland's assessment of the situation in Vietnam which he had given in November. General Westmoreland then reinforced the view of a vigorous enemy when it was reported on 10 March that he had requested an additional 206,000 troops.[30] His inexplicable lack of foresight on how the press would react to this request is truly astounding, especially given his determination in 1967 to exclude the press from knowing that intelligence had underestimated the enemy's guerrilla and self-defense forces. With the request for additional troops on the record, Westmoreland was hit from three directions – ridiculed for his optimistic reports in November, ridiculed for letting the enemy mass under his very nose, and now ridiculed for requesting an additional 206,000 troops in order to attain the victory which he had assured America of gaining in November against a foe whose numbers he said had been steadily decreasing.

George C. Herring described the situation in his book on Vietnam, *America's Longest War*:

> Televised accounts of the bloody fighting in Saigon and Hue made a mockery of Johnson and of Westmoreland's optimistic year-end reports, widening the credibility gap, and cynical journalists openly mocked Westmoreland's claims of victory. The humorist Art Buchwald parodied the general's statements in terms of Custer at Little Big Horn. 'We have the Sioux on the run,' Buchwald had Custer saying. 'Of course we still have some cleaning up to do, but the redskins are hurting badly and it will only be a matter of time before they give in.'[31]

Herbert Y. Schandler, in his book *The Unmaking of a President* offered this observation of the public's view on General Westmoreland:

> After the Tet offensive, General Westmoreland began to bear the brunt of congressional and press criticism for the Vietnam stalemate, primarily because of his optimistic public statements. He was identified in the public mind as the general who had predicted victory, had then been surprised by the enemy, and had requested 206,000 additional reinforcements.[32]

The very actions and words which had made General Westmoreland so credible were now his downfall. Ironically, his downfall and disrepute came at the very time when his military strategy of attrition had deeply hurt the Viet Cong forces. The enemy had done what Westmoreland's military forces could not do, mass their forces and stand and fight to the death. An attacking force of 84,000 lost over half their numbers, 45,000, not to mention the wounded and those who were to die later from their battlefield injuries, or the large numbers of defectors. The losses suffered were staggering. Militarily, the enemy had been dealt a significant setback.

Politically, the enemy's goal of fighting its own protracted war of attrition had the greatest impact during Tet. The goal of attrition was not one of the stated objectives of the enemy's Tet Offensive, but it had always been one of the consistent guiding principles of the enemy's efforts against the United States; send as many dead American sons home to the United States as possible. Tet met this enemy objective and General Westmoreland was the target of America's frustration.

General Westmoreland's continued tenure as Commander in Chief in Vietnam was becoming increasingly doubtful. At the outset of the Tet Offensive, President Johnson sent instructions to General Westmoreland:

> We are facing, in these next few days, a critical phase in the American public's understanding and confidence toward our effort in Vietnam. . . . To be specific, nothing can more dramatically counter scenes of VC destructiveness than the confident professionalism of the Commanding General. . . . Appearances by you, in the immediate situation, will make a greater impact here at home than much of what we can say.[33]

But President Johnson had played the credibility card once too often, and now, when it was needed the most, General Westmoreland's credibility was 'bankrupt.'

In February 1968, President Johnson expressed his full confidence in General Westmoreland, declaring 'I have no intention of seeing him leave.' One month later, on March 22, he announced that he would be bringing General Westmoreland home to become the Army's Chief of Staff. The two pillars of American involvement of Vietnam were to be gone by the end of the year 1968; the enemy's Tet Offensive effectively removed the opposition's political leader, President Johnson, and the military leader, General Westmoreland.

On the intelligence community: the scapegoat

The intelligence community was recovering from the bruising and confrontational battle over how to categorize and count the enemy in Vietnam. Hard feelings were still abundant on both sides. Then, Tet hit with an intensity unforeseen by anyone. The press, the public, and Congress wanted an accounting. How was this enemy, which was so decimated, with supply lines under constant bombardment, able to supply and mass such a force under our very noses? The natural scapegoat was intelligence, with many comparing the situation to Pearl Harbor, to the North Korean invasion of South Korea, and the Chinese entry into the Korean War.

Johnson convened the President's Foreign Intelligence Advisory Board (PFIAB) to investigate and determine if the military had indeed been surprised and if so, who was responsible. A working group was set up to assist the PFIAB. The group consisted of intelligence specialists from the Central Intelligence Agency, the Defense Intelligence Agency, the National Security Agency, the Joint Staff, and the State Department. The working group traveled to Saigon on 16 March 1968 and stayed until 23 March, gathering information, reviewing reports and interviewing personnel. The board summarized its findings to the President as follows:

> Although warning had thus been provided, the intensity, coordination, and timing of the enemy attack were not fully anticipated. Ambassador Bunker and General Westmoreland attest to this. The most important factor was timing. Few United States or GVN [government of South Vietnam] officials believed the enemy would attack during Tet, nor did the Vietnamese public. There was good reason for this: Tet symbolized the solidarity of the Vietnamese people.
>
> A second major unexpected element was the number of simultaneous attacks mounted. United States intelligence had given the enemy a capability of attacking virtually all of the points which he did in fact attack and of mounting coordinated attacks in a number of areas. He was not, however, granted a specific capability for coordinated attacks in all areas at once. More important, the nature of the targets was not anticipated. Washington and Saigon expected attacks on some cities, but they did not expect the offensive to have the cities, the civilian command and control centers, radio stations, and police headquarters as primary objectives.[34]

That a major enemy offensive was in the offing was foretold by military intelligence in Saigon. But, the offensive was viewed like any other offensive the enemy had cyclically launched throughout the war.[35] No special significance or purpose was attached to it. Five specific factors were missed by military intelligence: scope, coordination, timing, intensity, and target.

The scope, the extent and large target area of the Tet attacks were not thought possible. While it was given that the enemy could attack just about any place he chose, he was not credited with the ability to attack everywhere at once. The Tet attacks were across the entire breadth of the country against every major city and town by a force of 84,000 communist troops. An attack of such magnitude was not even considered possible by military intelligence because the enemy was not judged to have the capability to coordinate such a massive undertaking.

The coordination of this attack was deemed too complicated for such a novice and primitive foe. Brigadier General Phillip B. Davidson, Chief of MACV Intelligence during the Tet Offensive, admits, 'We looked with scorn on his primitive signal communications system and on (what we deemed) his amateurish staff work.' To get the word out to 84,000 Viet Cong (VC) and North Vietnamese Army (NVA) unit commanders, to preposition them and assure adequate supplies of food and ammunition, without alerting the

US and South Vietnamese was a monumental task which was accomplished without a reliance on radios and technology.

The timing of the attacks was a matter of degree. Both General Westmoreland and Brigadier General Davidson predicted an offensive either just before or after the Tet holidays. General Westmoreland believed there was a 65 percent chance the enemy would strike before Tet, while Davidson thought the odds were 60 percent likely that the enemy would use Tet to maneuver into position and then strike after the holidays.[36] However, when enemy units prematurely jumped the gun on 30 January in the central portions of South Vietnam, both General Westmoreland and Davidson agreed the attacks would occur on 31 January. That the enemy would attack on 'the most sacred of oriental holidays' amazed Davidson, as it did President Johnson who wrote, 'It was difficult to believe that the Communists would so profane their own people's sacred holiday.'[37] Davidson later pointed out that in 1789 the Vietnamese had launched a surprise attack on the Chinese during the Tet holidays.[38] More relevant recent history also showed that the Viet Cong launched attacks on Tet in 1960.[39]

The intensity of the enemy's Tet attacks caught everyone off guard. Even knowing that the enemy would be launching attacks that night, both General Westmoreland and Davidson returned to their billets. As Davidson later remarked, they were lucky the enemy didn't target their housing or they could have been easily captured.[40] The destructiveness and atrocities conducted by the enemy were most evident in the attacks on the old Vietnamese capital city of Hue. Over 2,800 civilians, civil servants, government officials, school teachers, and others were executed or buried alive in mass graves.[41]

That the focus and target of the enemy's Tet Offensive was to be the cities and towns of South Vietnam was so alien even to Maoist guerrilla warfare it was hardly even considered a possibility by military intelligence. Attacks against cities and towns were not uncommon, but to concentrate an entire offensive against all the cities and towns of importance was beyond the realm of credibility. As Davidson was later to tell General Westmoreland, 'Even had I known exactly what was to take place, it was so preposterous that I probably would have been unable to sell it to anybody. Why would the enemy give away his major advantage, which was his ability to be elusive and avoid heavy casualties?'[42] The enemy's major advantage to be elusive lay in his known realm, the countryside and the jungles. In the cities the enemy was trapped in unknown territory and subject to attrition at a terrible cost.

The enemy's 1968 Tet Offensive was a surprise. The degree of the surprise is still subject to much debate. A textbook once used at the United States Military Academy at West Point states: 'The first thing to understand about Giap's Tet offensive is that it was an allied intelligence failure ranking with Pearl Harbor in 1941 or the Ardennes offensive in 1944. The North Vietnamese gained complete surprise.'[43] Brigadier General Davidson, who has the unenviable distinction of being 'on watch' as an intelligence officer during three of the US military's most recent surprises (the North Korean invasion of South Korea, the Chinese entry en masse to the Korean War, and Tet), agrees with most of the PFIAB findings, but lessens the overall impact by insisting intelligence did give the warning and that even had he known everything, nobody would have believed it.[44] He further states that because the warning was given that the offensive would begin around Tet, the fact that it actually began *on* Tet was 'only a mild surprise.'[45]

What Lt. General Davidson later admits in his book, *Secrets of the Vietnam War*, that the US did not know is just as significant as the surprise:

> While we had some information about the enemy leadership and forces, we failed to appreciate fully such critical factors as Ho's resolution to unify Vietnam under communism, Giap's Strategy of Revolutionary War, the sacrificial valor of the NVA soldier, and the massive aid that China and the Soviet Union would furnish North Vietnam. We could have known these things, but we didn't.[46]

5   The Tet Effect

Intelligence and the public perception of war

> The press reaction to these inflated figures is of much greater concern.
> General Creighton Abrams[1]

Before Tet, America was willing to bear any burden to ensure the freedom of South Vietnam and protect that country from communist aggression. America, though wary, had faith in its military, intelligence, and leadership. After Tet, the American will was gone and the public questioned the credibility of their military, intelligence, and leadership. While the Tet Offensive was a dramatic enemy attack, the enemy was defeated. Tet, in and of itself, cannot adequately explain the dramatic change in the public's perception of the war.

The enemy's actions alone do not explain the change that occurred in America. There was a series of events, however, which served to amplify the Tet Offensive. When someone in a position of trust is found to have been disingenuous, that person will lose credibility. So it was with General Westmoreland and the intelligence community. In 1967, General Westmoreland, backed by the intelligence community, told the American public that the enemy was 'bankrupt' and the end of America's involvement in the Vietnam was in sight. The Tet Offensive revealed this forecast to be illusionary; the enemy was not 'bankrupt,' and America's military appeared to be stuck in an endless Vietnamese quagmire. General Westmoreland and the intelligence community lost credibility in the eyes of America. Their words were not trusted and their cause became suspect. The American people's perception of the war and their willingness to continue the fight changed.

This loss of the public's trust, as a result of leaders and intelligence appearing to be misleading, can be termed 'The Tet Effect.' The more dramatic the revelation, the greater the effect. In the case of Tet, the ferocity and scope of the attacks dramatically revealed the assessment of General Westmoreland and the intelligence community to be misleading. Further compounding the effect was the apparent manipulation of the intelligence community to conform to General Westmoreland's views.

The Tet Effect then is the result of a series of events in which those making decisions and policy co-opt intelligence to legitimize their views, then lose the trust of the people when those views are shown to be incorrect. General Westmoreland's flawed view that the crossover point signaled success was imposed upon the intelligence community, and with the legitimacy provided by intelligence, he shaped the public's perception of the war. When Tet revealed his view to be flawed, both he and the intelligence community lost the trust of the American public.

The Tet Effect is about leadership, intelligence, the public perception of war, and trust. When those in positions of leadership attempt to shape intelligence to conform to their views, the potential for a Tet Effect is initiated. When that intelligence is used to shape the public's perception, the Tet Effect is enabled. All that remains is a revelation that the perception is wrong, the Tet Effect is actuated, and the people lose trust in their leadership and the intelligence.

When leaders shape intelligence

Intelligence is information used by leaders to make decisions regarding adversaries and potential adversaries. The intelligence community gathers and analyzes information to assist leaders in their task to make decisions. Intelligence does not make the decision, does not wield the sword. People reluctant to make decisions do not rise to positions of leadership, leaders become what they are by making decisions, by wielding the sword. There is a delineation between the role of leader, those who make decisions, and that of intelligence, those who support the leader.

Intelligence is a difficult task. Gathering information the enemy holds secret, attempting to fill gaps in knowledge that defy profundity, trying to understand and think like an enigmatic enemy, these are the problematic affairs of intelligence. The enemy protects sensitive information and hinders access to anything that may reveal their capabilities and intentions. Further, the thought process and values of the enemy are often contrary and alien to American values and mores. To acquire secret information and to think like the enemy requires a high degree of objectivity. To accomplish its mission of providing information to leaders to assist them in making decisions, intelligence must remain above all else, objective.

To understand and think like the enemy, intelligence often finds itself at odds with the traditional American view. This often puts intelligence in an unenviable position of presenting information that is at odds with the concepts and values of American leaders. The mechanism by which intelligence is able to present contrary views is objectivity. Intelligence presented without bias, in a well thought out and logical process, is the best means of presenting contrary views.

Having no hidden agenda, being unbiased and objective also protects intelligence from the divisiveness of politics. There are always differing views and ways to solve a problem. The leader must discern the best view and decide upon the best solution. Leaders often have their own preferred method of looking at and solving a problem. Leaders rise to their positions in large part because of their ability to take on issues and solve them. Intelligence can have no preferred method, no special interest to serve. Leaders have their own views, and often intelligence can aid or hinder that view. Intelligence does not wield the sword, but neither can it be swayed by the wielder of the sword. Intelligence must be objective. Without objectivity, intelligence has no credibility, and no leader could trust the information given to them.

In Vietnam, the military leader, General Westmoreland, was convinced that in his war of attrition against the communist forces in South Vietnam the measure of success was the crossover point. In early 1967, he believed the crossover point had been reached. However, his intelligence organization did not entirely agree on nor support his viewpoint. Brigadier General Joseph McChristian never felt that manpower was a problem for the enemy. In McChristian's view of the enemy, the measure of success was a combination of capability, which included the enemy's numbers, and will.

The crossover point as a measure of military success was a fallacy. War is a contest of wills, and numbers do not confer any guarantee of victory. General Westmoreland, in gauging American success in Vietnam was ignoring the sage advice of both Sun Tzu, the ancient Chinese philosopher of war, and Carl von Clausewitz, the adept student of Napoleonic war. Both Sun Tze and Clausewitz warn against relying on numbers alone and both agree that war, above all else, is a contest of wills.

Throughout his tenure as General Westmoreland's Chief of Intelligence, McChristian believed that at current levels, the enemy had the capability and will to continue the war indefinitely. This assessment did not endear him to the rest of the Military Assistance Command, Vietnam (MACV) staff, nor did his inclusion of the enemy's self-defense forces in the order of battle. From the enemy point of view, the self-defense forces were an integral part of the communist strategy and constituted an element of their war-fighting capability. McChristian provided an objective, though unpopular, evaluation of the enemy.

Brigadier General McChristian finished his tour in Vietnam in June 1967, leaving a dilemma for General Westmoreland. McChristian's intelligence had found that the self-defense forces had been drastically undercounted. To now add the improved numbers to the order of battle would seem to contradict the crossover point assessment espoused by General Westmoreland. McChristian's replacement at the head of MACV intelligence, Brigadier General Phillip Davidson, found a solution for General Westmoreland – drop the self-defense forces.

The decision to drop the self-defense forces was politically motivated; motivated by the desire to avoid a seeming contradiction to the crossover point assessment. The justification provided by General Westmoreland for dropping the self-defense forces was twofold. First, he argued, the self-defense forces were not a combat force and should not be counted. This is a tenuous, though understandable argument; but why now? The self-defense forces had been carried without question from General Westmoreland in the order of battle from its inception in 1965, and by the South Vietnamese prior to that, and by the French even before that. The real justification lies in General Westmoreland's second argument, that the press would not understand.

The justification that the press would not understand became readily apparent during the National Intelligence Estimate (NIE) conference held at the Central Intelligence Agency (CIA) headquarters in August of 1967. In a message to the MACV representatives at the conference, Brigadier General Davidson said, 'I am sure that this headquarters will not accept a figure in excess of the current strength figures carried by the press.'[2]

The command position is clearly stated by General Westmoreland's deputy, General Creighton Abrams. In his message sent on 20 August 1967 to the Chairman of the Joint Chiefs of Staff and then passed on to the Director of the CIA, he states clearly that the command's overriding concern is the reaction from the press.

1 MACV representatives to the DIA [*sic*] conference dealing with Order of Battle strength for enemy forces in South Vietnam report that there is a continuing *controversy* regarding the inclusion of the strength figures for self-defense forces (*SD*) and secret self-defense forces (*SSD*) in the draft NIE 14.3–67. In General Westmoreland's temporary absence, I think it appropriate to make the *command position* on the inclusion of these strength figures clear.

2 *If SD and SSD strength figures are included in the overall enemy strength, the figure will total 420,000–431,000* depending on minor variations. This is in *sharp contrast to the current* overall strength figure of about *299,000 given to the press* here.

3 From the intelligence viewpoint, the *inclusion of SD and SSD* strength figures in an estimate of military capabilities is *highly questionable*. These forces contain a sizable number of women and old people. They operate entirely in their own hamlets. They are rarely armed, have no real discipline, and almost no military capability. They are no more effective in the military sense than the dozens of other nonmilitary organizations which serve the VC cause in various roles.

4 *The press reaction to these inflated figures is of much greater concern.* We have been projecting an image of success over the recent months, and properly so. Now, when we release the figure of 420–431,000, the newsmen will immediately seize on the point that the enemy force has increased about 120–130,000, *all available caveats and explanations will not prevent the press from drawing an erroneous*

and gloomy conclusion as to the meaning of the increase. All those who have an incorrect view of the war will be reenforced and the task will become more difficult.

5   In our view, the strength figures for the *SD and SSD should be omitted* entirely from the enemy strength tables in the forthcoming NIE. This will prevent the possibility that they can be added to the valid figures, and an erroneous conclusion drawn as to an enemy strength increase.[3] (Author's emphasis added.)

General Westmoreland who was in the Philippines vacationing with his family immediately endorsed the 'command position.'

I have just read Gen Abrams MAC 7849, and I agree. I do not concur with the inclusion of SD and SSD strength figures in the overall enemy strength. It distorts the situation and makes no sense. No possible explanations could prevent the erroneous conclusions that would result.[4]

To ensure the press came to no 'erroneous conclusions,' General Westmoreland and MACV dropped the self-defense forces and pressured the CIA to do the same. The fallacious crossover point assessment would not face scrutiny from intelligence, from the press, nor from the public. Policy concerns shaped the intelligence. Now the intelligence would shape the public's perception of the Vietnam War.

Intelligence and the public perception of war

By November of 1967 when General Westmoreland returned to the United States for his public relations campaign to bolster support for the Vietnam War, both the intelligence at MACV and at the CIA supported his crossover point assessment, allowing him to declare the enemy 'bankrupt' and predict that American troops could begin coming home in two years.

General Westmoreland was able to release figures which resembled those previously issued by MACV, thus raising no unwarranted concerns by those, who in the words of General Creighton Abrams, had an 'incorrect' view of the war. The numbers for the 'combat strength' showed a nice downward trend from just over 230,000 under the old accounting method used up until August 1967, down to just under 200,000 with the new figures released by General Westmoreland in October 1967 (see Figure 6). MACV even retained the old category of Viet Cong Infrastructure (VCI), and when these numbers were totaled all together with the Administrative and Service Troops which, like the infrastructure were not part of the combat strength, they matched nicely with the old figures used up until August (see Figure 7). The slight increase was easily attributed to the VCI, which clearly did not

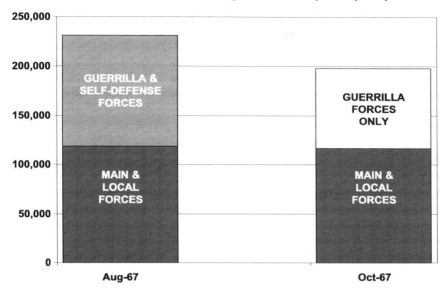

Figure 6 Communist combat strength for August and October 1967.

Source: Military Assistance Command, Vietnam (MACV) monthly order of battle for August and October 1967.

affect the combat strength and whose increase could easily explained away as the product of better intelligence. The VCI were not important, the important aspect was that the combat forces, unaffected by the VCI increase, had clearly been attrited and were decreasing as shown in Figure 6. Of course, if the self-defense forces had been included in the October 1967 figures, a more complicated explanation would have been required. For while the August and October 1967 figures are not too widely divergent, add in the self-defense forces and a totally different image emerges (see Figure 8).

If the self-defense forces had been included in the order of battle figures for October 1967, a more detailed explanation would have been required, as the discrepancy between the August total of 296,000 and the October total of 434,000, had the self-defense forces been included, would have been far greater. But, such a discrepancy was never presented to the press, and as demonstrated by Figures 6, 7, and 8, by dropping the self-defense forces, the figures appeared to fall in line with the previous numbers released by MACV. No elaborate explanations were necessary. By dropping the self-defense forces and presenting numbers represented in Figures 6 and 7, those who had an 'incorrect' view of the war had nothing to write about, other than that the combat strength was decreasing and better intelligence now showed that non-combat forces had increased modestly.

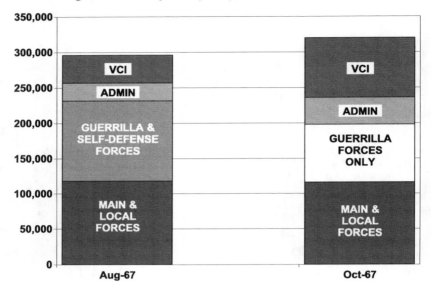

Figure 7 Communist strength totals for August and October 1967.

Source: Military Assistance Command, Vietnam (MACV) monthly order of battle for August and October 1967.

General Westmoreland, with his dilemma now solved, had both the tactical victories over the enemy and the intelligence evidence to back up his claim that the crossover point had been reached. Not only did his MACV intelligence figures show that the combat forces had reached the crossover point, but the CIA also verified it with the release of Special National Intelligence Estimate 14.3–67, *Capabilities of the Vietnamese Communists for Fighting in South Vietnam.*

The NIE backed General Westmoreland in two specific areas. First, that the enemy had reached the crossover point and their numbers were in decline, and second, the communists did retain the capability to continue for at least another year, but beyond that, the outlook was unsure.

> Manpower is a major problem confronting the Communists. Losses have been increasing and recruitment in South Vietnam is becoming more difficult. Despite heavy infiltration from North Vietnam, the strength of the Communist military forces and political organization in South Vietnam declined in the last year. . . . we believe there is a fairly good chance that the overall strength and effectiveness of the military forces and the political infrastructure will continue to decline. . . . Our judgment is that the Communists still retain adequate capabilities to support this strategy for at least another year. Whether or not Hanoi

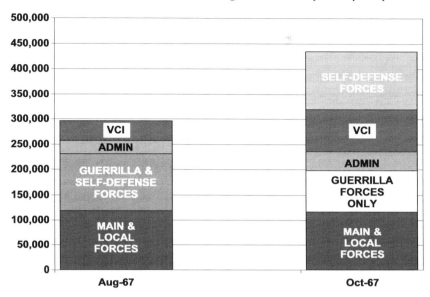

Figure 8 Communist strength totals if self-defense forces included for August and October 1967.

Source: Military Assistance Command, Vietnam (MACV) monthly order of battle for August and October 1967; self-defense figure from Phillip B. Davidson, *Secrets of the Vietnam War* (Novato, CA: Presidio, 1990), 43.

does in fact persist with this strategy depends not only on its capabilities to do so, but on a number of political and international considerations not treated in this estimate.[5]

While not released to the public, the essential tone of the NIE and its conclusions were likely released in background briefings to the press. Further, the NIE was undoubtedly one of the primary sources for the intelligence briefings that the President's Wise Men received in early 1967. Intelligence shaped by policy was shaping the public's perception of the war.

Backed by tactical victories and intelligence validation, General Westmoreland was now confident he could prognosticate the future of American involvement in Vietnam. During his public relations campaign tour to the United States in mid-November 1967, he told America that the end would be reached in two years. General Westmoreland had just laid his credibility on the line, and it rested squarely on the foundation set by intelligence. The intelligence foundation, unfortunately, was based upon information which was not dependable and did not tell the entire story. It certainly did not accurately portray the enemy and their will to continue the war. Such a foundation was likely to crack.

A matter of trust

The foundation not only cracked, it crumbled in the aftermath of the Tet Offensive. Tet was a shock in and of itself, but the enemy was decisively defeated at a tremendous cost, over 48,000 troops lost. However, with such staggering losses, Tet showed that the enemy was far from 'bankrupt,' and appeared willing and ready to accept even higher losses to attain their objectives. The confident predictions made in November were in stark contrast to the determination of the enemy demonstrated at Tet. From such contradictions arose the questions of credibility and trust.

When a democracy decides on war, the public looks to its national leaders for the justification, to its military leaders for accurate assessments of progress, and to intelligence for unbiased and objective information. The public has every right to expect to be able to invest full trust and confidence in its leaders, military, and intelligence to provide them with the information needed to decide issues of war. A democracy in war is demanding of information, its sons' and daughters' lives are at stake. If those in positions of trust and confidence are found to be less than truthful, found to be deceptive, or erroneous in their assessments, the public has every right to withdraw their trust and question the credibility of their leaders, their military, and intelligence.

In Vietnam after the Tet Offensive, the public had reason to doubt their leadership, the military, and intelligence. The public had been told the enemy was 'bankrupt'; this the enemy was not, as Tet so vividly revealed. Those who called the enemy 'bankrupt' were further tainted when it was revealed that intelligence had been pressured to keep the numbers low to avoid questions from the press. The military lost the trust of the public, it had misread the enemy and had been proven wrong, it had underestimated the enemy and been surprised, it had pressured intelligence to conform to its view, and it had tried to hide information from the press and the public; little wonder then that the military and intelligence lost the trust and confidence of a democratic public.

When a democratic nation decides on war, the trust the public holds in their leadership and the military is essential. Intelligence plays a critical role in this equation, for it is information upon which decisions of war are made. When intelligence is biased, the decisions made become suspect. Intelligence in Vietnam was biased to favor the assessment of the war made by the military. When this assessment was questioned, so too was the intelligence. The public was left questioning the military and intelligence, trusting the assessments of neither.

The Tet Effect shook the foundations of the war effort in Vietnam. A democracy, without trust in its military and the intelligence upon which decisions are made, cannot long continue the fight against a determined and capable enemy. The Tet Effect, the loss of trust by the public in their leadership when intelligence has been co-opted to support tenuous assessments that are then dramatically shown to be questionable, is a phenomenon democracies can ill afford. The intelligence community plays a crucial role in war and the decisions of war. The intelligence community is a major factor in the Tet Effect and must always guard against challenges to objectivity. Objectivity is the guardian to trust and the shield against the Tet Effect.

Part II

On intelligence and Vietnam

6   Setting the stage
The enemy's war

He who lacks foresight and underestimates his enemy will surely be captured by him.

Sun Tzu[1]

The Vietnam conflict has been called a strange war fought in a strange land. For the United States, it was a strange war for it was fought on the enemy's terms; fought in a strange land, the enemy's homeland. Nearly every aspect of the war was to some extent controlled by the enemy. It was the enemy's war. The United States was but an interloper, stepping in to assist an ally which was in danger of collapsing under the enemy's onslaught. To counter this enemy, the US adopted a strategy of attrition, and part of that strategy was finding out how many enemy there were to attrit. In the endeavor to count the enemy, the US was first faced with the task of deciphering the enemy's organization. The key to deciphering his organization lay in understanding the type of war the enemy was waging.

The enemy was engaged in an insurgency. The war was initially fought by South Vietnamese against South Vietnamese. The insurgents were South Vietnamese communists, closely aligned with their brethren in North Vietnam, fighting to take control of a fledgling Government of South Vietnam that was striving to establish democratic principles and was backed in that venture by the United States of America. The insurgents were conducting a guerrilla-style war, modeled upon the Chinese mold espoused by Mao Tse-Tung and refined by the Viet Minh of North Vietnam in their struggle and victory against the French.

Mao Tse-Tung on guerrilla warfare

Guerrilla warfare in the twentieth century is nearly synonymous with Mao Tse-Tung, the communist leader who, through guerrilla warfare, transformed China into a communist state. The world noted and took stock of Mao's methods, with guerrilla and soldier alike looking for lessons to employ or defeat his methods. The insurgents in South Vietnam looked upon his methods as an effective means to topple the Government of South Vietnam. The Government of South Vietnam and the US studied Mao to learn how to defeat them.

For Mao Tse-Tung, guerrilla warfare was a political undertaking. 'Military action is a method used to attain a political goal.'[2] The guerrilla was guided in his efforts by the political motive to subvert and take over the government. Every action taken by the guerrilla was guided by this political goal. Thus, the political organization was the foundation upon which all else was built. In typical communist style, political cells of three were the operating mode. Political proselytizing and recruitment were primary and ongoing activities for the insurgent. 'The revolutionary war is a war of the masses; it can be waged only by mobilizing the masses and relying on them.'[3] Everyone had a place and function to fulfill in the guerrilla war, whether that person be a farmer, a teacher, or a soldier. But to subvert a government, more than politicking is necessary . . . violence is required. 'Political power grows out of the barrel of a gun.'[4]

Violence against the government is the job of the guerrilla. Organized similar to the political cadre, in cells of three, the guerrilla organization starts out small and gradually becomes larger. 'All guerrilla units start from nothing and grow.'[5] The guerrilla operates in familiar territory and seeks to inflict violence at no cost to himself. Violent acts which expose the guerrilla to the least amount of danger, such as assassinations and terrorist acts, are the typical mode of operation.

With successful proselytizing and recruitment, and as local political foes are eliminated, the insurgent movement grows. With more and more guerrillas to operate, the movement can begin to challenge government forces more directly. Still operating in a mode which avoids direct, sustained contact, the guerrilla forces begin to wear down the government forces. Preferred actions include ambushes and hit and run tactics. 'The tactics of defense have no place in the realm of guerrilla warfare.'[6]

As the government forces become weakened and the proselytizing of the insurgents turns the people against the government, the guerrilla forces become even larger. Once restricted to localized areas, the guerrillas begin to take on the attributes of a more traditional military force. The guerrillas form larger and larger military units capable of deploying throughout the country. As the government forces become weaker and the insurgent stronger, the guerrillas become more willing to adopt tactics which call for them to stand and fight. This type of tactic is typically only undertaken when victory is guaranteed. 'Fight no battle unprepared, fight no battle you are not sure of winning.'[7]

The insurgency has now taken on the form of a traditional confrontation between two enemies. The insurgency now has the backing of the people and large, organized and equipped military units which are capable of defeating what remains of the government forces. The insurgency can now defeat the government with popular political support and on military terms. Mao Tse-Tung has conquered China.

In General Westmoreland's autobiography, *A Soldier Reports*, he described guerrilla warfare as consisting of three phases:

> In Phase One, the insurgents remain on the defensive but work to estab-lish control of the population and conduct terrorist operations. In Phase Two, regular military forces are formed, guerrilla attacks increased, and isolated government forces engaged. In the climactic Phase Three, large insurgent military units go on the offensive to defeat the govern-ment's large units and to establish full control of the population.[8]

Guerrilla warfare and the Viet Minh

While Mao Tse-Tung was establishing China as a communist nation, Ho Chi Minh was employing Mao's methods of guerrilla war, first against the Japanese in World War II, then against the French who were seeking to re-establish their colonial holdings in Southeast Asia. Ho Chi Minh began with a political cadre of about 30 and established a base camp in the remote mountains near the Chinese/Vietnamese border in 1940. This cadre formed the basis of the Vietnam Independence League, or the Viet Minh. The Viet Minh began proselytizing to convert the masses to their indepen-dence struggle. Ho Chi Minh soon had a 'self-defense' force, organized by Vo Nguyen Giap, which quickly grew and moved into the first phase of guer-rilla warfare, carrying out ambushes and assassinations.[9]

By 1946 when the French Empire was returning to Vietnam, the Viet Minh forces were larger, consisting of approximately 60,000 men and ready to conduct both Phase I and II operations against the French.[10] By the time of the collapse of the French at Dien Bien Phu in 1954, Giap and his guerrilla force had grown to 380,000 men and, as demonstrated at Dien Bien Phu, were capable of conducting sustained Phase III operations.[11]

Ho Chi Minh and the Viet Minh used the model of guerrilla warfare espoused and taught by Mao Tse-Tung. But they also brought their own nuances. A key aspect of the Viet Minh movement was their doctrine of the *dau tranh*, or struggle. The English translation of *dau tranh* as struggle does little to convey the emotion and highly charged nature of this term in Vietnamese. *Dau tranh* is a powerful and highly emotional term with conno-tations of sacrifice and dedication, a totality which is the revolutionary's world.[12] There is also a dualistic aspect to *dau tranh*, the political and the military which work in tandem, always together, as with a hammer and an anvil.[13]

The military struggle, *dau tranh vu trang*, encompasses the guerrilla insur-gency as described above in its three phases. The political struggle, *dau tranh chinh tri*, also has three components, or actions (*van*): *dich van*, or action among the enemy, which are non-military activities taken among the populace under control of the enemy; *dan van*, or action among the people, which are non-military activities taken among the populace in 'liberated' areas; and *binh van*, or action among the military, which are non-military activities aimed at the enemy's troops.[14] The political and military duality of the *dau tranh* takes on an almost religious fervor for the believer. Said one North Vietnamese, '*Dau tranh* is all important to a revolutionary. It shapes his thinking, fixes his attitudes, dictates his behavior. His life, his revolutionary work, his whole world is *dau tranh*.'[15]

Guerrilla warfare Viet Cong style

The Viet Minh were only partially victorious over the French in their *dau tranh*. The French were forced out of the country, but the Viet Minh only gained control over the northern portion of Vietnam. Under the Geneva Accords of 1954, Vietnam was divided along its thin waist at the 17th parallel, with the communists controlling North Vietnam and a non-communist government in control of South Vietnam. The *dau tranh* was incomplete. The communist faithful from the south trekked north to plot with their brethren, and in the late 1950s began to 'regroup' in the south. These 'regroupees' began to proselytize and lay the foundations of a new insurgency. On 20 December 1960, the National Liberation Front (NLF) was established by the *Lao Dong* (Worker's Party), the communist party of Vietnam, to carry out the communist strategy in the south. The *dau tranh* was underway in South Vietnam.

The NLF, a communist front with non-communist members, controlled the insurgency in South Vietnam through its central committee. The communists within the NLF controlled both the political and military *dau tranh*. The South Vietnamese communists were soon referred to as the Viet Cong, *cong* being a term for communist. While there was no organization or group claiming the title of Viet Cong, it was adopted by the press, military, and government to identify the insurgents.

By late 1964, the Viet Cong were well on their way to toppling the government, having moved from Phase I to Phase II. Seeing an imminent collapse of the South Vietnamese without intervention, the United States began to take an active role in the conflict. In reaction, a new twist was added to Mao's guerrilla warfare model: an outside force was introduced – the north began to send its own units south. Thus, as early as December 1964 at least one full regiment of the North's People's Army of Vietnam (PAVN) had infiltrated South Vietnam[16] and by December of the next year, nine PAVN regiments were suspected to be operating south of the 17th parallel.[17] Using tactics that bordered on Phase III, the North Vietnamese faced off against the United States in their first major confrontation from 14–16 November 1965 in the Ia Drang valley. In the face of rapid, mobile US reinforcements, the North Vietnamese followed standard Phase II guerrilla tactics and faded into the jungles.[18]

The collection of insurgent forces in South Vietnam were in a flux between Phase I and Phase II guerrilla operations, with the added North Vietnamese forces capable of staging Phase III operations. Thus, another nuance of guerrilla warfare was perfected in the countryside of South Vietnam, that of creating a synthesis (*chien tranh tong hop*) of the forces in the various phases of guerrilla operations. Instead of a progression from Phase I to Phase II and culminating in Phase III, the Viet Cong and the North Vietnamese forces used all the phases at once to support and enhance the operations of each other.[19]

Lieutenant General Phillip Davidson (promoted several times after his duty in Vietnam where he was a Brigadier General) in his book *Secrets of the Vietnam War*, described the strategy used by the communists as a 'mosaic.' 'In one area it may be in Phase III, conventional war, while nearby it may be in Phase II, and somewhere else it may be in a Phase I insurgency.'[20] He then gives the following example,

> In 1967–1968, the South Vietnamese I Corps area, also known as Military Region I (MR I), the northern five provinces of South Vietnam, had a Phase I insurgency in its southern coastal province of Quang Ngai, a Phase II (combination) in the two adjoining provinces to the north, and a good size conventional war (Phase III) in the two northern provinces of Quang Tri and Thua Thien.[21]

The United States and the Government of South Vietnam now faced a synchronized collection of forces in the form of the Viet Cong (VC) and the North Vietnamese Army (NVA). To defeat these forces the United States adopted a strategy of attrition. To measure the success of this strategy, the total number of the forces opposing them needed to be calculated. Having considered the type of war being waged by the enemy, the next task was to determine the enemy organization.

The military aspect

The organization of a guerrilla unit varies depending upon which phase the insurgency was fighting. In its infancy, the guerrilla forces are organized into small units at the village level. As the insurgency progresses, the guerrillas leave the village and move about the local area and provinces to ambush and attack where they can and to withdraw quickly as needed. As the insurgency moves into the later phases, the organization takes on a more traditional military look.

According to General Vo Nguyen Giap, military leader of the Viet Minh in their war against the French and generally credited as the military strategist behind the Vietnamese war effort against the United States, 'the people's armed forces consist of three categories of forces: the regular army, the regional forces, and the militia and self-defense forces.'[22] The US Military Assistance Command, Vietnam (MACV) viewed the Viet Cong military structure as main forces, local forces, and irregular forces.[23] With the insurgency at various phases throughout the country, the Viet Cong had sizable portions of all three types of forces.

The Viet Cong forces

The Viet Cong Liberation Army (*Quan Doi Giai Phong*) which led the *dau tranh va trang*, or armed struggle, can be described as a pyramid. The base of the pyramid provided the recruitment, indoctrination, and training ground. As a guerrilla's prowess in those things military progressed, he moved up the pyramid, first participating in only local area confrontations, then in district and regional engagements, to finally graduate to country-wide combat.[24] At each level, the guerrilla belonged to a particular type of organization, specializing in the type of fighting encountered by its forces. These forces on this pyramid were called:

1   irregular forces, making up the base of the pyramid,
2   local forces, occupying the middle of the pyramid, and
3   main forces, at the pinnacle of the pyramid.

   These forces making a pyramid also mirror the traditional administrative divisions within Vietnam. Moving from the smallest element, to the largest, the administrative divisions are:

1   hamlet,
2   village,
3   district, and
4   province.

   To better manage the *dau tranh va trang*, the Viet Cong added one additional layer, the military region, above the province (see Figure 9).

Viet Cong irregular forces

The irregular forces were composed of two types of troops, guerrillas and self-defense men. Often, the word 'secret' would precede these terms to indicate that the guerrilla or self-defense men were located and operated in South Vietnamese Government controlled areas. The irregular forces were the least understood by the US military, and as a result, underwent several name changes. Up until 1966, the irregulars were referred to as the militia forces and consisted of guerrillas and self-defense men. In 1967, at a conference to standardize names and methodologies, the militia forces became known

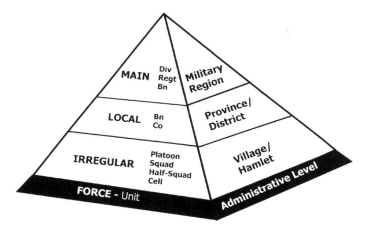

Figure 9 The Viet Cong Force Pyramid.

as the irregular forces, but still consisted of guerrilla and self-defense forces. In late 1967, the self-defense forces were dropped and the militia/irregular forces became just the guerrilla forces.

For the communists, both the guerrilla and self-defense forces were a part of their military organizational structure and 'irregular' best describes these two types of forces. The irregular forces occupied the lowest rung of the enemy military force structure and were found at the hamlet and village level. With 85 percent of the population of South Vietnam engaged in agriculture and living in the villages and hamlets of the countryside,[25] the Viet Cong had fertile ground in which to recruit. This rural life centered around the village, which was typically made up of several hamlets, or neighborhoods. The hamlet and village were the home of the irregular forces.

The communists had several venues to entice villagers to their cause. These venues ranged from political organizations, such as Farmer's Associations and Youth Leagues, which operated to mobilize the people against the government and the American 'invaders,' to hard-core guerrilla units which actively fought against the Americans and their 'lackeys.' The political cadre had many options to offer the potential recruit. Once drawn into the web, the cadre could work on obtaining increasingly active participation from the recruit, until the enlistee became an active insurgent.

In the early years of the insurgency, from 1960 to 1965, the guerrilla was the focus of Viet Cong military effort. As the war progressed, and the insurgency took on Phase II trappings, the focus turned to getting guerrillas trained and moved up to the regional and local forces. The guerrillas at the village level also took on more of a regular, full-time position. The self-defense force remained an option for unwilling recruits and the older population; becoming a larger and more encompassing force.

The difference between the guerrilla and the self-defense force has never been conclusively documented and understood. Part of the problem lies in the terms used, which changed over time and varied from region to region. Also, there was incomplete intelligence on these forces. Intelligence collected on the irregular forces was almost totally dependent upon human intelligence, with little or no technical intelligence collected on these forces. This was primarily due to the lack of radios at the guerrilla level, where communications were dependent upon humans.

In his defining book *Viet Cong*, Vietnam expert Douglas Pike describes the various types of forces making up the Irregular Forces in 1965. He talks of three different types of guerrilla (*du kich*): the village guerrilla (*du kich xa*), the secret guerrilla (*du kich bi mat*) and the combat guerrilla (*du kich dau*).[26] The village guerrilla typically was older, both in age and in arms and was limited in deployment, ranging only around and in the village. The secret guerrilla was similar to the village guerrilla except that in this case, the village was located in a Government of South Vietnam controlled area. The combat guerrilla was typically younger, had better arms, and participated in military activities outside the village. As such, this type of guerrilla actually fell under the category of local forces, which means this type of guerrilla was receiving the training that marks his advance up the pyramid. Pike also mentions paramilitary or self-defense forces, but reports that the nature and type of activities of these forces were unknown at that time. He said these forces included self-defense men (*tu ve*), self-defense combat men (*tu ve chien dau*), secret self-defense men (*tu ve bi mat*), and people's self-defense men (*tu ve nahn dan*).[27]

By 1966, a CIA analyst named Sam Adams had begun his quest to understand the enemy's numbers. In a trip to Vietnam in 1966, he visited a *Chiue Hoi* (Open Arms) camp for Viet Cong who had switched sides, giving up their associations with the communists and swearing their loyalty to the Government of South Vietnam. Adams found a guerrilla/self-defense force similar to that described by Pike, but with a few changes. Adams found three types of guerrillas and two types of self-defense forces. The guerrillas were:

- village guerrillas (*du kich xa*),
- hamlet guerrillas (*du kich ap*), and
- secret guerrillas (*du kich mat*).

The self-defense forces he found were the:

- self-defense men (*tu ve*) and
- secret self-defense men (*tu ve mat*).[28]

Both Pike and Adams describe village and secret guerrillas. Pike does not give a special category for hamlet guerrillas, but he does note that the guerrilla units were found at the hamlet level in cells of three men, half-squads of six men, or even up to an entire squad of twelve men.[29] Both also describe the militia as self-defense forces. What is significant is that both Pike and Adams describe two distinct entities – the guerrillas and the self-defense force. The self-defense men were poorly armed and seldom used in direct military action. The self-defense forces were the first stepping stone into the Viet Cong military organization, and if a recruit showed any promise, as any able-bodied man would, they quickly moved on to the guerrilla forces and began their journey up the pyramid.[30] Thus the self-defense force was left with mostly elderly and otherwise unfit people. They would participate in road-cutting and other acts of sabotage,[31] as well as the construction of numerous types of booby traps, the bane of infantry patrols everywhere in Vietnam.[32]

Lieutenant General Phillip B. Davidson, described the self-defense forces thus:

> They were undisciplined, composed largely of old men, women, and children whose age, health, or sex rendered them unfit for any of the other categories in the VC force structure. Their function is even now a matter of dispute. They operated only in their own villages, and had a few antique weapons which they rarely used. They never attacked and rarely defended even their own villages. Since the SD [self-defense force] was made up of women, children, the aged, and the cripples, they could not even be used as a recruiting base for the combat elements of the Communist forces.[33]

Davidson, like Pike in describing the secret guerrillas, goes on to explain that the word 'secret' denoted the self-defense forces which were located in Government of South Vietnam controlled areas, with the principal function of gathering intelligence.[34] The production of booby traps could also be assumed to be a function they retained even though they were in government controlled areas. While General Davidson claims the self-defense forces could not be used as a recruiting base because they were composed only of older and unfit personnel, as was pointed out earlier, any recruit generally starts out in the self-defense force,[35] and it is because they are fit that they spend little time in the self-defense force, quickly moving up the pyramid. In estimating the number of self-defense forces, however, it is fair to assess that the greatest bulk of their numbers would have been unfit for the rigors of guerrilla warfare. Also in support of Davidson, it was projected that after the 1968 Tet Offensive, because of critical manning shortfalls at the higher levels of the pyramid, increasing numbers of recruits (but not all) were sent directly to the local and main forces without the benefit of self-defense and guerrilla activity.[36]

The real question, however, is whether the self-defense force was militarily significant. General McChristian and Sam Adams thought they were, while

General Davidson thought not. This fact should be noted here: any force capable of inflicting casualties (booby traps accounted for one-third of US casualties)[37] or impacting on military operations (road-blocks, booby traps, mines) is militarily significant. These things the self-defense forces could do.

More importantly, the self-defense forces were viewed by the communists as an integral part of their political and military war against the Government of South Vietnam and the US military. The self-defense forces have been a component of guerrilla warfare from the beginning, being used by Mao Tse-Tung in his guerrilla efforts.[38]

The irregular forces were the foundation of the pyramid which describes the Viet Cong military structure. It was here that recruits were first drawn into the military *dau tranh vu trang* struggle. The self-defense force, or *tu ve*, seldom participated in actual military acts and served only as the introduction and initial training for recruits. The physically fit quickly moved on to guerrilla units at the hamlet (*du kich ap*) or the village level (*du kich xa*). The guerrillas were organized into cells of three, like most things communist. At the hamlet level, the guerrillas could be found in groups as small as a cell of three members, to a half-squad of six, or sometimes up to a full squad of twelve guerrillas. At the village level, the guerrillas were organized into platoons of three to four squads (36 to 48 guerrillas).[39] These guerrillas lived, worked, and operated in their village and hamlet areas. Those which showed promise, or as the war took its toll on personnel, those who were simply fit, were moved up the VC pyramid to the next level, the local forces.

The Viet Cong local forces

The administrative levels in Vietnam ran from the hamlet, to the village, to the district, then to the province. With irregular forces found at the village and hamlet, the next level up on the VC pyramid was to the district and province level. Here, the forces were given more training and indoctrination, as well as better arms. They also were organized into larger units which moved and operated within their district or province. The Viet Cong referred to these types of units as regionals or territorials (*Bo Doi Dia Phuong*),[40] while the US military called them local forces.

The district level, located immediately above the village, and below a province, was typically organized into a company of three or four platoons. They specialized in operations into nearby enemy territory to stage propaganda meetings, assassinate local leaders, and destroy strategic hamlets established by the Government of South Vietnam.[41] They were under the operational control of the district party committees and operated as independent companies (*dai doi doc lop*),[42] and should not be confused with the companies which make up the battalions associated with the provincial local forces or of the main forces.

The provincial forces were also considered part of the local forces, being the next level above the districts. Under the Government of South Vietnam, there were 44 provinces within South Vietnam in 1965. The Viet Cong also broke the country into provinces, roughly corresponding to the government's, but only containing 37 provinces. The Viet Cong Province Head-quarters typically had one or two battalions.[43] In a study conducted by the Rand Corporation in 1967, researchers documented the Viet Cong units operating in the Dinh Tuong province, located in the heart of the Mekong Delta south of Saigon, from 1964 to 1966.[44] The researchers identified one provincial battalion, the 514th. The 514th Province Battalion was first organized in 1961 with a single platoon of 30 men and by August of 1962 consisted of two companies, each with three platoons of 30 men each and a reconnaissance squad of 10 men. By 1965, the battalion had grown to five companies. Prior to 1965, the companies had operated independently in the various districts of Dinh Tuong province; they now came together as an independent battalion.

The first three companies of the 514th Battalion were infantry units consisting of 225 men each. Each company specialized in a specific type of activity. The first company specialized in performing raids, the second company in attacking posts, while the third company's specialty was ambushes. Each company had three platoons of infantry with approximately 40 men armed with assorted rifles and submachine guns. They were supported by six support platoons of 15 men each which were armed with machine guns, mortars and recoilless rifles, and a twelve-man reconnaissance squad. In addition, the battalion had one reconnaissance/intelligence squad of twelve men and a headquarters staff of three. This gave the 514th Battalion a strength of nearly 700 men in June of 1964.

Two additional companies were also attached to the 514th Battalion. The fourth company was an anti-aircraft unit armed with machine guns, recoil-less rifles and about 80 men. The fifth company was a special operations-type company with only about 90 volunteers and soldiers with proven combat records assigned.

Lieutenant General Davidson relates that a wealth of intelligence data was available on the local forces and describes them as follows:

> The local forces were armed and disciplined full-time Viet Cong units, organized by province and district. While they were not of the high caliber of the main forces, they were battle worthy units similar to the unfederalized units of our National Guard.[45]

The local forces, while deployed in their own districts and provinces, could not live and work in their home villages and hamlets like the irregular forces. This meant they had to develop training areas, deployment areas, and safe havens. They were basically deployed in the field for the duration of the war, although being deployed in their home province allowed them close access for visits home, provided they were not moved up the pyramid to the main forces.

The Viet Cong main forces

With battalion-sized forces now at the provincial level, the Viet Cong forces continued their expansion into more of a traditional-type military organization, creating regimental and divisional units. To manage the military struggle, the Viet Cong by 1965 had divided South Vietnam into six military regions referred to as MR-1 through MR-6. (These regions for the most part remained unchanged through the war, but some additions and name changes were made later.) These military regions were controlled by the regional party committees operating within the regional communist front organization. It was within these military regions that the main forces operated. The main forces (*Quan Doi Chu Luc*), often referred to as the 'hard hats' for the helmets they wore, were a collection of independent battalions (*tieu doan co dong*), regiments (*trung doan*), and eventually, divisions.[46]

In their study of insurgency operations in the delta province of Dinh Tuong from 1964 to 1967, the Rand Corporation researchers noted that there were two regiments, the 1st and 2nd Dan Thop Regiments, operating in the Viet Cong Military Region-2 in which the Dinh Tuong province was located. Two battalions of the 1st Dan Thop Regiment, the 261st and 263rd battalions, spent a considerable amount of time in the Dinh Tuong province and their organization and activities were documented by the Rand researchers. The researchers also note that according to Military Assistance Command, Vietnam (MACV), a typical Viet Cong infantry battalion consisted of 300–600 personnel, organized into three infantry companies, a heavy weapons company, and specialized units such as reconnaissance, signal, and sapper.[47]

In August of 1964, the 261st Battalion consisted of six companies (three infantry, two heavy weapons, and one sapper) of over 500 men. Its commanding officers were said to be 'regroupees,' South Vietnamese who had gone to North Vietnam after the 1954 Geneva Accords split Vietnam and who then returned to organize the *dau tranh* against the South Vietnamese Government. It had a good fighting reputation with most of its platoon leaders boasting over ten years of combat experience.[48] The 263rd Battalion had five companies of nearly 600 men in December of 1965. These five companies consisted of three infantry and two heavy weapons companies. The battalion was composed of mostly new recruits, with some guerrillas and local district troops from Long An, Dinh Tuong, and Kien Hoa provinces. It received two months of training before deploying for military operations.[49]

In 1964, the first Viet Cong division was formed and outfitted with modern AK-47s, 7.62 mm machine guns, rocket launchers, mortars, and recoilless rifles.[50] The 9th Viet Cong Division wasted no time moving into action, attacking and holding the Binh Dinh provincial capital of Binh Gia for four days beginning on 28 December 1964. In the process, the 9th ambushed and destroyed the South Vietnamese 33rd Ranger Battalion and 4th Marine Battalion, then stood and held their ground, inflicting heavy losses on South Vietnamese forces sent to relieve the 33rd and 4th battalions. This signified a change in operations often associated with the move from Phase II to Phase III insurgent warfare.[51]

The Viet Cong were ready to take over South Vietnam. The only thing standing in their way was an ever-increasing US military presence. To counter the US, the North Vietnamese *Lao Dong* communist party called in their heavy hitters, the People's Army of Vietnam (PAVN) or as the Military Assistance Command, Vietnam called them, the North Vietnamese Army (NVA).

The North Vietnamese Army (NVA)

Guiding the insurgency in the south against the government had been the North Vietnamese communist party, the *Lao Dong*. Content to provide leadership, guidance, arms, and supplies to their communist brothers in the south, the *Lao Dong* was forced to increase their level of participation with the deployment of NVA units in 1965 to counter the increasing US presence and military operations.

North Vietnamese Army (NVA) main forces

Beginning in late 1964 and early 1965, the NVA began to infiltrate its own main force units across the 17th parallel to bolster their Viet Cong brothers and provide a counter against the growing US military forces. By November of 1965, MACV intelligence estimated there were nine NVA regiments in South Vietnam.[52] The NVA main forces remained under the control of and received their orders from the North.[53]

Like the VC main force, an NVA battalion typically consisted of three infantry companies, a heavy weapons company, and specialized units like reconnaissance, signal, and sapper platoons.[54] The infantry companies were armed with the latest and best communist armaments, including the AK-47, SKD rifles, RPD 7.62 mm light machine guns, and rocket propelled grenade (RPG) launchers. The heavy weapons company included 81 mm and 82 mm mortars, 57 mm and 75 mm recoilless rifles, and 12.7 mm machine guns. In 1968, tanks were an added weapon in the NVA main force arsenal with PT-76 amphibious tanks participating in the battle for Khe Sanh.[55]

By January of 1968, the number of NVA battalions had surpassed the number of VC battalions, with the NVA operating 99 battalions in South Vietnam while the Viet Cong had 98 battalions. Just five months later, the

NVA had increased to 113 battalions while the VC, badly hurt by their debilitating Tet Offensive, were down to 91 under-strength battalions. These figures show the ascendancy of the North Vietnamese forces in the conduct of the war in South Vietnam. After the Tet Offensive, the Viet Cong became secondary players in their own war; the North was taking over.

North Vietnamese in Viet Cong units

Another indicator that the North was taking over the war was the number of North Vietnamese assigned to Viet Cong units. In 1966, MACV estimated that no more than 10 percent of Viet Cong battalions were made up of North Vietnamese personnel. By mid-1968, the North Vietnamese personnel making up Viet Cong battalions had increased to nearly one in three.[56]

In looking at the war effort of both NVA and Viet Cong main and local forces (excluding the irregular forces), the North only accounted for just over 5 percent of the battalion strength in early 1965. By 1966 this had tripled to nearly 20 percent, and doubled again to approximately 45 percent in 1967. By the start of 1968, North Vietnamese battalions constituted over half of the battalions found in South Vietnam (99 NVA to 98 VC), and with the 10 percent North Vietnamese manning found in the Viet Cong battalions, the North accounted for a full 60 percent of the enemy battalion strength facing the United States and the Government of South Vietnam. After the Tet Offensive, this increased further to over 70 percent.[57] North Vietnam was poised to take over South Vietnam.

Administrative and service troops

A war can not be prosecuted without supplies, communications, and processed 'paperwork.' This was just as true of the enemy as it was of the US forces. The enemy had a much shorter support 'tail' than did the United States, but without these types of troops, the enemy could not operate.

A key contribution to the enemy's war effort was made by the communication-liaison troops which ran the Postal Transportation and Communications Service. These troops were responsible for the transmission of mail, official orders and correspondence, intelligence information, medicine, and money, as well as guiding troops unfamiliar with the area.[58] The commo-liaison troops were organized at the regional, province, district, and village level. In Military Region 2, there were four regional stations in 1965, each with approximately 50 men. At the province level, there were typically 20–35 commo-liaison personnel. At the district and village levels, commo-liaison personnel were only responsible for postal communications. There were about 10–15 personnel at the district level, while the village level manning varied depending upon size, but seldom had more than 10 commo-liaison personnel.[59]

The commo-liaison function was a critical link in the Viet Cong organization, providing the communications channel in a secure mode from the top levels of the central committee within the National Liberation Front, down to the lowest levels at the village and hamlet. It not only provided information flow downward, but also provided the conduit for the upward flow of intelligence information. Without such an organization, the command and control of the insurgency would have been severely hampered.

Another key element was the logistical troops which kept the forces supplied with food and ammunition. Self-sufficiency was a hallmark of the guerrillas, but without supplies flowing in from North Vietnam down the Ho Chi Minh Trail and from shipments through the port at Sihanoukville in Cambodia, the guerrilla movement would have been slowed to a near standstill. One of the principal units providing this logistical service was Group 559 which built, maintained, and ran the supply route known as the Ho Chi Minh Trail. The trail grew from a collection of way stations placed a day's march apart, to twelve consolidated complexes. The size of Group 559 also grew from a contingent of just a few hundred to over 50,000 plus 50,000 NVA engineering troops and another 12,000 NVA infantry and anti-aircraft artillery troops who provided defense.[60]

Group 559 and the Ho Chi Minh Trail were the essential links between the insurgency in the South and the guidance, control, and vital supplies which emanated from the North. As the North's share in the war increased, so too did the importance of the Ho Chi Minh Trail and the troops which kept it operating.

The military aspect in summary

The enemy faced by the Government of South Vietnam and the United States had many facets. The insurgency was fighting a synchronized war of Phase I, II and III with a collection of forces that included irregular self-defense and guerrilla forces, regular troops organized locally at district and province level employing guerrilla tactics, and more traditional main battle forces, which used semi-conventional tactics when it suited them, or the tried and true hit-and-run guerrilla ruse. These forces were joined by the even more conventionally armed and battle tested battalions of the People's Army of Vietnam (PAVN), or as they were referred to by MACV, the NVA or North Vietnamese Army.

This collection of forces was supported by a dedicated and extensive network of service and administrative troops which kept the deployed forces supplied with food and ammunition, letters from home, and orders from headquarters. While nowhere near matching the technological prowess of the United States, these back country soldiers frustrated and outlasted their military superiors.

The enemy can thus be categorized as follows:

- main forces (VC and NVA)
- local forces (provincial and district)
- irregular forces (village and hamlet)
- administrative and service troops.

This then was the military *dau tranh vu trang* struggle; what of the political *dau tranh chinh tri* struggle?

The political aspect

The insurgency in South Vietnam had been controlled from the North from the beginning. The *dau tranh*, which had begun initially against the Japanese in World War II and then continued against the French colonialists, was incomplete with the signing of the 1954 Geneva Accords and the North Vietnamese communist party, the *Lao Dong*, had not lost sight of this fact. They controlled but half of what they considered their country. To remedy this flawed situation, the *Lao Dong* began sending back those South Vietnamese who had fled North with the division of Vietnam in 1954. These 'regroupees,' as detailed in the preceding section, began to recruit and instigate the military *dau tranh vu trang* struggle which gave birth to the Viet Cong main, local and irregular forces. These 'regroupees' also began the political *dau tranh chinh tri* struggle and formed the basis of what became known as the Viet Cong infrastructure or VCI, those elements which formed the 'Viet Cong shadow government' and which directed the Viet Cong military forces.

The National Liberation Front

As the name advertises, the National Liberation Front (NLF) was a group set up as a front for organizations, associations, and political parties which advocated the downfall of the government in South Vietnam and reunification with the North. The controlling element of the NLF was the *Lao Dong* communist party of North Vietnam, through its Southern branch, the People's Revolutionary Party, or PRP (*Dang Nhan Dan Cach Mang*).

The NLF was established by the *Lao Dong* on 20 December 1960 with the purpose of inciting the population of South Vietnam to revolt in a *Khoi Nghia*, or General Uprising (literally means 'to stand up and fight for a just cause').[61] To accomplish this goal required an extensive organization which relied heavily upon proselytizing and agitation. The NLF was organized at all Vietnamese administrative levels, starting at the hamlet and village levels, to the district and provincial echelons, up to the regional offices and the central committee.

The focus of the NLF effort was at the village. Douglas Pike, in his work *Viet Cong*, captures the importance of the village in any endeavor:

> The central fact about Vietnam is the village. For two thousand years it has been so, and although the two cities of Saigon and Hanoi may have been regarded abroad as Vietnam, to the Vietnamese the village was his land's heart, mind, and soul. Surrounded by its high bamboo hedge, itself possessing a mystic quality, the village has bound the inhabitants into close communal and kinship relationships and, at the same time, separated them from the rest of the world. It was a haven and a defense. When he left, a villager was expected to return in pilgrimage each lunar new year; and no matter how far he traveled or how long he stayed away, his village was always home, and there he wished to be buried.[62]

Thus, it was at the village that the NLF sought to bring in and convert the people to their cause. To convert the people, various associations were formed for which the people would feel an affinity. Villagers could join simply as a spectator, and then through proselytizing be converted to the NLF program and ultimately, be brought into the communist web, either by joining the PRP and themselves becoming agitators under the political *dau tranh chinh tri* struggle, or if young and fit, joining the military *dau tranh vu trang* struggle and becoming a guerrilla and a part of the insurgency's force pyramid.

The associations run by the NLF included Liberation Associations for Farmers, Women, Workers, Youth, Student, and Cultural. These Liberation Associations acted as the foundation for the entire insurgency[63] as it served to mobilize the population through propaganda and agitation.[64] The NLF was open to all, and many non-communists joined, but the NLF was the creation of the North Vietnamese and internal control was exercised through the communist People's Revolutionary Party of South Vietnam.

The People's Revolutionary Party

Originally called the Southern branch of the *Lao Dong* communist party, the People's Revolutionary Party (*Dang Nhan Dan Cach Mang*) carried out the *dau tranh* in South Vietnam. Founded on 1 January 1962, its Central Committee became known to the military community as the Central Office, South Vietnam, or COSVN. The People's Revolutionary Party (PRP) was the guiding force behind the insurgency in South Vietnam and was itself tightly controlled by the *Lao Dong* in the North.

A PRP training manual from October 1965 listed the Party's goals and objectives,

> The Party [objective] . . . is to overthrow imperialism, colonialism, and feudalism, to build a life of peace, prosperity, and happiness without

oppression and extortion . . . Once independence is obtained, the next step is unification, constructed and consolidated in every way to make the country powerful and rich, a stronghold of peace. Then will come the social re-organization, along socialist-communist principles, without land demarcations, cooperating in rural electrification, re-education of individuals, nationalization of private property, cultural and scientific education for everyone, progressing day by day to better and better things in all fields. Also, helping other small weak countries to struggle against imperialism and rid the world of conflict and to help provide everyone with freedom, legality, warmth, food, and happiness . . .[65]

The PRP was also the driving force behind the National Liberation Front, with PRP committees running the NLF at every echelon, from regional to the hamlet.[66] At the top of the PRP was the Central Committee, which had three primary responsibilities:

1   military commissar,
2   NLF control and
3   general administration.[67]

The military commissar was naturally responsible for the Viet Cong forces. He also coordinated with the North to synchronize the operations of the Viet Cong forces with those of the NVA, which remained under the control of the North Vietnamese.[68] The NLF controlling agent oversaw recruitment, organization, proselytizing, and indoctrination, while the general administration function ran the financial, intelligence, communication, and liaison programs.

At the bottom of the organization was the traditional communist three-man cell. One to seven of these cells were grouped into the basic PRP unit called the *chi bo*. The *chi bo* was the PRP's 'link with the masses,' and was also referred to as the hamlet branch or street branch of the PRP.[69] Anywhere from three to twelve *chi bo* received their direction and leadership from an executive committee of the PRP located at the street zone in the city, or at the village level. This was the lowest echelon with any type of decision-making authority and its executive committee typically consisted of five to seven members.[70] This was also the lowest level at which a military affairs function was found. It was also here that the NLF had its extensive organization of Liberation Associations.

An unidentified publication in both English and Vietnamese published in December 1968, probably in Saigon, contains the following description of how the PRP takes over a village:

As the Party cadres gain power over the villages they begin to regulate all aspects of each resident's life. Movement to and from GVN [government] controlled areas is strictly monitored; government papers and identification cards are frequently destroyed; government administrators are neutralized or executed and replaced by elements of the party structure; heavy taxes are levied; fortifications are constructed in order to establish 'combat villages'; the Military Affairs Section organizes local guerrilla forces; the youths are urged or forced to join the Liberation Youth Association or the People's Revolutionary Youth Association; through propaganda and indoctrination, leaders are recruited and trained to act on behalf of the Party and/or the Front; men are recruited or drafted for the Liberation Army; news media are strictly controlled so that all events are reported from the Party's point of view; security agents control visitors and prosecute 'spies'; villagers are forced to house and feed VC troops as they move through the area; women are urged to participate in face-to-face struggles (demonstrations against GVN authorities); families of ARVN (Army of South Vietnam) soldiers are constantly plagued to order their men back home; villagers are forced to provide bearer services for supplies and ammunition; and a constant barrage of propaganda vilifying 'the American imperialists and their Saigon puppet government' is repeated so often even by school children that neither thought nor free action seem possible.[71]

Such was the power of the PRP and its NLF organization at the village level, carrying on the political *dau tranh chinh tri* struggle while guiding the military *dau tranh vu trang* struggle. It was not a questionable matter then, that the people controlling the PRP and NLF were considered to be the enemy also; referred to as the Viet Cong Infrastructure or VCI. The VCI were considered the enemy and a special effort, often referred to as the 'Phoenix Program,' was specifically operated to eliminate this threat.[72]

Summary of the political aspect

The continuation of the *dau tranh* led the *Lao Dong* communist party of North Vietnam to establish the National Liberation Front in 1960 to complete the struggle and reunite all Vietnamese under the banner of Ho Chi Minh. The National Liberation Front encompassed the political struggle of *dau tranh* and was open to all who opposed the Government of South Vietnam and sought reunification with the North. To establish communist party control of the NLF, the *Lao Dong* also set up the People's Revolutionary Party, the communist party of South Vietnam, to manage the NLF and also provide guidance to the Viet Cong forces engaged in the military struggle of *dau tranh*. The close integration of the military and political struggle can best be illustrated by depicting the organizational relationship of the PRP, NLF, and VC Forces (see Figure 10).

The PRP and the NLF were the political instruments of the *dau tranh* and as such were considered the enemy, referred to as the Viet Cong infrastructure. The VCI, along with VC/NVA main forces, VC local forces,

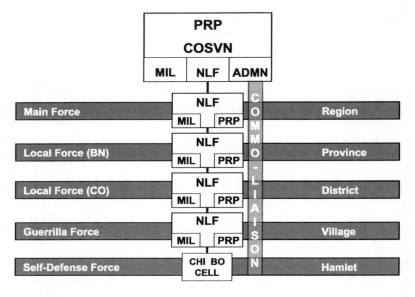

Figure 10 Relationship of the communist political and military organizations.

VC irregular forces, and administrative and service troops constituted the categories which were counted by military intelligence as the enemy.

The enemy: our own biases

The enemy's war and his forces – both military and political – were not well understood by American intelligence. The surprise which came on Tet 1968 threw intelligence under intense scrutiny. There were numerous explanations for why Tet came as a surprise, such as the excuse that the enemy had acted irrationally and in a way that nobody could have predicted. Yet, the signals were there, the US just did not understand them because they did not understand the enemy.

In 1967, on the eve of the Tet Offensive, US intelligence had lost its way. First, intelligence lost its objectivity, succumbing to the command viewpoint that the enemy was moving into conventional war, leaving guerrilla and insurgency warfare behind. While viewed by those in command as intelligence finally joining the team, the loss of objectivity hindered intelligence efforts to understand the enemy organization and motives. This loss of objectivity was aided by a predilection toward ethnocentrism, the natural tendency to view the war in terms of one's own references. 'The American Way of War,' was conventional warfare with conventional arms, this was the type of war the American military had been trained for, the type of war they wanted to fight. Further, compounding the inability to understand the enemy was the over-reliance of intelligence on technology. The enemy, especially at the lower levels of the irregular forces, seldom used radios and blended in with the local populace or hid in the jungles, thus rendering them invisible to the US technology of radio-intercept and aerial photography.

If the basics of the enemy's organization was not well understood in Vietnam, how could intelligence hope to unravel the enemy's plans and strategy, or even begin to comprehend what motivated the enemy and what would make them succumb to the US will? Intelligence in Vietnam did not know these things, and worse, intelligence in 1967 was about to become embroiled in a bitter internal battle amongst themselves. A true drama of tragedy was about to unfold.

7 Setting the stage
Vietnam intelligence in 1967

(MACV Deputy Commander General Creighton) Abrams grinned widely, slapped me on the back, and said, 'That's the stuff I want to hear.'

General Phillip Davidson[1]

Brigadier General Phillip Davidson was ready to join the MACV team when he arrived in the summer of 1967 to take over as the J2, Assistant Chief of Staff for Intelligence. Whereas his predecessor, Brigadier General Joseph McChristian was professionally, and coldly, referred to by General William Westmoreland as 'my intelligence chief,' Davidson was on a first name basis with General Westmoreland.[2] Davidson brought a new view of the Vietnam War to MACV intelligence, a view that more closely mirrored those in command. McChristian had not endeared himself to the rest of the MACV staff with his assessment that the enemy had the will and capability to continue the war indefinitely. Nor did General Westmoreland appreciate the dilemma McChristian left him upon the J2's departure in June of 1967; increased enemy numbers based upon improved intelligence, at a time when Westmoreland believed the crossover point had been reached and the enemy's numbers, improved or not, were on the decline.

McChristian's view of the enemy also differed from the rest of the MACV staff. For McChristian, any force that could hamper the MACV mission was included in the order of battle, this included the old men, women, and children of the country's hamlets organized by the enemy into self-defense forces. MACV wanted big-unit warfare, battalion against battalion, division against division, mano e mano. General Davidson dropped the self-defense forces from the order of battle and believed the enemy was moving into big-unit warfare, the 'American Way of War,' as so aptly named and described by Russell F. Weigley in his seminal work, *The American Way of War, A History of United States Military Strategy and Policy*.[3]

To better understand the enemy, McChristian initiated a program to collect information from more traditional sources of intelligence, the human.

Relying on captured documents, interrogation reports, and informants, McChristian's intelligence organization found it had undercounted the self-defense forces and the political infrastructure running the communist war effort. General Davidson belittled this effort and insisted any information had to be confirmed by another source, preferably 'technical intelligence.'

Intelligence under McChristian was a frustrating experience for many at MACV. His assessment of the enemy, that they had the will and capability to continue the war at current levels, prompted Major General William DePuy, the MACV/J3 or Director of Operations, to remark, 'If McChristian is right in what he's saying, we're losing this war.'[4] The measure of success in the war for McChristian was the enemy's will. Not so for his replacement. Brigadier General Davidson believed the enemy was hurting and with their numbers on the decline, the crossover point had been reached; in a war of attrition, numbers counted as a measure of success.

The summer of 1967 marked a change in the intelligence perspective in Vietnam. Under Brigadier General Joseph McChristian, intelligence supported the MACV staff with assessments of the enemy using all sources of intelligence to determine their will and capability to affect the MACV mission. With the arrival of Brigadier General Phillip Davidson, intelligence was a team player on the MACV staff, assessing the enemy's ability to affect MACV's 'American Way of War,' using the latest technology to count the enemy as the measure of success. In short, MACV intelligence was a team player, supporting the 'American Way of War' with the latest technology to count the enemy as the measure of success.

A team player

Intelligence at MACV in the latter half of 1967, was a fully integrated member of the MACV team. While General Westmoreland had been presented with a dilemma by his previous J2 in the form of higher numbers at a time when he was projecting declining numbers, his new J2 provided him with solutions, not dilemmas. General Davidson offered up the self-defense forces to be cut from the order of battle. By eliminating these forces, the overall improved numbers appeared to reflect the continued decline of the enemy with no jumps or gaps that would catch the eye of the press.

Not only did General Westmoreland's new J2 provide the solution, he was a key to implementing the explanation. When the CIA proved reluctant to accept MACV's view of the enemy strength totals, General Davidson led the full-court press to pressure the CIA to conform to the MACV perspective. In two acrimonious conferences, one at the CIA headquarters in Virginia and the other at the MACV headquarters in Vietnam, General Davidson stone-walled and refused all compromise on the enemy strength totals. In the end, his MACV team won and the CIA dropped the self-defense forces from the enemy's order of battle strength totals.

Supporting the 'American Way of War'

The enemy faced by the United States in Vietnam took on a myriad of forms. The enemy fought in small guerrilla units, ambushing then fleeing, never staying to fight. The enemy fought in small combat units, attacking isolated outposts and villages, but again, seldom staying to fight. The enemy also fought as regular combat units, engaging the Americans in isolated areas, such as Khe Sanh, and staying to fight it out until forced to retreat. The preferred 'American Way of War,' in which the full brunt of American power could be brought to bear on the enemy, was when the enemy used regular combat units and stayed to fight. This was the best way to kill the most enemy in this war of attrition.

Intelligence under McChristian had focused on the regular type of enemy units initially. But having received a good estimate of these units' strength, he then turned to the guerrillas, the militia-type forces known as the self-defense forces, and the political infrastructure. MACV showed little interest in these types of units, and under Davidson, the self-defense forces were dropped. For General Davidson, the war was swiftly moving to more conventional type engagements with regular combat units. Here, he was in full agreement with General Westmoreland and the rest of the MACV staff who 'sensed, largely by intuition,' that the enemy was quickly moving to a more conventional type of war with regular combat units.[5] The enemy was going to fight the 'American Way of War' – this was the assessment of the new MACV/J2.

With the latest technology

For General McChristian, 'The greatest source of intelligence in the world is an individual who knows what you want to know and that you have access to. I think that in this type of war you have to put the main reliance on human intelligence and that means interrogations and documents.'[6] To General Davidson, such information was 'low-grade intelligence.'[7] Such intelligence was unreliable and subject to deception. Besides, America had more advanced and technical means to gather intelligence, and technology was much more reliable and less susceptible to deception.

The 'American Way of War' entailed large-scale confrontations where superior firepower and technology could devastate the enemy. The American Way of Intelligence was very similar, technology could snoop where humans dared not tread. America's forte was technology, and technology had proved its worth in the world of intelligence. Using sophisticated sensors, America could listen in on the enemy's communications and take pictures of the enemy's movements and support structure. Intelligence derived from technical means was not subject to the establishment of a source's bona fides, technical means were non-biased and objective.

Intelligence derived from technical sources required greater protection, and thus carried higher classification levels. Human intelligence, was typically only Confidential or Secret and carried no caveats, it was 'low-grade.' Intelligence derived from technical means, however, carried higher classifications with caveats, restricting their dissemination to only those with the proper, 'high-grade' clearances. In the Vietnam War, intelligence was graded, and for General Davidson, it was technical intelligence that received the highest grade.

To count the enemy as the measure of success

For General McChristian, the enemy's will and capability were the measures of success in the Vietnam War. In a war of attrition, General Davidson saw the enemy's numbers as the gauge for success. With the battlefield successes of 1967, the enemy must be hurting, so assessed General Davidson in his briefing to the Secretary of Defense in July 1967. General Davidson also had the figures to back him up. The enemy's numbers were on a decline in 1967, and the order of battle summaries prepared by both General McChristian and General Davidson showed the decline graphically.

Where Davidson and McChristian differed was in the importance of the decline. To McChristian, even though the numbers were in a decline, the enemy still had the will and capability to continue. For Davidson, this was a 'pat' assessment. More important to Davidson was how to kill more enemy; he focused on trying to divine what the enemy planned to do next. With such information, US forces could be prepared to meet and fix the enemy, thus furthering the 'American Way of War,' and advancing the strategy of attrition.

To support General Westmoreland in his public relations campaign to bolster public support for the war, General Davidson was very aggressive in making sure that the downward decline of the enemy's numbers was properly graphed. Here, to continue the image of a steady, unbroken decline, the self-defense forces were eliminated from the order of battle summaries. And to ensure unbroken ranks within the intelligence community, General Davidson was the front-man in pressuring the CIA to highlight the decline in the enemy's numbers and remove any possible glitches that might give those who viewed the war 'incorrectly,' any reason to question the figures. The figures showed success, and declining enemy numbers signaled that an end to the war was in the offing and that the enemy was 'bankrupt.'

The differences between the two men who held the position of MACV/J2 in 1967, General McChristian until June, and General Davidson thereafter, are stark and clear. Intelligence at MACV in 1967 went through a transition with the change in intelligence leadership. Such a change was dramatic, and from the CIA's perspective, it marked a transformation from a possible meeting of the minds to a confirmed, all-out confrontation. Vietnam in 1967 was ripe for a dramatic intelligence war.

8 An intelligence drama
The protagonists

> What is called 'foreknowledge' cannot be elicited from spirits, nor from gods, nor by analogy with past events, nor from calculations. It must be obtained from men who know the enemy situation.
>
> Sun Tzu[1]

The Vietnam War in 1967 had become an American War, with an American strategy – attrition. To accomplish this strategy, the tactics of search, find, fix, and destroy the enemy were honed. By 1967, the strategy was showing encouraging results. General Westmoreland told President Johnson in a meeting in Washington, DC in April 1967, that he believed the crossover point had been reached, and the enemy's numbers were on the decline. The Secretary of Defense, Robert McNamara, was not convinced. The Secretary, who had always been suspicious of the military and their optimistic reporting, had ordered the Central Intelligence Agency in April 1967 to cross-check the numbers coming out of General Westmoreland's headquarters at the Military Assistance Command, Vietnam (MACV).

The beginnings of a bureaucratic drama were in place. The bureaucracies were the intelligence organizations of the MACV Assistant Chief of Staff for Intelligence (J2) and the Central Intelligence Agency. The issue of contention was the order of battle, the official listing of enemy numbers and units. This was the natural territory of the military forces, but the war also included a political aspect as an insurgency. Both MACV/J2 and the CIA felt they were justified in being considered the experts in this area. There was no 'chain of command' for the various intelligence organizations in Vietnam and each had free rein to pursue whatever they felt was within their purview.

The protagonists in this intelligence drama were Brigadier General Joseph A. McChristian, US Army, the MACV/J2 from June 1965 to June 1967; Brigadier General Phillip B. Davidson, US Army, the MACV/J2 from June 1967 to May 1969; and Mr. Sam Adams, an analyst working in the office of the Special Assistant for Vietnam Affairs (SAVA) at CIA. Each of these protagonists brought their own unique views on the war and experiences in the various ways and means of intelligence to the task of determining who was the enemy and how to count that enemy. All three developed strong and unshakable 'estimates' on the enemy's order of battle. Though expressing widely differing views and opinions and rarely reaching consensus, all three were intelligence professionals.

Brigadier General Joseph A. McChristian

Brigadier General McChristian arrived in Vietnam on 29 June 1965 and had a grand total of 102 military intelligence personnel assigned under his command. By the time he left, over 2,466 were under the operational control of the MACV/J2.[2] Immediately upon his arrival he began bringing in the intelligence resources he felt were needed to provide MACV with the most accurate, timely, adequate, and usable intelligence on the enemy's strength, capabilities and vulnerabilities.[3] By October of 1965 he had also established the nucleus of his intelligence effort by creating four centers, composed of both American and South Vietnamese intelligence professionals. These four centers were:

1   The Combined Intelligence Center, Vietnam (CICV),
2   Combined Military Interrogation Center (CMIC),
3   Combined Document Exploitation Center (CDEC), and
4   Combined Material Exploitation Center (CMEC).[4]

The Combined Intelligence Center, Vietnam (CICV) was the main analytical organization, looking at order of battle, area analysis, targets, imagery interpretation, and material intelligence. Being a 'combined' center meant that the highest classification of the data used was typically Secret. Technical intelligence, such as that intelligence gathered on enemy radio communications, was highly classified and was seldom available to the CICV. Thus, the primary sources of information were interrogations and documents.

The Combined Military Interrogation Center and Combined Document Exploitation Center were critical sources of intelligence for McChristian and his CICV. 'I have always considered the greatest source of information a person who is knowledgeable on the subject and the second greatest source a document containing such information.'[5] The Combined Material Exploitation Center produced intelligence on the enemy's weapons and equipment based on analysis of materials captured during the war.

McChristian and the 'American Way of War'

McChristian tended to view the war from the enemy's perspective, but with few intelligence resources available to MACV/J2 in 1965, he had to prioritize and this meant emphasizing the enemy forces that could cause the most harm. 'As resources came in I put them on the most important enemy capabilities first, their regular forces.'[6] The North Vietnamese Army (NVA) and the South Vietnamese communist Viet Cong (VC) main and local forces were the top priority as they could have the most immediate effect upon the accomplishment of the MACV mission. McChristian, while putting the regular forces as the top priority, also recognized guerrilla, self-defense (SD) forces and the Viet Cong infrastructure (VCI) as threats which also had to be dealt with as resources became available.

By late 1966 and early 1967, McChristian felt he had enough intelligence capabilities in country to begin allocating collection efforts against the guerrilla, SD forces, and the VCI. He initiated two collection programs, CORRAL to gather information on the VCI, and RITZ to amass data on the guerrilla and SD forces.[7] McChristian recognized the VCI, SD force, and guerrillas as threats to the accomplishment of the MACV mission in South Vietnam. 'Any forces that could adversely affect the accomplishment of the mission should be in the Order of Battle,' he stated, even the Viet Cong infrastructure, because 'they controlled the military.'[8]

> Even though a guerrilla may not carry a weapon, he certainly knows how to sharpen and replace a pungi stake or to use a hand grenade made from a beer can. A good intelligence officer must avoid preconceived ideas when it comes to estimating the enemy. In Vietnam, it was necessary to discard temporarily many of the conceptions that our military education and experiences had engendered. Our enemy's school was 'the bush' – to quote General Giap – and his strategy, tactics, and organization fitted a revised Maoist view of protracted war. For this reason I realized that military intelligence in Vietnam had to adapt if it was to be successful against this enemy.[9]

To help his subordinates comprehend the necessity of not adopting an American viewpoint in analyzing the enemy, he would often tell the story of a mission he undertook in Ecuador to conduct a study on the potential for insurgency in that country in the early 1960s. He encountered an indigenous Indian with a blowgun and asked him if he wouldn't rather use a gun. The Indian replied that when he used his blowgun to hunt piglets, he could kill many without scaring the others away. A gun, the Indian explained, would scare all the piglets away after the first shot. Further, it cost the Indian nothing to make his blowgun and darts, while a gun would be expensive and he would constantly have to buy ammunition. No, the Indian wouldn't part with his blowgun.[10] McChristian was not focused on only the main and local forces; he recognized and counted all the forces the enemy used. He recognized that the enemy was not going to ape the 'American Way of War' and would use all the resources available to them.

McChristian and technology

During a briefing to Secretary of Defense Robert McNamara in July 1966 to justify the funds MACV needed to build an intelligence organization, McChristian stated: 'The greatest source of intelligence in the world is an individual who knows what you want to know and that you have access to. I think that in this type of war you have to put the main reliance on human intelligence and that means interrogations and documents.'[11] McChristian received the go ahead from McNamara to build the Combined Interrogation Center and the Combined Document Exploitation Center, the foundation of his intelligence efforts.

McChristian did not eschew technical intelligence even though he held human intelligence in the highest regard. He recognized the impact technical intelligence would have on locating the enemy and the need to pass on such information in a timely fashion. He worked out an agreement with the National Security Agency where he could task their assets and pass sanitized information immediately to the US forces on the ground.[12] He also salvaged ground-based direction-finding equipment and put it to use in tracking the Headquarters of Military Region 4, just north of Saigon. As a result of this effort, and the use of other intelligence resources such as pattern analysis and imagery interpretation, McChristian recommended an attack be made on the Headquarters in January 1967.[13] This operation, dubbed Operation CEDAR FALLS, was a multi-division attack by the US and resulted in 750 enemy dead, the capture of 280 prisoners, 540 defectors, and 3,700 tons of rice, in addition to over 500,000 pages of enemy documents.[14]

> Every scrap of information, every written report, is to the intelligence officer as nickels and dimes are to a banker. It takes a lot of them to make the business profitable. Every piece of information must be accounted for like money and confirmed or refuted as genuine or counterfeit. When an intelligence analyst receives an unconfirmed report, he cannot let it go. He must confirm or refute it.[15]

Brigadier General McChristian did not discount any type of information; he recognized the importance of human intelligence, especially in the primitive environment in which the enemy operated. But he also used technical intelligence to get relevant and timely information to the field where it was needed.

McChristian and numbers

When McChristian asked his predecessor for a brief on the MACV order of battle for the enemy forces, Marine Brigadier General Youngdale replied, 'What do you mean by Order of Battle?'[16] In June 1965, MACV had no order of battle. The new J2 turned to the South Vietnamese for help and they provided the numbers which became the basis for the MACV order of battle, but these figures were 'very, very inadequate.'[17] With limited resources, McChristian set out to accurately account for the main and local forces. With more NVA battalions infiltrating and VC battalions being formed, the Combined Intelligence Center, Vietnam was able to accurately identify and account for these units and their personnel. The order of battle on the main and local forces was never doubted. The same could not be said of the figures for the irregular forces and VCI.

In the first iteration of the order of battle by the CICV, a caveat was placed on the figures for the irregular forces and VCI, stating that these figures were based solely upon information given by the South Vietnamese and were unverified. Subsequent issues of the order of battle carried no such caveat,[18] contributing to some of the confusion and reluctance on the part of certain individuals to suddenly change these numbers once more accurate figures became available. More accurate information on the irregular forces and VCI did become available by May 1967, based on collection programs specifically initiated to more accurately account for the irregular forces and VCI.[19] The new data on the irregular forces and VCI substantially increased their numbers over the figures originally provided by the South Vietnamese and carried in the MACV order of battle for nearly one-and-a-half years. The numbers increased from the 112,800 carried in the order of battle from May 1966 to August 1967[20] to a revised estimate of 190,100 that was presented by MACV at a conference in August 1967.[21]

The revised figures came out well after McChristian had departed Vietnam and only after much debate and discussion within MACV.[22] The new figures were not included in the MACV Order of Battle Summary until October 1967, after a contentious debate with the rest of the intelligence community. Even then, not all of the 190,100 figure was used as the SD force (117,900) were dropped from the Summary.

McChristian as a team player at MACV

Brigadier General Joseph A. McChristian was referred to by some of the MACV staff not by name, but as Brigadier General Phillip B. Davidson's 'predecessor.'[23] He was not viewed as team player, which was later borne out by his role as the most senior officer to testify not for, but against, General Westmoreland in a libel case brought by Westmoreland against CBS in 1984. General Westmoreland always referred to McChristian as 'my intelligence chief' or 'my intelligence officer' in his autobiography, *A Soldier Reports*.[24] In the acknowledgments to his book (written eight years before the trial), Westmoreland conspicuously neglects to mention Major General McChristian, but does include Brigadier General Phillip B. Davidson,[25] to whom he refers as 'Phil Davidson' in the text of his book.[26]

General Westmoreland and the staff of MACV, however, never questioned the accuracy of McChristian's intelligence. Several operations, such as CEDAR FALLS in January 1967, were the direct result of recommendations by McChristian. Further, General Westmoreland spent several pages of his book expounding the accuracy and thoroughness of McChristian's intelligence on supplies coming from Sihanoukville, Cambodia.[27] While his credentials as 'my intelligence chief' were never questioned, he never endeared himself with the rest of the MACV staff with his assessment that 'the North Vietnamese and Viet Cong have the will and the capability to conduct a protracted war of attrition at current levels of activity indefinitely.'[28] Major General William E. DePuy, while the J3 at MACV in 1966, once remarked after a briefing in which McChristian gave his assessment on the enemy's will and capability, 'If McChristian is right in what's he's saying, we are losing this war.'[29]

McChristian described his relationship with General Westmoreland as very military and professional. He said Westmoreland was confident in the intelligence he received from McChristian and never disagreed or questioned his assessment that the enemy had the will and capability to continue at current levels.[30] However, General Westmoreland could not have shared McChristian's assessment; in April 1967, just over one month before McChristian was to leave Vietnam, General Westmoreland told President Johnson that he believed the 'crossover point' had been reached.[31] Such a view would never have come out of the Combined Intelligence Center, according to McChristian, who maintains that manpower was never one of the enemy's vulnerabilities.[32] Brigadier General McChristian was not on General Westmoreland's team.

McChristian as a team player with the CIA

Brigadier General McChristian had built a sizable intelligence organization in Vietnam, but he had competition. The CIA was also in country, and fell outside of General Westmoreland's operational control. McChristian felt all intelligence in Vietnam should have fallen under General Westmoreland. He said, 'One of the long-accepted principles of war – unity of command – was violated in Vietnam because of the nature of the insurgency. In this conflict, all US intelligence organizations were not centralized under the MACV commander.'[33]

McChristian felt that the CIA was less than forthcoming in passing on intelligence. 'I can't remember the CIA bringing me any information and saying, "Here, you might find this useful".'[34] While the CICV was compiling information on the VCI, McChristian sought input from throughout the intelligence community; none was forthcoming from the CIA. Yet when the MACV published their VCI study, CIA demanded that responsibility for the VCI be taken over as a project of the CIA. McChristian spurned them, replying, 'They can influence adversely the accomplishment of our mission; I feel I'm responsible for that.'[35]

When an Order of Battle Conference was convened in Honolulu, Hawaii in February 1967, Brigadier General McChristian let the CIA and everyone else present from the intelligence community know who was in charge in Vietnam:

> Gentlemen, I heard some loose remarks earlier in the day that we are here assembled to arrive at a new number for the order of battle. I would like to use this opportunity to inform anyone who harbors this notion to drop it, and to drop it at once. The Vietcong order of battle is MACV's business, which is to say, my business. Don't tread on me.[36]

Brigadier General Phillip B. Davidson

Taking over as MACV/J2 on 1 June 1967, Brigadier General Davidson immediately found himself at odds with his West Point classmate, Brigadier General McChristian. He relates in his book, *Secrets of the Vietnam War*,

> Joe's basic operating principle – at least as I saw it – was to throw the maximum amount of manpower, machines, buildings, and money at the intelligence problem, and by sheer weight of effort overpower it. . . . Now, let me say candidly that I disagree with this approach to military intelligence. Somewhere along the line, increased numbers of people just get in each other's way. Excess personnel lower the effectiveness of an intelligence organization; they don't raise it. And, while I accept that a sizable organization is required to collect and produce basic intelligence data, concentration on sheer numbers of people obscures the fact that the really valuable intelligence is produced by a few talented analysts and estimators.[37]

Brigadier General Davidson also found fault with McChristian's assessment of how the war was progressing, deriding his estimate that the enemy had the will and capability to continue indefinitely, describing it as 'pat.'[38] McChristian had left a briefing for Brigadier General Davidson to give to Secretary of Defense Robert McNamara who was to arrive in just a week. Davidson was unsettled by the short notice and felt uneasy giving a briefing he did not write to a Secretary of Defense notorious for his probing questions. Even more unsettling for Davidson was that he did not agree with the assessment at all. 'As I read it my spine turned cold.'[39] Fortunately for Davidson, the Arab/Israeli War of 1967 intervened and McNamara's visit was put off for one month.

In Davidson's view, McChristian was not offering any indication of what the enemy's intentions were; no predictions on future enemy plans or operations. Davidson felt that, given the facts, it is the intelligence officer's responsibility to forecast future enemy operations, plans, and trends; to answer the commander's 'eternal' question, 'What the hell is the enemy going to do?'[40] To assist him in answering this question, Davidson immediately fired McChristian's estimators, whom he thought were 'hopeless,' and brought in his own experts, Colonels Daniel O. Graham (later Lieutenant General) and Charles A. Morris. Davidson, Graham, and Morris became the MACV estimators.[41] 'The lesser ranks may do the research and even write the first drafts, but "the man," the J-2 himself, must get into the estimate early. It is his estimate, and he will have to defend it against all assailants and skeptics – of which there is always an ample supply.'[42]

In the briefing he eventually gave to Secretary McNamara in July 1967, Davidson dropped McChristian's 'pat' assessment that the enemy could continue at the present levels indefinitely. Instead, Davidson offered the following insights:

> Overall, the enemy must be having personnel problems. His losses have been heavy, and his in-country recruiting efforts unsatisfactory. He is probably attempting to make good his losses by heavy infiltration, but we cannot conclusively prove this, nor do we know how successful he has been. We hear frequently of the so-called 'Crossover point' – that is, when we put out of action more enemy per month than we estimate he brought into country and recruited for that month. This is a nebulous figure, composed as you have seen of several tenuous variables. We may have reached the 'crossover point' in March and May of this year, but we will not know for some months.[43]

The difference between McChristian's assessment, that the enemy had the will and capability to persist indefinitely at current levels, and Davidson's estimate that in all likelihood the 'crossover point' had been reached, was stark. A new era in MACV/J2 was definitely underway, and Davidson was on Westmoreland's team.

Davidson and the 'American Way of War'

Davidson viewed the war from a strictly American perspective, but in later years recognized the hazards of ethnocentrism. When discussing the 'surprise' of Tet in his book, *Secrets of the Vietnam War*, he spends several pages talking about ethnocentrism and the fact that everyone suffers from its effects. He admits that his own ethnocentrism, and that of the South Vietnamese, did not allow them to foresee the enemy attacking during the Tet period of 1968. He further explains how he failed to appreciate the enemy's ability to orchestrate the Tet attacks: 'We looked with scorn on his primitive signals communications system and on (what we deemed) his amateurish staff work.'[44]

Davidson and the rest of the MACV staff were focused on the American Way of War, which meant concentrating on the enemy's main and local forces which most resembled conventional forces. Davidson explains that 'Westmoreland and the MACV staff sensed, largely by intuition, that the war had already progressed from a Phase I insurgency into Phase II (a combination insurgency and conventional war) and was swiftly moving towards Phase III (conventional war).'[45] Read ethnocentrism for 'sensed' and 'intuition.'

The conventional war 'sensed' by Davidson and the MACV staff never fully materialized, except for battles such as Khe Sanh. By mid-1968, as Davidson explains in his acclaimed and monumental work, *Vietnam at War*, the *Lao Dong* politburo in Hanoi instructed the military forces to revert back to 'guerrilla-type small-unit action.'[46] The communists flirted with conventional-type warfare again in early 1969 with two regimental-size attacks and 16 battalion-size assaults, but again quickly reverted to guerrilla-type operations, with a directive issued in April 1969 stating, 'Never again, and under no circumstances are we going to risk our entire military force for just an offensive. On the contrary, we should endeavor to preserve our military potential for further campaigns.'[47] This meant guerrilla, not conventional, warfare.

The *Lao Dong* also began to reiterate that NVA main units should mix with Viet Cong guerrillas to create a more flexible offensive capability.[48] In the view of Gabriel Kolko, in his book, *Anatomy of a War*:

> For its strength [the enemy's strategy] was not numbers or arms but mobility, and its decisive flexibility was wholly based on the willingness of thousands of committed local guerrillas and political cadres to improvise, muddle through, and persist for long periods in the fashion that kept RVN [Republic of Vietnam] and American forces distracted and vulnerable. This critical distinction between *revolutionary and conventional warfare* was to prevail until the war's end.[49] (Author's emphasis added.)

Davidson and technology

According to Davidson, in Vietnam 'the main source of intelligence was just the same old hard-nosed things that you get in any war: prisoners of war and documents. If you get the right one, they'll tell you anything.'[50] Of course, the question then becomes, is 'anything' just anything to please the interrogator or is it reliable data? For that and other reasons, Davidson referred to this type of data as 'low-grade intelligence.'

> A bunch of people who were working on these documents and seeing what they considered to be large infiltration, or this, that, or the other thing, were people working on a *low grade of intelligence*, compared to the leadership, very restricted in numbers, who were working on not only this *low-grade intelligence*, relatively speaking, but on all

sources of intelligence. So a lot of times when people would come to you with something that they had gained from the Secret [data] only, you'd know it might be only partially true or it might literally be untrue. They didn't have the whole picture.[51] (Author's emphasis added.)

Davidson favored intelligence which could be collaborated by more than a single source, or what is called 'all-source' intelligence. Generally, no single source of intelligence was given credence unless another source could back it up.[52] For conventional types of forces which used radios, this was typically not a problem as technical intelligence was readily available, as were the more traditional types of intelligence, such as prisoners, defectors, and documents. For non-conventional forces, however, this became a problem. Davidson explained, 'The guerrillas didn't operate radios.'[53]

Davidson, like McChristian, advocated the use of all intelligence resources and placed great emphasis on the collection of human intelligence. Where the two differed was on the acceptability/credibility of intelligence resources. Davidson felt humans and documents were automatically suspect on several accounts, and thus required verification from other sources. Davidson saw humans and documents as unreliable because of problems with:

- translation
- truthfulness
- terms, and
- validity.[54]

McChristian, on the other hand, accepted the analytical capability of his analysts to develop and refine sources, and did accept evidence which was referenced by at least two sources, even if both sources were derived from the same type (human or technical) of intelligence.[55]

On occasion, Davidson did allow the use of evidence that was 'low grade' and not 'all-source.' In describing how his estimators tracked the infiltration of NVA units into South Vietnam, Davidson related how the interrogation of a prisoner or defector would reveal a unit designator:

> Then on that one source alone – it was picked up as a possible infiltration source – now, an infiltration figure was possible. If we got another PW or another document which confirmed largely what he's said, it was picked up as probable or confirmed, I've forgotten now. But it took two to really make sure of it.[56]

Davidson immediately added, 'And then, of course, normally beyond that you'd get additional confirming evidence,' i.e. technical intelligence. Davidson felt best when his data was backed up by technical intelligence, and not solely reliant on 'low-grade' human intelligence. This view put those intelligence analysts following the guerrilla and SD forces at a distinct disadvantage. Nearly all the intelligence gained on these forces was 'low-grade,' thus easily disregarded and subject to various interpretations by the estimators.

Davidson and numbers

With an emphasis on conventional forces and because 'guerrillas didn't operate radios,' the order of battle as it had been compiled by McChristian and his CICV staff was due for an overhaul. Although McChristian's RITZ program, a collection effort specifically focused on the guerrilla and SD forces, was beginning to provide solid numbers, Davidson felt the data was 'soft.'[57] The Order of Battle Summary continued in its old format while MACV debated on how to present the RITZ data. MACV/J2 continued to use the old numbers until October 1967, when the decision was made to drop the SD forces from the order of battle. The figures on the guerrilla forces were retained, but were considered 'soft' and subject to negotiation.[58]

The guerrilla and SD forces were 'irregulars,' unlike the 'regular' conventional-type units found in the main and local forces. Further, while the guerrillas did carry guns and were considered a threat, the SD forces were largely composed of old men, women, and children who were mostly unarmed, and if they did have any weapons, they were antiques and seldom used.[59]

The main and local forces were organized in typical military fashion, with squads, platoons, companies, battalions, regiments, and divisions. These units used modern weapons and equipment, including radios, which made them subject to intelligence collection methods of a technical nature. The guerrillas were never organized in units larger than perhaps a company, most being in squads and platoons. They had older weapons and seldom had access to radio equipment. This made them much harder to confirm with 'all-source' intelligence. Further, being organized at the village and hamlet level, there were literally thousands of such squads and platoons, with no chance of collecting timely, valid intelligence data on every single guerrilla squad or platoon. Accounting for the guerrilla force was a continuing intelligence dilemma, one which the RITZ collection program had attempted to resolve.

Accounting for the guerrillas was tough enough; the SD forces were even more difficult to count. Also found at the village and hamlets, they were typically formed into groups of three to make a cell, and could be found in units as large as a squad (12 people in 4 cells). Further, they were seldom involved in any type of offensive military operation and if unarmed, as they almost always were, they were not, could not, be engaged and shot at by US military forces.

For the sake of expediency, just removing the momentous task of trying to count the SD forces, which some on his staff maintained could not be done,[60] and because they were a force of no military consequence,[61] Davidson decided to remove the SD forces. Further, the SD force were not only dropped, but they were totally eliminated as even a consideration in the order of battle, not even mentioned or footnoted.

Such a decision, not to mention or even footnote the SD forces, gives an indication that this decision was motivated by more than just intelligence concerns. Of far greater concern was the press reaction. A 'command decision' had been made to drop the SD forces and Davidson carried it out. The overriding concern was not an accurate accounting of the enemy forces, but concern over the press; intelligence had been politicized.

Davidson as a team player at MACV

Brigadier General Davidson was more outgoing and interacted to a larger degree with the MACV staff than had Brigadier General McChristian. Whereas McChristian was on professional military terms with General Westmoreland and was always referred to as 'my intelligence chief, Brigadier General McChristian,' Davidson was known more personably as 'Phil Davidson' by General Westmoreland. McChristian also had a less amicable J3 to operate with in the form of Major General William DePuy, who often did most of the intelligence work himself and objected to many of McChristian's recommendations.[62] Davidson had 'a real close friend'[63] in Major General Carter Townsend as the J3 under General Creighton W. Abrams, who replaced General Westmoreland as the Commander of MACV in June of 1968. Davidson also got along well General Abrams.[64]

Beyond the friendships, Davidson also saw the Vietnam War in more conventional terms than did McChristian. This put Davidson more in tune with the rest of the MACV staff. Davidson relates how General Westmoreland viewed pacification as a 'bore' and looked to fight the 'big unit' war.[65] When it came to the order of battle, Davidson was a team player, agreeing with General Westmoreland's view that the SD force should not be counted.

General Westmoreland had not questioned the inclusion of the SD force in the order of battle until McChristian's RITZ program had produced higher numbers. Higher numbers complicated the view that he had just expressed to President Johnson, that the 'crossover point' had been reached; and further, Westmoreland just did not feel the press was sophisticated enough to understand that the numbers were the result of refined intelligence, not a sudden influx of new troops.[66]

Davidson as a team player with the CIA

Davidson, like McChristian, had a formal relationship with the CIA. He passed MACV intelligence data to the CIA, and the CIA passed intelligence to MACV. Beyond this formal relationship, MACV and the CIA seldom agreed on the analysis of the intelligence data. MACV believed they were impacting North Vietnam with their bombing campaigns but the CIA disagreed. MACV believed a major supply route now ran from Sihanoukville in Cambodia to Vietnam, but the CIA disagreed. MACV determined the SD force were not a significant military factor and should be dropped from the order of battle, the CIA disagreed.

All of these disputes generated debate and discussion, but the contention over the order of battle was particularly acrimonious, with name-calling, finger-pointing and ultimately, the accusation by one of the CIA analysts of a 'conspiracy' by the MACV intelligence leadership. That CIA analyst was Sam Adams.

Mr. Sam Adams

Sam Adams never rose to a supervisory position within the CIA, yet this national intelligence organization certainly came under his influence as his Vietnam estimates became the CIA's estimates. And when the CIA 'caved in' to the MACV view, Sam Adams sought to unseat the head of the CIA, Richard Helms, seeking an Inspector General investigation against him. His conviction that he alone had the correct figures on the guerrilla and SD forces in Vietnam eventually led to his departure from the CIA in 1973. Yet his departure did not end his quest to prove he was right. Adams contacted the Army Inspector General and provided his information, suggesting they look into bringing court martial charges against General Westmoreland. He wrote an article in *Harper's Magazine* in May 1975 which argued that the enemy's true numbers had been hidden. The article resulted in a Congressional investigation, known as the Pike Commission, named after Congressman Otis Pike, the chairman. Even this was not enough, for he then served as a paid consultant and primary accuser in a CBS documentary aired on Saturday, 23 January 1982, entitled *The Uncounted Enemy: A Vietnam Deception.* Complete with Mike Wallace relentlessly firing pointed questions at an ill-prepared General Westmoreland, the program alleged a conspiracy by the MACV/J2 to purposely deceive the American leadership with regard to the true number of enemy faced in Vietnam, and came libelously close to implicating Westmoreland as the man in charge who gave the order to MACV/J2 to lie about the numbers. For a lone analyst sitting within the isolated walls of CIA's Headquarters in Langley, Virginia, just outside Washington, DC, Sam Adams and his numbers had become a force with which to be reckoned.

Adams and 'The American Way of War'

If it is possible that anyone could become so immersed in the primitive aspects of guerrilla warfare, becoming so enthralled with that aspect that they ignore the more conventional views, then Sam Adams represents that possibility. In his first days at the CIA, Adams worked as an analyst following the post-colonial confusion in the African Congo. In this environment of primitive tribal clans and families, Adams made sense and logic out of the varying alliances and influences among the clans, developing an elaborate system of notecards to track and analyze the complex situation.[67]

When Adams moved to the Vietnam branch in August of 1965 to study the Viet Cong morale, he brought this same empathy to his understanding of the situation. He also brought his means of tracking and monitoring a primitive enemy system. Employing his notecards and poring over the voluminous amounts of captured documents, prisoner of war interrogations, and defector reports, Sam Adams compiled an extensive understanding of the enemy's guerrilla and SD forces.

Adams and technology

Sam Adams relied almost exclusively on the volumes of data coming out of the Combined Document Exploitation Center and the Combined Military Interrogations Center, as well as the reports coming out of CIA's own interrogation centers and intelligence stations in Vietnam, all of which were basically non-technical intelligence. Because guerrilla and SD forces operate at a primitive level, below the threshold for collection by technical intelligence resources, Sam Adams had little choice in this regard. To understand, monitor, and account for the guerrilla and SD forces in Vietnam, one had no choice but to rely on intelligence derived from humans and documents. Thus, when Sam Adams came girded for combat he was armed only with 'low-grade intelligence,' making him susceptible to attack by those who disdain non-technical intelligence, and MACV contained many such detractors.

Adams and numbers

When Sam Adams joined the Vietnam branch of the CIA in August of 1965, he began a study on the morale of the Viet Cong forces.[68] He found these forces were defecting in astoundingly high numbers, numbers too high not to have some sort of explanation; it meant something but he couldn't find a satisfactory answer. Exhibiting what was to become a recurring theme, he thought perhaps the numbers were faked.[69] Adams undertook to resolve the mystery and departed to Vietnam in January 1966 for a three-month mission of discovery. There he compiled extensive data on his notecards on the defection figures for all of Vietnam's 44 provinces. He found an 'average' province in Long An, located south of the capital city of Saigon, and traveled there for a more exhaustive examination of their defection figures. Again, his figures were extremely large; in a four-month period, 146 Vietnamese had defected under the *Chieu Hoi* (Open Arms) program. Of the 146, 58 belonged to the Viet Cong Infrastructure and 88 were soldiers. Of the soldiers, 6 were main and local force troops, while 41 were guerrillas and 41 were SD forces.[70] To gauge the impact of these defections, Adams referenced the MACV Order of Battle Summary for Long An province; 100 guerrillas and 80 SD forces were listed.[71] In four months, nearly half of Long

An's guerrilla and SD forces (82 of 180) had defected. Something was wrong. The next day Adams queried the province chief, 'Could you tell me how many VC guerrillas and militiamen your intelligence people carry for Long An?' 'Two thousand,' was the reply.[72] Something was definitely wrong.

Being an analyst driven to answer the incongruent, he tackled the voluminous papers generated by the interrogation and document centers in Vietnam. The reports showed that not only were defections a problem, but even more troublesome to the enemy were desertions. With defections, desertions, killed in action and wounded, the number of enemy just didn't add up.[73] Adams sought the advice of George Allen, the CIA expert on Vietnam, who cautioned him about statistics, 'There's nothing wrong with them per se, but they're only a tool, not an end in themselves. See how they stack up against other evidence. If they don't fit, something's the matter.'[74]

Adams returned to the United States after three months in Vietnam and continued his review of MACV captured documents and interrogations in his office at the CIA headquarters. By late August of 1966, he had compiled a vast database of notecards, folders, and calculations which he summarized in a draft paper he forwarded for coordination in which he asserted the MACV holdings for guerrilla and SD forces of 100,000 were 'too low' and 'should probably be at least doubled,' and suggested that MACV take responsibility for resolving the discrepancies.[75] Adams displayed symptoms of self-aggrandizement, fantasizing that he would soon be called by the President on his remarkable findings that only he had deduced.[76] This was to be the first of many disappointments and roadblocks that hindered him in getting his story told; his draft was returned with no comments. Adams, in true Quixote form, didn't quit, but began to preach to anybody that would listen. Through his doggedness and preaching, Adams developed many followers and converts, both at CIA and at MACV, including George Carver, the Special Assistant for Vietnam Affairs to the CIA director, Richard Helms. Also, unknown to Adams at the time, Carver had arrived at his conclusion that the guerrilla and SD forces were half of what they should be, independent of the RITZ collection program which was netting similar results for Brigadier General McChristian and his analysts at the Combined Intelligence Center in Vietnam.

Adams as a team player at the CIA

Sam Adams had his admirers and detractors at the CIA. He was recognized as the expert during the Congo episodes of the mid-1960s, and his work on the guerrilla and SD forces in Vietnam was also affirmed as remarkable by his bosses. His troubles with the CIA began when the CIA accepted a compromise with MACV regarding the exclusion of the SD forces from the order of battle. His boss at the CIA at the time, George Carver, was the chief architect of the compromise and while Carver marveled at Adams' analytical capabilities, he would not back him on his quest to include the SD forces in the order of battle.

Adams, who had filed an Inspector General complaint against the Director of the CIA, managed to retain his job, but his career with the Agency had reached its apex. While tolerated by the CIA, he was going nowhere. He made the most of his quixotic reputation, uncovering a large Viet Cong spy network and revealing higher communist rebel strength in Cambodia. Even Adams recognized the futility of his quest, but he made the most of it, 'One of the problems with this thing is, besides being quixotic, it was also an awful lot of fun.'[77] He eventually retired from the CIA in 1973, but never relented in his quest.

Adams as a team player with MACV

Not all within MACV disdained non-technical intelligence, and Sam Adams developed several relationships, some even close, with analysts at MACV. These analysts at MACV tended to work on the same issue of guerrilla and SD forces as Adams. In particular, the chief of the order of battle section within the Combined Intelligence Center, Vietnam (CICV), Colonel Gains Hawkins, became friends with Adams and was a primary source of information on the handling and alleged suppression of the numbers on guerrilla and SD forces within MACV. While not a friend, he found an ally even in the head of MACV/J2 from June 1965 to May 1967, Brigadier General Joseph A. McChristian.

General McChristian shared an appreciation for intelligence derived from humans and documents, as related in the preceding section of this chapter dealing with McChristian. Adams and McChristian also shared the view that the SD forces were a factor and threat against US military forces and their ability to carry out their mission.

The problem for Sam Adams was that McChristian left in May of 1967, just when the issue of the SD force was being discussed and debated at the CIA and MACV. His replacement, Brigadier General Phillip B. Davidson, did not share McChristian's view of the SD force nor his view on the validity of non-technical intelligence.

With McChristian's departure, Sam Adams and his 'low-grade intelligence' were, in the words of one MACV/J2 colonel, 'full of shit.'[78] Sam Adams became even more disdained at MACV than non-technical intelligence. 'He has a mental problem or something,' said another MACV/J2 colonel.[79] Brigadier General Davidson never took Adams seriously and characterized him as a 'Don Quixote' on a misguided quest.[80] Thus, in his quest to prove his rectitude, Sam Adams felt few qualms in directing the salvos of accusations he levied at MACV in his *Harper's* article and the CBS documentary for which he served as a paid consultant. He didn't care for them, and they didn't care for him. Somewhere, the focus of intelligence seems to have become orphaned. Both sides of the issue had merit, but neither side was willing to begrudgingly bestow the courtesy of professional acceptance of disagreement on the impact and import of the other's views. This dismal display was played out in an intelligence drama, a tragedy in three acts fought on three battlefields.

9 An intelligence drama

A three-act tragedy

> The Vietcong order of battle is MACV's business, which is to say, my business. Don't tread on me.
>
> Brigadier General Joseph McChristian[1]

Sam Adams, Brigadier General Phillip B. Davidson, and Brigadier General Joseph A. McChristian were on a collision course. These three protagonists, strong in their convictions and uncompromising in their views, were about to take the entire US intelligence community onto several bitter and acrimonious battlefields to see whose view would be the last one standing.

This drama contained three acts, taking place on three battlefields in the form of three conferences held in 1967. All three conferences – February in Honolulu, Hawaii, August in Langley, Virginia, and September in Saigon, South Vietnam – revolved around the order of battle, who was responsible for the numbers, and just who constituted the enemy. Early on, it appeared the Military Assistance Command, Vietnam (MACV) and the Central Intelligence Agency (CIA) had reached a meeting of minds, but with a change of leadership within the MACV intelligence organization, the battle was soon joined.

Act One: The Honolulu Conference

Rumors had been circulating in both Washington and Saigon of potential changes in the order of battle, of the 'doubling' of some enemy forces. At the White House, the National Security Advisor to the President, Walter W. Rostow, heard the rumors and sought to bring them to an end. He suggested to the Chairman of Joint Chiefs of Staff that a conference be held to discuss the order of battle with all concerned parties to work out definitions and establish responsibility. The result was *The Conference to Standardize Methods for Developing and Presenting Statistics on Order of Battle Infiltration, Trends and Estimates* held at Camp Smith in Honolulu, Hawaii from 6–11 February 1967.

The MACV position: a round peg

From the very beginning of the conference, it was clear who was running it: Brigadier General Joseph A. McChristian, who told the attendees, 'The Vietcong order of battle is MACV's business, which is to say, my business.'[2] Under McChristian's leadership, the attendees identified four conference objectives:

1   To establish agreed definitions, criteria and methodologies for the computation of statistical data on order of battle, infiltration and related matters, and to establish procedures for coordinating changes.
2   To establish an agreed system for reporting data on these subjects and to establish procedures for coordinating changes.
3   To develop guidelines for the interpretation and dissemination of statistical data on VC/NVA order of battle, infiltration, and related matters.
4   To develop a program which will keep the consumers of the statistics fully apprised of the derivative methodology and limitations on the use of this information.[3]

The conference agreed on the terms and definitions of the enemy they faced and on what enemy strengths to measure. It was agreed that there were four components of the enemy strength:

1   combat strength, measured by the number of VC and NVA main and local forces and their combat support units;
2   administrative service strength, which included the administrative, logistics, repair and service-type troops;
3   irregular strength, measured by the number of guerrilla and self-defense (SD) forces; and
4   political order of battle strength, which was all the members of the Viet Cong Infrastructure (VCI) down to the hamlet level (members who served both in a military force and in the VCI were only counted in the military force.)

The enemy totals carried in the order of battle represented a compilation of the combat, administrative, irregular, and political strength figures.

Each of the enemy forces described above is controlled and directed by the Communist political apparatus in South Vietnam, known as the 'Viet Cong Infrastructure'. The political order of battle strength which comprises this infrastructure is a vital segment of the insurgency. It includes individuals who devise military plans and operations (particularly in the area of logistical support), issue the orders, and ensure that these orders are carried out. In many cases, these individuals also serve as military commanders. As such, they are included in the military strength categories of the order of battle. This is particularly true at the village and hamlet level where one of the local political bosses will be the leader of the guerrilla platoon or squad. In short, the political infrastructure is an integral part of the total enemy strength and should be included in the order of battle.[4]

Trying to measure these forces was a monumental challenge. The combat strength and administrative service strength were the easiest to measure as they were organized along conventional military lines. Information on these types of units could be extrapolated based upon the known organizational structure for these units. Thus, if a VC battalion was identified, it was a simple matter to extrapolate the number, as a typical VC battalion consisted of three infantry companies, a combat support company, and platoons of signal, reconnaissance, and sappers with 300 to 600 personnel.[5]

The same could not be said of the irregular strength, the guerrilla forces. The numbers varied widely depending upon the village and hamlet, whether the area was under VC or Government of South Vietnam control, what province it was located in, the strength of the political organization within the village, the lack of contact with US military forces, and the sheer number of villages and hamlets on which data had to be collected. The lack of data was even more restrictive on the SD forces.

To resolve this lack of data and bring the irregular forces into sharper focus, MACV informed the conference that a special collection program had been undertaken.

During the past few months, the groundwork has been laid through coordination with all GVN [Government of South Vietnam] and US agencies from the national to the subsector level, to obtain a more valid estimate of irregular strength by means of a combined collection program. This program places the focus on collection at the sector level, and uses all combined GVN and US assets available at that level. The combined estimates and supporting information developed at the sector level will be forwarded to Saigon for review and comparison with total information available in Saigon. Preliminary indications point to a sharp increase in the number of irregulars to be carried in the order of battle. This will not, however, indicate that actual irregular strength has jumped, but only that we have refined our knowledge of it, and that strengths will be retroactively adjusted.[6]

The same type of collection on the nebulous Viet Cong infrastructure was also undertaken by MACV to better represent their strength in the order of battle.

An intensive community-wide intelligence collection program against these segments of the infrastructure and a refinement of previous data has been initiated and probably will result in a substantial increase in the total number carried in the political order of battle.[7]

MACV/J2 made a commitment at the conference to develop and disseminate the results of their collection efforts on the irregular forces 'as a matter of high priority,' and that newly identified strength in the political order of battle will be 'added to the order of battle as soon as possible.'[8] The intelligence which MACV had inherited from the South Vietnamese in 1965 when Brigadier General McChristian took over as J2 was finally prepared to provide an accurate picture of the enemy they faced.

The CIA position: a round hole

Sam Adams attended the Order of Battle conference in Hawaii with some trepidation. His own studies on the guerrilla and SD forces had finally been accepted at the CIA. He had transferred out of his original office working Vietnam in the Southeast Asia Branch and now worked for the Special Assistant for Vietnamese Affairs (SAVA) to the CIA director. His boss, George Carver, had direct access to Richard Helms, the CIA director, and he also frequently worked directly with members of President Johnson's staff.

George Carver thought highly of the diligence and sense of discovery that Sam Adams brought to his analysis. He felt Adams had found something and was ready to back Adams' figures at the conference. As it turned out, MACV and CIA had both come to the same conclusions, independently of each other. The guerrilla and SD forces were not accurately accounted for under the current order of battle, and armed with a better understanding of these forces and a more accurate method for enumerating these forces, both MACV and CIA were ready to substantially increase their numbers.

Sam Adams had initially thought he was in for a rumble at the beginning of the conference when Brigadier General McChristian made his unbridled assertion that the order of battle was his and not to harbor any thoughts to the contrary. However, this feeling soon faded when McChristian continued:

> In the last few months, certain individuals in certain organizations have raised questions about three of the four categories of the MACV order of battle. Colonel Hawkins of my OB branch has made a preliminary investigation into these categories. This investigation shows that each of them will need drastic upward revision.[9]

As the conference progressed and he heard of the MACV collection programs against the irregular and political order of battle he felt reassured that CIA and MACV were in agreement.[10] He was particularly heartened when Colonel Gains Hawkins proclaimed to the conference, 'You know, there's a lot more of those little bastards out there than we thought there were.'[11]

The result: a meeting of minds

The conference ended amicably. The primary combatants were in agreement. The numbers carried for the irregulars and political order of battle were low and based upon the outcome of MACV's collection efforts, would be revised higher for a more accurate accounting of these forces. MACV left the conference with the edict to quickly incorporate its collection results into the order of battle. CIA left the conference confident that it could now proceed with a new National Intelligence Estimate (NIE) that accurately projected a unified intelligence position on the true nature and strength of the enemy forces the US faced in Vietnam.

The only ominous sign coming out of the conference was noted by George Allen, a CIA expert on Vietnam, who also worked in the SAVA for George Carver. Allen noted upon reviewing the conference report that the attendees had taken Brigadier General McChristian at his word and had given sole responsibility for the order of battle figures to MACV. Allen explained to Adams, 'Now Westy can do any damn thing with them that he wants.' [12]

Adams waited expectantly for the next edition of the MACV order of battle summary; it arrived with no changes to the irregular or political order of battle. [13] The same was true for the May, June, July and August editions of the MACV Order of Battle Summary.

Act Two: The Langley Conference

The combatants, who had appeared to have had a meeting of minds in Honolulu in February of 1967, gathered again to discuss the order of battle in August of 1967. This time the subject of scrutiny was the National Intelligence Estimate (NIE) which was being prepared for the signature of Director of Central Intelligence, Richard Helms. The location was not Honolulu, but Langley, Virginia, at the CIA's headquarters just outside of Washington, DC. The carefree Hawaiian Islands were replaced by the political backwaters of the Potomac. The initial battlefield at Honolulu had been cleared and the combatants had left in agreement; now in Langley, the real battle was enjoined.

The MACV position: a square peg

The higher figures for the irregular forces and political order of battle that Brigadier General McChristian had agreed to get into the order of battle 'as a matter of high priority,' never materialized. While the collection programs he referred to at the conference did indeed yield the expected higher figures, these higher figures ran into a wall of political reality. Two objections were raised over the new figures. First, the new figures raised the order of battle numbers from about 300,000 to nearly 500,000, and while this was simply a more accurate reflection of the enemy's force and did not represent a sudden increase in the number of enemy, the leadership at MACV feared that the press would seize only upon the increase and ignore any explanations offered by the military. As General Westmoreland attempted to explain to Mike Wallace years later in 1982, 'the people in Washington were not sophisticated enough to understand and evaluate this thing, and neither was the media.'[14] With the large number of press in Vietnam covering the war unfettered, there was fierce competition for headline-making news.[15]

The second consideration was a hesitancy by the MACV leadership to include increased numbers in a category which was not considered to be a combat force. The SD forces were the bottom of the VC/NVA military pyramid. Able-bodied personnel hardly ever remained in the SD forces for any length of time and, as such, these forces consisted mainly of the old or very young. They were seldom armed and hardly ever took part in any offensive activities. However, these forces had been counted in the order of battle by the French in their war against the Viet Minh, by the South Vietnamese when the insurgency undertook to topple their government, and by the United States. The inclusion of these forces had never been seriously challenged; and so long as their numbers had remained constant, without changes, they likely would have remained in the order of battle. But in early 1967, with an emphasis on collecting a more accurate accounting of these forces, the Irregular's (both the guerrilla and SD forces) numbers nearly doubled, from about 120,000 to almost 200,000.

Brigadier General McChristian believed the SD forces were capable of impacting the mission of MACV and therefore were a factor to be included in the strength figures of the order of battle. But in May 1967, when the improved figures were coming in on the SD forces, McChristian was preparing to leave Vietnam. His replacement, Brigadier General Davidson, did not share McChristian's view that the SD forces could impact the MACV mission. Davidson viewed the SD forces as militarily insignificant and felt no obligation to continue the practice that the US had inherited from the French and South Vietnamese. The SD forces were not a combat force and, under Davidson, these forces would not be included in the order of battle. By taking such a position, Davidson was able to avoid having to explain any increase in the order of battle to the press.

Thus, as the CIA began the process of writing a new National Intelligence Estimate, the seemingly innocuous task of adding up the enemy became a monumental challenge. Expecting MACV to provide better and more accurate data for the guerrilla and SD forces, the CIA instead received from MACV a new position that the SD forces should be taken out of the order of battle completely.

The CIA position: a round hole

The CIA position had not changed during the interim between the February Honolulu Conference and the National Intelligence Estimate Conference held at their own Headquarters in August. The CIA was aware of the adjustments undertaken with the change in MACV/J2 leadership and the CIA's George Carver, made a trip to Saigon in July in an attempt to head off an impasse in the writing of the NIE. He met with the new MACV/J2, Brigadier General Davidson, and the two soon came to an agreement. The SD forces would not be counted as a combat force; the order of battle would be divided into two separate categories, combat forces consisting of the main, local and guerrilla forces and non-combat forces which included the SD forces and Viet Cong infrastructure. The impasse which had been feared appeared to have been resolved. However, although MACV agreed to two categories, they did not agree to put a hard and fast number on the SD forces, as related in a message on 10 July 1967 to the CIA from Carver while he was in Saigon: 'On non-military, Hawkins supported 80,000 political cadre as good estimate, but reserved on self-defense figure saying evidence here very inconclusive (which true), and perhaps verbal statement on this category might be preferable to number.'[16] The Hawkins referred to in the message was Colonel Gains Hawkins, the chief of the CICV order of battle office.

When the MACV delegation arrived in August at the Langley NIE conference, it became immediately apparent that the conference was headed for an impasse over the SD force figures. The MACV delegation refused to include any reference to a number for the SD force in the order of battle, articulating the position that the SD forces were not a military threat and, since there was not enough data to quantify them, it was impossible to count them. The CIA disagreed on both counts; they felt because the war was an insurgency, forces such as the SD were important and should be counted, and they had an analyst in Sam Adams who had counted them.

The result: no fit

After the Honolulu Conference, both the CIA and MACV were in agreement on the order of battle, but after the Langley Conference a definite impasse had developed with the MACV change of heart on the question of the SD forces. The National Intelligence Estimate on Vietnam was in disarray; a process which had normally taken several weeks, perhaps a month, had now dragged on for months. The NIE was a product of the Director of Central Intelligence, Richard Helms. An NIE was also to be a consensus of the national intelligence community, with all major intelligence organizations having a voice, including the State Department, and the Defense Intelligence Agency representing the military. Being signed by Richard Helms, however, meant the CIA had the last word, although if another intelligence agency disagreed, their opposition and the reason for it would be footnoted in the NIE.

MACV was not officially a member of the committee drafting the NIE, but attended as the experts brought in by the Defense Intelligence Agency. Further, they were the organization 'on the ground' in Vietnam and were the authority on the order of battle; after all, it was their personnel whose lives were on the line and they were facing the enemy depicted in the NIE. As described by Thomas Powers in his book on Richard Helms, *The Man Who Kept the Secrets*, Helms did not want to step into what was a traditionally military matter. Helms addressed the leaders working on the NIE:

> Look, said Helms, this is the most important disagreement about the war. There is a total split between the civilians and analysts on a subject the military is supposed to know something about. We've got to come to an agreement; you fellows go back and work this out.[17]

The CIA applied a great deal of pressure on the MACV delegation to agree to a number being put on the SD forces. The head of the MACV party sent a message to Brigadier General Davidson on 19 August 1967 relaying that the CIA was still planning on putting a figure in the NIE for self-defense forces, and that with them an overall total of 420,000 for enemy strength would be the result.[18] Brigadier General Davidson immediately responded in a message on 19 August 1967 in which he stated:

> Further consideration reveals the total unacceptability of including the strength of the self-defense forces and the secret self-defense forces in any strength figure to be released to the press. The figure of about 420,000, which includes all forces including SD and SSD, has already surfaced out here, this figure has stunned the embassy and this headquarters . . . In view of this reaction and in view of General Westmoreland's conversations, all of which you have heard, I am sure that this headquarters will not accept a figure in excess of the current strength figure carried by the press.[19]

In the next few a days a flurry of messages came out of Saigon, criticizing the CIA and insisting that the inclusion of the SD forces was totally unacceptable. From Robert Komer, General Westmoreland's chief for pacification, came a message on 19 August 1967 to George Carver in which he stated:

> MACV is determined [to] stick by its guns, and you can well imagine ruckus which would be created it if [sic] came out as everything tends to on Vietnam that agency and MACV figures were so widely different. Any explanation as to why would simply lead press to conclude that MACV was deliberately omitting SDF/SSDF category in order [to] downgrade enemy strength. Thus credibility gap would be further widened at very time when in fact we are moving toward much more valid estimates.[20]

General Creighton Abrams, the deputy commander in Vietnam, made his view very clear in a message sent to the Chairman of the Joint Chiefs of Staff, who then passed it on to the Director of the CIA:

1 MACV representatives to the DIA [*sic*] conference dealing with order of battle strength for enemy forces in South Vietnam report that there is a continuing *controversy* regarding the inclusion of the strength figures for self-defense forces (*SD*) and secret self-defense forces (*SSD*) in the draft NIE 14.3–67. In General Westmoreland's temporary absence, I think it appropriate to make the command position on the inclusion of these strength figures clear.

2 *If SD and SSD strength figures are included in the overall enemy strength, the figure will total 420,000–431,000* depending on minor variations. This is in *sharp contrast to the current* overall strength figure of about *299,000 given to the press* here.

3 From the intelligence viewpoint, the *inclusion of SD and SSD* strength figures in an estimate of military capabilities is *highly questionable.* These forces contain a sizable number of women and old people. They operate entirely in their own hamlets. They are rarely armed, have no real discipline, and almost no military capability. They are no more effective in the military sense than the dozens of other nonmilitary organizations which serve the VC cause in various roles.

4 *The press reaction to these inflated figures is of much greater concern.* We have been projecting an image of success over the recent months, and properly so. Now, when we release the figure of 420–431,000, the newsmen will immediately seize on the point that the enemy force has increased about 120–130,000, *all available caveats and explanations will not prevent the press from drawing an erroneous and gloomy conclusion* as to the meaning of the increase. All those who have an incorrect view of the war will be reenforced and the task will become more difficult.

5 In our view, the strength figures for the *SD and SSD should be omitted* entirely from the enemy strength tables in the forthcoming NIE. This will prevent the possibility that they can be added to the valid figures, and an erroneous conclusion drawn as to an enemy strength increase.[21] (Author's emphasis added.)

General Westmoreland, who was visiting his family in the Philippines, immediately endorsed the message sent by General Abrams, saying:

I have just read Gen Abrams MAC 7849, and I agree. I do not concur with the inclusion of SD and SSD strength figures in the overall enemy strength. It distorts the situation and makes no sense. No possible explanations could prevent the erroneous conclusions that would result.[22]

By 29 August 1967, even the US Ambassador to Vietnam, Ellsworth Bunker, had weighed in with an eyes only message to President Johnson's National Security Advisor, Walter W. Rostow. In this message, Ambassador Bunker states:

1   Bob Komer and I wish [to] bring to your attention potentially serious problem created by new NIE now on verge of completion.
2   Despite thorough re-analysis by now massive MACV intelligence machine which has brought MACV position much closer to that of CIA, the latter's experts appear insistent on bringing out an estimate which will make enemy strength 430,000 to 490,000 instead of the range centering on 298,000 developed by MACV.
3   CIA does this chiefly by adding to strength figures some 120,000 so-called self-defense and secret self-defense forces, which are not organized military units at all but rather mostly unarmed, part-time hamlet defense element of women, children, and old men on which we have very little evidence and which is so inconsequential and rarely encountered by us as not to warrant inclusion in enemy strength. In last analysis only armed men plus structure controlling and support them should validly be included.
4   I need hardly mention the devastating impact if it should leak out (as these things so often do) that despite all our success in grinding down VC/NVA here, CIA-figures are used to show that they are really much stronger than ever. Despite all caveats, this is inevitable conclusion which most of press would reach.
5   Westy has gone back hard at Buss Wheeler [Chairman, JCS] on this and I intend to mention it to the President in my coming weekly. NIE credibility gap created would be enormous, and is quite inconsistent with all the hard evidence we have about growing enemy losses, declining VC recruiting and the like.[23]

The pressure which the CIA had brought to bear on the MACV delegation came back in full force. Now, the CIA was under pressure to compromise with the MACV position. It was imperative to arrive at a consensus between the major contending parties, CIA and MACV, both as a matter of presenting a unified position to the US leadership and so as not to provide any fodder for the media. Recognizing the potential for catastrophe should an agreement not be found and exerting his leadership as the man 'on the ground,' General Westmoreland invited the combatants to Saigon to resolve the matter.

Act Three: The Saigon Conference

The combatants gathered one more time in Saigon on 9 September 1967 for another round. The next six days saw the most acrimonious and caustic debate, calling into question not only the analysis and conclusions drawn by the participants, but their character and competence as well. For the CIA, both George Carver and Sam Adams were present. For MACV, Brigadier General Davidson was present on his home turf, with immediate back up from both General Westmoreland and his Pacification chief, Robert Komer. The pressure was definitely on the CIA this round.

The MACV position: square peg

Brigadier General Davidson would hear of no alternative to his position which was now practically set in stone – no change in the number currently given to the press. The easiest way to accomplish this was by not including the SD and secret SD forces. This position could be justified by the questionable military nature of these forces, the fact that there was little or no technical intelligence available on these forces, and only sparse intelligence from captured documents which were difficult to verify and did not provide a complete picture of these forces without extrapolating, using the figures for several provinces to arrive at a figure for all of the provinces.

Brigadier General Davidson had all of the Saigon leadership behind his position and evidently the backing from Walter W. Rostow, the influential National Security Advisor to President Johnson. Further, CIA director Richard Helms was wary of imposing the CIA view on what 'the military is supposed to know something about.' Davidson was not going to allow the SD forces into the order of battle; as a category of the enemy he was intent on them becoming extinct. No number, not even a mention of them was to be made in the order of battle (OB) period.

> To throw Adams's figure of 120,000 to 200,000 of these people into the OB, and then merge them with such troops as the NVA and the VC Main Force units, local force units, and guerrillas, would be like adding diamonds, pearls, garnets, and pebbles to arrive at an overall figure for stones. This overall figure would be misleading when presented to the American people, who could not be expected to sort out the various categories of enemy strength and appreciate their varying combat capabilities.[24]

Brigadier General Davidson also felt that the CIA representatives were smug in their approach, appearing to MACV as 'arrogant and overbearing – the experts come to show these military intelligence neophytes how to "do" Order of Battle.'[25] The impasse was not only over figures and press, but was becoming personal.

The CIA position: 'the circle is squared'

The CIA came to Saigon with the intention of reviewing the methodology and analysis of each of the categories, without regard to any final outcome of the figures.[26] The question as to how the press would accept the figures was of secondary concern for the CIA and they reminded MACV that the NIE was the responsibility of the Director of Central Intelligence, Richard Helms. The CIA still wanted some type of quantification of the SD forces and argued that some mention of them must occur within the NIE, but they did allow that any figures for the SD force would not be counted toward the total for the enemy's combat strength.

The CIA delegation felt that MACV was 'stonewalling' and George Carver, in his messages to keep Mr. Helms informed of the proceedings, described the first days of the conference as 'frustratingly unproductive.'[27] Even the Defense Intelligence Agency representatives, who had argued strenuously on the side of MACV at the Langley conference, became irritated and upset with the attitude displayed by MACV. Said one DIA analyst, 'We did not travel 8,000 miles to be insulted.'[28]

Carver felt the key to breaking the impasse was to talk with General Westmoreland. 'If I can budge Westmoreland, this whole matter can be resolved to everyone's satisfaction in a few hours of serious discussion. If I can not, no agreement is possible,'[29] Carver relayed to Helms on 11 September 1967. Westmoreland had been on vacation when the conference began, but was expected back that day and Carver was hoping to make his case to Westmoreland as soon as possible. What Carver hoped to sell Westmoreland on was the previous agreement he had tentatively worked out with Brigadier General Davidson back in July – not to count the SD force in any strength category, but to mention them only in textual form. This compromise met MACV's condition that the SD force in no way be quantified and CIA's insistence that the SD force be explicated in some way as a factor in the enemy's strategy; the circle could be squared.

The result: a fit of sorts

The 'stonewalling' by MACV and the CIA 'arrogance' was getting nowhere. After days of literally haggling over the numbers, Brigadier General Davidson gave Carver a white card with the following figures:

Main and local forces	119,000
Administrative services	25–35,000
Guerrillas	75–95,000
Total	219–249,000 (mean 234,000)
Political cadre	70–90,000
Self-defense and secret self-defense	No quantification[30]

Carver again suggested that analysts from both sides sit down and go through the numbers category by category. Brigadier General Davidson refused, saying it was MACV's final offer, 'not subject to discussion,' a 'take it or leave it' proposal.[31] CIA, DIA and the intelligence representatives from the State Department then convened their own mini-conference and for the next six hours worked out their own numbers and presented them to Brigadier General Davidson as a united front.[32] The numbers presented the forces as follows:

Main and local forces	119,000
Administrative services	35–45,000
Guerrillas	75–95,000
Total	229–259,000
Political cadre	58–90,000
Self-defense, secret self-defense and assault youth	Textual explanation[33]

Brigadier General Davidson accepted the figures, but balked at the 'textual explanation' of the SD forces. In the several paragraphs offered by Carver, one of the 'textual explanations' said:

> Our current evidence does not enable us to estimate the present size of these groups with any measure of confidence. Some documents suggest that in early 1966 the aggregate size of the self-defense group was then on the order of 150,000.[34]

This was seen by Brigadier General Davidson as an oblique attempt to quantify the SD forces, and this Davidson would not accept. He told Carver, 'Let's just accept the fact that we are in terminal disagreement – you use your figures, and we'll use ours.'[35] Davidson also felt that General Westmoreland was of the same opinion and would not accept the 'textual explanation.' Carver had dinner that evening with Robert Komer and met with General Westmoreland the next day. Westmoreland accepted the compromise with some minor changes and Carver reported to Helms on 13 September 1967, 'Circle now squared.'[36]

General Westmoreland formally accepted the figures on 14 September 1967 when he sent a message to the Chairman of the Joint Chiefs of Staff with the following figures:

Main and local forces	119,000
Administrative services	35–40,000
Guerrillas	70–90,000
Total	224–249,000 (mean 236,500)
Political infrastructure	75–85,000[37]

Accentuating the positive, General Westmoreland did not reference the 'textual explanation,' but did mention, 'The Washington representatives agree with MACV that the NIE should not quantify the categories of self defense, secret self defense and other similar VC organizations.'[38]

In his message to Richard Helms on 14 September 1967, George Carver noted that General Westmoreland had formally reported the agreement to the Chairman of the Joint Chief of Staff and that he had endorsed the results. Carver also said, 'Only remaining task is mending of personal fences with General Davidson.'[39] This would prove to be even more daunting task than 'squaring the circle,' but it was not General Davidson who was to hold a grudge, but the CIA's own Sam Adams who viewed the compromise as a 'CIA collapse.'[40]

Adams was amazed that not only had the SD forces been dropped from the order of battle, but also felt that all the numbers were patently too low. His memoir explained:

> The militia [SD forces] had marched out of the estimate in exchange for only fifteen thousand guerrillas, not the great many more that Colonel Hawkins and I agreed there were. The service troops, although higher than MACV's earlier numbers, were still 'scaled down' on the order of 50 percent. Even the regulars had dropped a couple of thousand . . . Finally, the political cadres had flown off to a separate perch.[41]

The battlefields of the order of battle and National Intelligence Estimate conferences were cleared and the smoke settled. But, the war was far from over. Sam Adams pursued the issue and this culminated in the CBS documentary, *The Uncounted Enemy: A Vietnam Deception*, and the subsequent libel suit by General Westmoreland against CBS and Sam Adams. The courtroom trial was a virtual replay of these battlefields, with the same warriors, though older, still holding to their positions. Nothing had really changed. However, the figures did have an impact. The press reaction MACV had so much feared became a reality when the enemy attacked on Tet.

10 From tragedy, four morals
Intelligence principles

> Now the reason the enlightened prince and the wise general conquer the enemy whenever they move and their achievements surpass those of ordinary men is foreknowledge.
>
> Sun Tzu[1]

Intelligence in Vietnam played out a drama in 1967 that ended in tragedy. When the communists attacked with a ferocity that belied their 'bankrupt' characterization, the Tet Effect ensued and the trust that the American public had placed in its leadership, military, and intelligence crumbled, as did their will to continue the war. Intelligence was at the center of the drama and a key contributor to the Tet Effect. A close examination of the intelligence drama of 1967 and the ensuring Tet Effect tragedy reveals four important morals, guiding principles for intelligence. Given the tremendous trust the American public places in intelligence to provide accurate information, it is essential that the lessons of this drama guide future endeavors and that these principles guard against another Tet Effect.

The principles under which intelligence operated at MACV in late 1967 were, to all appearances, appropriate. Intelligence was an integral team player, supporting the American Way of War with the latest technology to count the enemy as the measure of success. In all aspects, the way in which intelligence operated in Vietnam was wrong. As a team player, intelligence lost its objectivity, advancing the 'command position,' against all those who had an 'improper view of the war.' Intelligence succumbed to ethnocentrism as it 'intuitively' viewed the enemy as moving into a more conventional, American type of warfare, when in fact, the enemy was waging its own war, using its own, unique strategy. Intelligence employed all the latest technology in Vietnam and held such information in the highest esteem, yet this primitive enemy rendered this technology mute. And in the final accounting, the enemy's numbers, though declining, by no means signaled the end of his determination or any flagging of his will to see Vietnam united under the communists.

The morals gained from this intelligence drama and the principles to be learned are fourfold. First, intelligence must be objective, any hint of bias taints the analysis and plants the seeds of distrust and suspicion. Second, the only way to understand the enemy is to think like the enemy; ascribing American values and ideals to the enemy only serves the enemy's cause, to the detriment of our own. Third, technology is a tremendous benefit, but it is not the be-all and end-all, especially when dealing with a primitive enemy. The only way to truly know the enemy, to know what they are thinking, to understand their intentions, is to spy in the old-fashioned way, using humans. And fourth, the measure of success in war is not numbers, but will. It was the enemy's will, not his numbers that frustrated General Westmoreland's strategy of attrition. As General Davidson later writes, 'While Westmoreland's strategy of attrition could inflict casualties and drive large enemy units from South Vietnam, it could not reach that magical level which was so painful that Ho (the leader of North Vietnam, Ho Chi Minh) would cease his aggression.'[2]

On intelligence and objectivity

The intelligence drama of 1967 centered around how to quantify the militia forces of the Viet Cong. MACV argued that these forces were insignificant militarily, consisting of old men and women, or young children, poorly armed if at all, who seldom, if ever, engaged US military forces. Taken at face value, the argument has merit. It was accepted as policy by MACV in September 1967. After that time, the militia were never again mentioned in the order of battle at MACV. It was a policy decision.

Unfortunately, it was a policy decision that will forever be tainted with the implication that it was instituted to present a consistent image to the press, to present numbers which showed no dramatic increase over any other previous month. The messages from MACV, in particular the message from General Creighton Abrams on 21 August 1967, clearly demonstrate that MACV's overriding concern was the press. General Abrams eloquently lays out the MACV position, and as the Deputy Commander to General Westmoreland, he has every right to do so.

> 2   If SD and SSD strength figures are included in the overall enemy strength, the figure will total 420,000–431,000 depending on minor variations. This is in *sharp contrast to the current* overall strength figure of about *299,000 given to the press* here.
>
> [. . .]
>
> 4   *The press reaction* to these inflated figures *is of much greater concern*. We have been projecting an image of success over the recent months, and properly so. Now, when we release the figure of 420–431,000, the newsmen will immediately seize on the point that the enemy force has increased about 120–130,000, *all available*

caveats and explanations will not prevent the press from drawing an erroneous and gloomy conclusion as to the meaning of the increase. All those who have an incorrect view of the war will be reenforced and the task will become more difficult.[3] (Author's emphasis added.)

General Abram's first concern was the press, his second, the justification for removing the militia. Again, in his operational capacity, he has the right and obligation to do so.

The most disturbing aspect was the message that Brigadier General Phillip B. Davidson sent to the MACV delegation attending the Langley NIE conference in August 1967. In that message he reiterates the unacceptability of including the militia forces in any figure on the enemy's strength. He then states, 'I am sure that this headquarters will not accept a figure in excess of *the current strength figure carried by the press.*' (Emphasis added.) This intelligence decision was influenced, if not dictated by, concerns over the press. No matter how trivial some have portrayed the militia forces as being, no matter how strong their argument might have been for not including the militia in the order of battle, the decision was tainted; the final and overriding concern was the press, not an accurate accounting of the enemy.

The pressures to present an optimistic and upbeat image of the success in Vietnam were enormous. The CIA came under virtual attack from MACV for their continued insistence on including all aspects of the enemy's forces. The volleys emanated from throughout the Saigon hierarchy, with messages not only from Brigadier General Davidson and General Abrams, but from General Westmoreland as well, from the MACV chief for pacification efforts, Robert Komer, and even from the US Ambassador to South Vietnam, Ellsworth Bunker. A unified front was desired to present a solid image of success. MACV/J2 succumbed to operational considerations and the CIA did all it could do, arriving at a creative compromise which did appear to have accomplished the impossible by 'squaring the circle.'

This was not the first time MACV had been in this situation. In July of 1964, just one month after General Westmoreland took over as Commander of MACV, the figures for the enemy order of battle were revised upward to reflect more accurate intelligence. The press release stated:

The seeming increase, the spokesman emphasized [on] July 29, is not the result of a recent build-up in Viet-Cong strength, but of a more realistic estimate of the size of the communist force in South Viet-Nam in the light of evidence now available.[4]

While the increase in 1964 was minuscule (from a range of 23,000–27,000 to a higher range of 28,000–34,000, an increase of only 5,000–7,000) compared to the large increase due to better intelligence in 1967 (from 299,000 to over 400,000), the fact is that the situation was not new, unknown, uncommon, or unthinkable in Vietnam. Given the environment, it was understood that intelligence never really had a firm grasp on the total number of the enemy faced in Vietnam. Reports also circulated attesting to the fact that even the Viet Cong and North Vietnamese themselves had no firm accounting of the total numbers under their control. While the press was tough in Vietnam, given the precedent that as intelligence gained better information it had periodically revised its numbers, that even the enemy was unsure of its total strength, and that this war was an insurgency fought in the most primitive of conditions, the MACV intelligence organization should never have allowed concerns about press reaction to have entered into any intelligence decision, no matter how trivial they judged it to be.

Of all the intelligence episodes recorded during the Vietnam War, even the shortsightedness of missing the various aspects of the enemy's Tet Offensive does not approach the low point that intelligence reached as it allowed concern over the press to influence the intelligence estimate on the enemy's order of battle. This was not how an intelligence estimate should be crafted. Even if the intelligence decision to drop the militia was justified, the decision is forever tainted and any explanation suspect.

On intelligence and ethnocentrism

Ethnocentrism was described by General Phillip B. Davidson in his book *The Secrets of the Vietnam War* as the grand dragon which all intelligence officers must face.[5] While he does not discuss ethnocentrism in reference to his decision to drop the militia from the MACV order of battle, the bias of ethnocentrism was present and had an influence on his decision. He even hints that he may have been mistaken in removing the militia forces from the order of battle accounts. His view that the enemy was rushing into 'big unit' warfare was to prove unfounded. Ethnocentrism was also to bias his own views as he tried to discern in which phase of insurgency the enemy was fighting. In his later years, he found that one of the 'secrets' of the Vietnam War was that the enemy was fighting in a mosaic incorporating all the phases.[6]

Militia forces count

The center of the intelligence drama of 1967 was how to account for the enemy's militia, the self-defense and secret self-defense forces. These forces had been carried by the French in their order of battle, had been carried by the South Vietnamese, and when the US began its order of battle on the enemy, these forces were included. In early 1967, analysts from the Defense Intelligence Agency (well before the decision became tainted by concerns over the press) challenged MACV and its then J2, Brigadier General Joseph

A. McChristian, on whether the militia forces should be in the order of battle.

In a message dated 1 April 1967, a delegation of DIA representatives meeting in Saigon to discuss order of battle issues with MACV/J2 reported back to the director of DIA the following:

> DIA team remains at odds with MACV/J2 on several points, including battalion-contact statistics, irregular and political OB, and in-country recruitment/conscription. DIA team want lower figures in each case.
>
> Concerning irregulars, DIA team plans recommend to both General McChristian [MACV/J2] and General Carroll [DIA director] that 'irregular' figure be scrapped and only 'guerrillas' carried as part of the military force figure. . . . MACV will probably push for 198,000 figure for irregulars unless DIA team sells idea of breaking out guerrillas.[7]

The debate on the militia forces was an ongoing affair that passed through several phases. The final outcome was highly dependent upon the philosophy of the current MACV/J2. Under Brigadier General McChristian, the militia were viewed as a component which, no matter how trivial, could affect MACV plans and operations. As such, they should, McChristian believed, be included in the enemy order of battle. Brigadier General Davidson was more concerned with the 'big unit' war, and he carried with him a 'scorn' for the primitive efforts of the Viet Cong. The militia, Davidson believed, were not militarily significant and, as such, could be dropped from the order of battle. A difference of philosophy, but which one was right?

The important question here, is not how *we* viewed the self-defense forces, but how the *enemy* viewed the self-defense forces. If the enemy believed these forces were a part of his military organization, then they should be reported by intelligence as such. The ethnocentric impulse to report only on forces that conform to our version of the threat removes vital information that a commander, his planners, and his soldiers need to understand the adversary.

The concept of self-defense forces has its roots in Mao Tse Tung's guerrilla warfare philosophy. In guerrilla warfare, the entire populace is to be mobilized, every skill and capability used. As Mao explained:

> There are those who say: 'I am a farmer,' or, 'I am a student;' 'I can discuss literature but not military arts.' This is incorrect. There is no profound difference between the farmer and the soldier. You must have courage. You simply leave your farms and become soldiers. That you are farmers is of no difference, and if you have education, that is so much the better. When you take your arms in hand, you become soldiers; when you are organized, you become military units.[8]

For the Viet Cong and their Viet Minh predecessors a guiding tenet established from their very beginnings in the late 1930s was: 'There must be total mobilization of the people – organizing millions to rush into battle – a task only the Party is capable of handling.'[9] Everyone had a place and task to perform in support of the *dau tranh* struggle.

An enemy document dated 18 August 1966 and written by the Current Affairs Section of the Central Office of South Vietnam, the equivalent of a standing committee to the People's Revolutionary Party (communist party in South Vietnam), was captured during Operation CEDAR FALLS on 12 January 1967. The document was a policy paper intended for use and implementation by Party members in the villages and hamlets. It discussed guerrilla and militia forces and the role of all people in the struggle.

> When following the Party chapter's resolution to create a people's struggle movement in the hamlets, it is very important to build, properly assess and *use the militia and guerrilla forces as the core* of the people's war movement. . . . Our present policy is to strengthen our present *militia and guerrilla* forces and increase these forces by recruiting more troops from the liberation association members and paying more attention to the forces for women and youth.
>
> In carrying out guerrilla warfare, *we have many ways of fighting in which all age groups can participate* if they have the spirit and resent the enemy. Thus we can extensively develop the guerrilla and militia forces by including old people's guerrilla units, teenage guerrilla units, women's legal guerrilla units in liberated areas and women's illegal guerrilla units in disputed areas. The movement can be strong only when we organize many guerrilla units and spur them on to compete with each other in achieving merit . . .
>
> Guide all Party members and association members to join the guerrillas so as to step up the military study movement among the people, so that when the enemy comes *each person, in his own way, can take part in the common task of fighting* him.[10] (Author's emphasis added.)

Each individual had a place and duty to perform in fighting the enemy, regardless of their sex, age, or experience. Professor Douglas Pike, one of the foremost experts on Vietnam studies, noted in his book on the army of North Vietnam, *PAVN: People's Army of Vietnam*, that the US military could never seem to agree on who to count as a member of the enemy's military forces. Pike notes, 'By the enemy's own definition there was no such thing as 'non military.'[11] Professor Pike then further chastises the intelligence community for inventing terms and categories to delineate the enemy instead of using the enemy's own organizational structure.

The enemy's organizational structure does conform fairly closely with the categories used by MACV and the intelligence community to categorize the enemy. Pike provided the following People's Army of Vietnam organizational philosophy:

> Traditionally, the Vietnamese Communists have organized their fighting forces as a troika. Earliest references to PAVN speak of three types of troops. Such usage continues today. The three are:
>
> 1 The Main Force, that is, the regular army, navy and air force, what elsewhere would be called the standing armed forces.
> 2 The Regional or Local Force, consisting of infantry companies with limited mobility and organized geographically, what elsewhere would be called a national guard or standing reserve.
> 3 The Militia/Self-Defense Force, a semi-mobilized element organized along social structure lines (village, urban precinct) or economic enterprise (commune, factory, work site) which elsewhere would be termed a reserve force or simply a registered military manpower pool.
>
> . . . The PAVN Main Force is composed of regular troops; PAVN Local Force of provincial, regional, territorial local and district local troops; PAVN Self-Defense Force is composed of militia troops, mobile militia troops, Assault Youth groups, Self-Defense troops and village troops.[12]

The concept and use of the term 'self-defense force' as the bottom foundation in the enemy's military pyramid predates the Viet Minh, the Viet Cong, and the People's Army of Vietnam; it can be traced back to Mao Tse Tung. When Mao was leading the Chinese against Japanese imperialism he wrote:

> All people of both sexes from ages of sixteen to forty-five must be organized into anti-Japanese *self-defense* units . . . Their responsibilities are: local sentry duties, securing information of the enemy, arresting traitors, and preventing the dissemination of enemy propaganda. When the enemy launches a guerrilla-suppression drive, these units, armed with what weapons there are, are assigned to certain areas to deceive, hinder, and harass him. Thus, the *self-defense* units assist the combatant guerrillas. They have other functions. They furnish stretcher-bearers to transport the wounded, carriers to take food to the troops, and comfort missions to provide the troops with tea and rice. If a locality can organize such a *self-defense* unit as we have described, the traitors can not hide nor can bandits and robbers disturb the peace of the people. Thus the people will continue to assist the guerrillas and supply manpower to our regular armies. 'The organization of *self-defense* units is a transitional step in the development of universal conscription. Such units are reservoirs of manpower for the orthodox forces.'[13] (Author's emphasis added.)

Thus spoke Mao in 1937, and so the Viet Cong organized in their *dau tranh* struggle even as the United States intelligence community fought amongst themselves, not trying to understand the enemy, but instead seeking to create an enemy in their own image. Even as they argued, more evidence of the self-defense force strength and place in the enemy's organization accumulated.

The *Chieu Hoi* (open arms) program was designed to induce the Viet Cong to desert, and the success of the program was another measure of determining success in this war without fronts. The figures were collected monthly and included in progress reports. In October 1968, J.M. Carrier, working for the Rand Corporation, published *A Profile of the Viet Cong Returnees: July 1965 to June 1967*. His data contains a wealth of statistical information on self-defense force defectors, which in turn sheds some light on the self-defense forces themselves. Carrier provided a description of the Viet Cong in the mold of a pyramid. 'The general movement upward of personnel in the VC military is from militia to guerrilla units, guerrilla to inter-village units, inter-village to district units, districts to province units, and province to main force units.'[14]

Carrier presents a wealth of statistical data, which was typically broken into 'VC Classification' categories. His 'VC Classification' entailed four categories; regular force, guerrilla, militia, and civilian. It is the militia category which would have been of interest to the military intelligence analysts arguing their theories in August and September 1967.

One interesting table that Carrier presented was labeled 'VC Strength Versus Returnees (Oct–Dec 1966)' in which he listed the percentage of returnees as compared to the overall VC strength estimate. No source is given for his chart data, but his breakdown of the VC force strength was 26 percent regular force, 21 percent guerrillas, 34 percent militia, and 19 percent civilian.[15] Certainly somebody had information estimating the make-up and apportionment of the enemy's forces.

Carrier noted that Viet Cong village and hamlet militia forces were the third most numerous type of returnee, ranking behind guerrillas and regular force troops.[16] During the period of Carrier's profiles, July 1965 to June 1967, 4,528 *Chieu Hoi* returnees identified themselves as belonging to the militia forces; this out of a total of 41,671 returnees, or slightly over 10 percent.[17]

One of the most interesting statistical findings that Carrier presented on the militia forces was that these forces were not made up mostly of old men and women and youth. Carrier studied the ages of returnees during two quarters, the first October–December 1965 and the second October–December 1966. He found that of those militia members who defected in the last quarter of 1965, nearly 44 percent were in the age group 18–29. Thirty-three percent were in the same age group in the same quarter for 1966. Those in the age group 30–41 made up 44 percent of the last quarter of 1965 militia defectors and 53 percent of the last quarter of 1966 militia defectors. Less than 10 percent of the militia defectors were ever under the age of 18 or over the age of 41.[18] Clearly, some of the militia were of prime military age, unless they had all defected.

Women were also part of the militia forces that defected, with 25 *Chieu Hoi* returnees identifying themselves as belonging to the militia. This is a relatively small figure compared to the 101 women returnees who identified themselves as belonging to local forces and the 404 who said they were part of the guerrilla forces.[19] Women were a part of the enemy force structure, but they were not singled out and deleted from the order of battle strength figures. The militia forces, according to the *Chieu Hoi* statistics were a part of the enemy force structure, and they should not have been removed from the order of battle strength figures.

The military effectiveness of the militia forces was a key factor in arguing to remove the militia forces from the order of battle. However, as Sam Adams was fond of pointing out, fully 20 percent of the casualties suffered by US forces in Vietnam came from booby traps and mines.[20] He also testified under oath and was not challenged by General Westmoreland's lawyers:

> And I remember when I visited the Vietnam Memorial, I asked myself, as sort of an analyst, how many of those 45,000 who were on those slabs of marble – it isn't marble, it's granite – of granite, how many of those were killed probably by people who weren't listed in the official order of battle or who belonged to organizations that weren't in the order of battle, and I said to myself, trying to figure the odds, that it was probably at least a third were killed by people not in the OB.[21]

The official numbers seem to back up Adams's contention. Of the 47,322 casualties due to hostile action in the Vietnam War, the largest cause of death was 'gunshot or small arms fire,' accounting for 18,468 or nearly 40 percent. The next highest was 8,455 listed under multiple fragmentation wounds, such as those suffered from booby traps, and another 7,432 due to grenades and mines, favorite weapons of the militia. These two categories account for 15,887, or 35 percent of the total casualties.[22] No definitive figure lists how many of the small arms fire, fragmentation, or grenade and mine casualties came from the militia forces, but an estimate of one-fifth to one-third would not seem unlikely.

Micheal Clodfelter published a book entitled *Vietnam in Military Statistics*. In this book Clodfelter breaks out the statistics in a slightly different format. He lists 18,396 casualties to small arms fire, slightly smaller than the 18,468 listed in official figures. He also has a specific category for 'booby traps,' in which he lists 8,464 US casualties, or almost 20 percent of his total of 46,323 casualties.[23]

The predominant theme of these casualty statistics is that they did not come from the 'big unit' conflicts that were envisioned to be the direction in which the war was heading by General Westmoreland and his intelligence chief, Brigadier General Davidson. One of the concessions that Davidson later made was that he would have included the militia forces in the order of battle had the war in Vietnam been in Phase I insurgency.

> Their [McChristian and Adams] insistence, then, in including the Communist political infrastructure and the impotent SD and SSD in the Enemy Order of Battle made sense if the war was, *in reality*, a Phase I insurgency. In fact, in such an insurgency these civilian/political elements should have been emphasized over the enemy's main force and local force units.[24] (Emphasis is Davidson's.)

It is interesting to note that General Davidson chose to highlight, *in reality*, because the premise of his book, *Secrets of the Vietnam War*, was that the biggest 'secret' of the war was the communists' 'Strategy of Revolutionary War,' which incorporated all phases of revolutionary warfare, from Phase I insurgency through Phase III conventional warfare. He has revealed that the enemy's 'Strategy of Revolutionary War' was *in reality* a 'mosaic' of Phase I, II and III. General Davidson insists that the Vietnam War did encompass Phase I operations; is he also insisting that the 'impotent' militia forces should have been included in the order of battle? Davidson seems to further hint that he would have included the militia when he later talks about the 'numbers' dispute. He says, 'a debate about the controlling essentials [the "Strategy of Revolutionary Warfare" mosaic] would have clarified the positions of both antagonists [MACV and CIA].' In other words, a discussion of the Phases of Revolutionary Warfare would have convinced both MACV and the CIA that the militia forces were a part of the enemy's revolutionary warfare and thus should have been included in the order of battle.[25] General Davidson had finally come to the same realization that Mao Tse Tung, the Viet Minh, and the Viet Cong all understood: the militia forces were a part of the struggle. (Unfortunately, General Davidson could not confirm these conclusions as he passed away on 7 February 1996.)

Main force envy

The United States forces in Vietnam were well versed in Mao and could elaborate on the phases of guerrilla warfare by rote. US leaders had studied the Viet Minh struggle against the French and could readily recognize the many ruses the enemy put forward. But for all this knowledge, the strategy of guerrilla warfare remained an alien concept, unless the enemy was in Phase III. Phase III, where the enemy took on the weakened government forces with conventional forces, was the type of warfare the American military knows best: force on force, destroying the enemy.[26] With its technology and vast industrial base, this was the type of warfare America had used in the defeat of Germany and Japan in World War II, and it had worked.

Our ethnocentric tendencies would not allow us to pursue and understand the war as an insurgency which consisted of three phases. Even though Phase III involved conventional type forces, the purpose of these forces was the completion of the insurgency. In South Vietnam, even though some units were engaged in Phase III activities, most were still operating at a Phase II or even Phase I level. Further, a force operating in Phase III can drop back and begin operations at Phase II at any time. Vietnam was not a conventional war, no matter how hard some tried to make it so.

In Vietnam, the enemy enticed the US military with trappings of conventional warfare. The Viet Cong and North Vietnamese Army both deployed battalions that aped conventional military units. Like a conventional force, these battalions formed regiments and the regiments formed divisions. The enemy's main forces gave the outward appearance of a conventional foe, they appealed to our ethnocentric view of what an enemy force should look like. Yet, these main forces still employed the tactics of guerrillas, refusing to stand and fight, staging ambushes, and attempting to set traps. However, these main forces were what the US could most relate to; these were the units which offered the greatest opportunity to attrit the enemy. It was on these forces that the US military focused its attention and resources.

A good illustration depicting the US focus on main force units occurred in 1967 in a dispute between the US Marines operating in the northern portion of South Vietnam, and General Westmoreland. The Marines wanted to deploy Combined Action Platoons (CAPs) permanently at villages alongside the local South Vietnamese militia to protect the villages and deter guerrilla attacks. General Westmoreland objected to this strategy, principally because such a deployment allowed the larger main forces in the north of South Vietnam to 'move at will.'[27] General Westmoreland urged the Marines to seek out the enemy main forces and destroy them. 'I believed the marines should have been trying to find the enemy's main forces and bring them to battle, thereby putting them on the run and reducing the threat they posed to the population.'[28] From the Marine viewpoint, the enemy forces had the initiative and could not be forced into battle. However, the Marines could defeat the enemy's objectives of controlling the population with their CAPs; the main forces could stalk their prey all they wanted, but the Marines would not allow the enemy to attack the prey.

The strategy of attrition itself forced the US military to focus on the larger main forces. It would be inefficient to seek out small platoons or even companies of enemy guerrillas when there were larger battalions, regiments, and divisions to be sought out and destroyed. The body count of a battalion engaged for even a short time far exceeded the number killed in a guerrilla squad.

A cursory review of General Westmoreland's portion of *Report on the War in Vietnam (As of 30 June 1968)*, in which he gives an accounting of his activities in Vietnam from 1964 to 1968, reveals numerous graphs, charts, and statistics. A good contrast of the focus on main forces and guerrilla/ militia forces can be found in the charts for 1968. There are three charts listing the changing numbers of both friendly and enemy battalions and a fourth chart showing the increasing number of North Vietnamese battalions and their manning in Viet Cong battalions. All these charts show changes and fluctuations and reveal the progress of US forces in attriting the Viet Cong.[29] Yet, the most telling graph was one which showed the populace under Viet Cong control. In 1964, the Viet Cong had outright control of 20 percent of the villages in South Vietnam. This percentage shows only a slight downward trend and in 1968 was near 15 percent. Four years of war and the Viet Cong still controlled over 75 percent of the territory they held in 1964.[30]

Perhaps the best example of the fixation on main forces was the build-up leading to the Tet Offensive and the siege of Khe Sanh. In late 1967 and early 1968, US intelligence closely monitored the build-up of NVA main forces near the Marine outpost at Khe Sanh.[31] At the same time, intelligence noted prisoners talking of the upcoming 'final victory,' as well as increased enemy strength, and an increase of over 200 percent in the number of truck sightings on the Ho Chi Minh Trail. All of this was interpreted by Westmoreland as signs of an upcoming main force attack in the northern provinces of South Vietnam, with minor attacks throughout the rest of the country as diversions to tie down US forces.[32]

Intelligence meticulously plotted and followed the deployment of the NVA 325C and 304 Divisions around Khe Sanh as Westmoreland and his staff put the final touches on coordinated artillery, tactical air, and B-52 strikes.[33] MACV waited in anticipation of the chance to attrit these main force units. When the massive Tet Offensive occurred, not with main force units, but with the local and guerrilla forces, not against a fortified military post, but against the cities of South Vietnam, Westmoreland still looked upon them not as the primary attack, but as a diversion.[34]

Another example of this fixation on the main forces was the decision in late 1967 by MACV military intelligence to drop the militia as a category of the official order of battle, because they were militarily insignificant. The chances of engaging the militia in a military operation were practically nil. Why waste resources trying to count that which you will not kill? General Davidson explains in his book *Secrets of the Vietnam War:*

> Seeing a conventional war in the offing, the MACV staff emphasized the enemy's main and local forces units as the key elements of enemy strength. The guerrillas and the civilian elements of the enemy force structure were remnants of a past phase and were of minor relevance to the conventional war which was fast approaching.[35]

The focus of the war was on the main forces; they were much easier to count.

The faces (phases) of insurgency

One of the most apparent areas of ethnocentrism during the Vietnam War was the constant search for the point at which the enemy crossed over into Phase III of guerrilla warfare, where the guerrilla military units take on an orthodox organization and stand and fight the 'big unit' battles. In 1967, Westmoreland and the MACV staff were convinced that the war had moved out of Phase I insurgency into Phase II, a combination of insurgency and conventional warfare. They were further convinced that the war was moving swiftly to Phase III conventional warfare.[36]

General Westmoreland and the MACV staff had come to this conviction more by intuition than by any factual or statistical evidence.[37] That is to say, their conviction was based upon their own ethnocentric grand dragons and the hope that the enemy would fight the 'American Way of War.' For General Westmoreland, pacification was a bore, and it was the 'big unit' war that he longed to fight.[38] The enemy did entice General Westmoreland, several times offering him tidbits and whiffs of conventional fights, such as at Khe Sanh, but the overall tone of the war remained guerrilla.

During the entire war in Vietnam, less than 10 percent of the battles involved VC/NVA units of a battalion or larger size. A full 90 percent of the attacks conducted by the VC/NVA were by company or smaller-sized units. From 1965 to 1968, of the 7,966 reported attacks, only 297 were conducted by a battalion or larger sized unit, and from 1969 to 1971 only 49 attacks were made by VC/NVA battalion or larger sized units.[39] The war in Vietnam was not conventional.

In his book *Secrets of the Vietnam War*, General Davidson reveals that one of the greatest 'secrets' of the war was the enemy's 'Strategy of Revolutionary War.' He listed several characteristics of the strategy, three of which are of particular importance in determining within which Phase the war in Vietnam was fought. The first of these characteristics was: 'It is *total war*. It mobilizes all the people whom the revolutionists control. It uses to the utmost every available facet of its power.'[40] Here again, Lt. General Davidson's own words argue for the inclusion of the militia forces.

The second characteristic which defined the 'Strategy of Revolutionary War' and its phases was: 'It is a *changing war*, featuring a constant shift between the Phases with consequent changes in the mix and importance of military and political *dau tranh*.' The war was not a linear progression from Phase I to Phase II to Phase III. It incorporated a shifting panorama of these phases.

The third and most important characteristic that General Davidson listed as defining the enemy's 'Strategy for Revolutionary War' was:

> Revolutionary war is a 'mosaic' war. In one area it may be in Phase III, conventional war, while nearby it may be in Phase II, and some-where else it may be in Phase I insurgency. For example, in late 1967 a

large-scale conventional war (Phase III) raged along the Laotian border
of northern South Vietnam and around the DMZ. At the same time, a
Phase II situation (conventional/insurgency) prevailed in mid-South
Vietnam, while a pure Phase I insurgency existed in the Mekong Delta
of southern Vietnam. . . .

The three different phases of revolutionary war could exist in even
closer proximity to each other. In 1967–1968, the South Vietnamese I
Corps area, also known as Military Region I (MR I), the northern five
provinces of South Vietnam, had a Phase I insurgency in its southern
coastal province of Quang Ngai, a Phase II (combination) in the two
adjoining provinces, and a good sized conventional war (Phase III) in
the two northern provinces of Quang Tri and Thua Thien.[41]

The 'big unit' war that the US wanted to fight was not to be. The ethnocentric tendencies which sought out the evidence at every chance to predict
a move by the enemy into Phase III conventional warfare was never to
materialize; it was a mirage constantly just on the horizon but never fully
coming into view. The intuition of General Westmoreland and the MACV
staff was a symptom of their ethnocentric impulse to bring the firepower
of superior American technology to bear. The image of an elephant stamping
on ants is an appropriate metaphor for our indulgence in our ethnocentric
egoism.

Ethnocentrism and the Tet surprise

The US forces in Vietnam were gearing up for a conventional fight. Their
intuition and instincts told them the enemy was moving out of Phase II
insurgency warfare and would soon confront them as conventional
Phase III forces. The US focus was on the Viet Cong and NVA main
forces. In a wargame conducted in late December 1967 and early January
1968, MACV analysts predicted the likely enemy course of action would
be to attack in the northern provinces with main and local forces in an
attempt to gain control of the northern section of South Vietnam.[42] Thus,
when the enemy began massing NVA divisions in the vicinity of Khe Sanh,
the natural conclusion was that they had correctly divined the enemy's intentions. Even as the Tet Offensive on the cities and towns of South Vietnam
began, General Westmoreland remained convinced that these were simply
diversion attacks designed by the enemy to bring US forces in from the
periphery where he expected the main attacks to occur.[43]

General Westmoreland's concern with Khe Sanh as the primary attack and
attacks on the interior of the country as diversionary was expressed in a
message he sent to both the Commander in Chief of the Pacific Forces and
the Chairman of the Joint Chiefs of Staff on 23 January 1968. In this message,
General Westmoreland cautions, 'It is prudent to expect that enemy activities

may be initiated simultaneously elsewhere in RVN in an attempt to divert and disperse our strength to levels incapable of country wide success.'[44]

This belief that Khe Sanh was the main objective fitted the ethnocentric view that the enemy was intent on fighting a conventional battle with the United States. The focus of intelligence since June 1967 had been on the more conventional enemy forces since the departure of Brigadier General Joseph A. McChristian. Khe Sanh and the NVA divisions surrounding it represented the type of war the US was prepared and equipped to conduct. When the premature attacks on the cities in central South Vietnam occurred on 30 January 1968, General Westmoreland and Brigadier General Davidson both agreed more attacks would be occurring on the night of 30 January and morning of 31 January. But, both thought these were diversionary attacks, not the main offensive which they both still viewed as imminent at Khe Sanh. It was no wonder then that they both returned to their billets; neither expected these attacks to be anything more than diversionary, the enemy would be saving his main forces for Khe Sanh.

In preparation for the anticipated attacks on Khe Sanh, General Westmoreland diverted intelligence resources to the Khe Sanh area. He used 'every available means to pinpoint the enemy by patrols, reconnaissance planes, radio intercepts, and electronic sensors.'[45] While providing valuable intelligence for Khe Sanh, James J. Wirtz argues in his book *The Tet Offensive: Intelligence Failure in War*, that this effort diverted valuable intelligence resources away from the other areas in South Vietnam. The result, Wirtz suggests, was increased surprise when the Tet assaults on the southern cities materialized.[46]

General Davidson spends a great deal of time in his book *Secrets of the Vietnam War* talking about ethnocentrism. 'Underlying all of the other sources of American surprises at Tet – and this is particularly true of faulty perceptions – lies that grand dragon awaiting all intelligence officers and commanders – ethnocentrism.'[47] Davidson blames ethnocentrism for the US unwillingness to accept the risks that the North Vietnamese were willing to take. 'One never attributes folly to his enemy – but then, as we shall see, of such assumptions are surprises made.'[48]

On intelligence and technocentrism

Technology came of age in Vietnam. The first 'electronic battlefield' was deployed along the Ho Chi Minh trail, picking up the rumblings of passing trucks, relaying the information via aircraft orbiting high above to computers safely monitoring and plotting the information in Thailand. The information was passed to attack aircraft, sometimes within 30 minutes, which could then drop their bombs on the unsuspecting convoys. The same sensors were deployed around Khe Sanh during its siege by the North Vietnamese. The data from the sensors was used for artillery and aircraft strikes against the enemy.[49] Technology was making significant inroads and Vietnam was a hard learning ground. Technology offers many advantages and it assisted in many areas which otherwise held no other solution. But technology could not solve the riddle of what the enemy intended and how long he could sustain the carnage.

In the realm of technical intelligence, signals emanating from enemy radios provided a wealth of information, but not all of the enemy's forces used radios. Plentiful intelligence information was available on main force units, thanks in large part to technical intelligence. Local force units also had a good deal of intelligence gathered on them, again thanks to technical intelligence. But, for the guerrilla and militia forces, which operated without radios, intelligence information from technical means was negligible.

Technology is most useful against a technologically savvy enemy. But against a primitive foe, technology's usefulness wanes. With no radios or electronic signals emanating from a primitive force, intelligence collection via technical means yields only silence.

The lack of any indication from technical intelligence sources of an enemy offensive other than the cyclical attacks to be expected in the February to May time-frame serves as a clear warning against over-reliance on technology. During the lead-up to Tet, technology was actually used to paint a deception as US intelligence became 'mesmerized by the electronic image' of the NVA massing along the borders of South Vietnam.[50] At the same time, the Viet Cong and North Vietnamese forces inside South Vietnam were massing around and infiltrating the cities that were the true targets of the Tet Offensive. Technology rendered the US intelligence efforts deaf and blind to the upcoming Tet attacks.

Olde fashioned intelligence

Sun Tzu marveled at the delicate art of espionage. 'Delicate indeed! Truly delicate! There is no place where espionage is not used.'[51] And it was Sun Tzu who also counseled, 'Secret operations are essential in war; upon them the army relies to make its every move.'[52] The truly effective intelligence which can counter either a primitive or technical environment is still good, old-fashioned, hard-nosed intelligence from a source who knows the information sought. In Vietnam, there was no shortage of enemy to debrief and interrogate. Prisoners and defectors were constantly flowing through the districts and huge amounts of data and information were gained. Of course, the problem lay in the sheer amount of data, and in determining whether the source was being truthful or not, and, if truthful, whether the information was actually valid or a plant or simply wrong. 'Delicate indeed! Truly delicate!'

The same was true for the next best thing in the absence of a living human who knew the information sought, and that was a document containing the information sought. Huge amounts of captured enemy documents were processed through MACV daily. The enemy had a propensity to write; young soldiers to their loves or mothers, the political cadre to their supervisors, the platoon and company commanders to their battalion commanders. And to service all this mail were the commo-liaison troops who served as the postal service for the enemy, organized from the lowest hamlet to the inner sanctum of the *Lao Dong* Central Committee in Hanoi.

Like the interrogation and debrief reports, the data from captured documents was overwhelming. Unfortunately, there was little glamor in working with these types of sources. The real-time ability to provide information on a timely basis to make a difference in a combat situation was non-existent. Working with documents and reports was not the way to catch the attention of your supervisors. The glamorous world of intelligence lay on the technical side.

An acceptance of not moving in the intelligence fast lane and a determination to ferret out the nuggets of valid and pertinent information did have rewards of its own. Sam Adams of the CIA was able to discern a great deal of information and build a basis for understanding the enemy. He did this while working the Congo crisis and built a good reputation for himself. He also built a reputation while analyzing the Viet Cong, and undoubtedly would have had a successful career with the CIA had he not become so fanatical about proving that he was correct in his own assessments.

Another CIA analyst, Joe Hovey, working with interrogation and debrief reports and captured enemy documents, was able to accurately forecast the enemy's Tet Offensive. His report was forwarded to the CIA and even passed on to Walt W. Rostow, the President's National Security Advisor, who then passed it on to President Johnson.[53] Hovey's report contained caveats as to its accuracy and CIA headquarters downplayed the significance and validity of the information contained in the analysis. However, Hovey, relying on good, old-fashioned intelligence was able to decipher the enemy's plans and intentions, while the technophiles at MACV chased the 'mesmerizing' electronic ghost images of the enemy wisping along the periphery.

Another old intelligence officer was also able to discern the enemy's Tet Offensive based upon reports and documents. Lieutenant General Fred Weyand was a former intelligence officer who had been promoted from commander of the 25th Division to commander of the II Field Force, roughly a Corps-sized unit responsible for the Saigon region. On 10 January 1967 he told General Westmoreland he had disturbing intelligence that indicated the enemy was attempting to draw his forces to the border areas and had actually planned attacks on the urban centers. He convinced General Westmoreland to cancel several operations along the border and to allow him to draw his forces in closer around the Saigon area.[54] General Weyand only had intelligence on his area of responsibility and was unable to ascertain the entire scope of the enemy's offensive.

Adams, Hovey and Weyand all demonstrate that properly trained, determined and skilled intelligence officers can gain useful and critical information from reports and documents. General Davidson was not impressed with these types of intelligence sources and did not trust them. If he had put more faith in his officers working with these types of intelligence sources, perhaps he would not now be saddled with the reputation of having been 'on watch' when the enemy surprised the US forces during Tet 1968.

If it's not technical, it's not 'real' intelligence

One of the primary reasons that it was easier to count the main forces than those of the guerrilla/militia forces, was the use of technical intelligence. America's intelligence community has a rich history of using technology in the realm of espionage. World War II is replete with examples of how our technical prowess allowed the US to anticipate our enemy's plans. In the Pacific theater, Naval Intelligence was able to decipher Japanese war plans, while in the European theater, 'ULTRA' was feeding a steady flow of deciphered German message traffic. The force of this technical intelligence prowess was also brought to bear in Vietnam. There was only one problem: the Vietnamese fought a primitive war and not everyone brought a radio.

'The guerrillas didn't operate radios,' explained General Davidson to an interviewer in June of 1982. As a result, 'We didn't have a much better hold on the thing [guerrilla numbers and activities] from some peculiar, secret source of intelligence.'[55] In other words, technical intelligence was of little value in documenting the numbers, activities, plans, and intentions of the guerrilla forces. The only sources available to chronicle the guerrilla forces were captured documents and interrogations. To Davidson, these sources were suspect due to the following:

1 problems with translation,
2 inability to easily ascertain whether the figures listed were goals or actual strengths,
3 inability to easily determine if the information was accurate, misleading, or simply false, and
4 the information was seldom timely, especially in comparison with the near-instantaneous reporting of technical intelligence.[56]

Davidson insisted on 'all-source' intelligence,[57] meaning that more than just a human or documentary source was needed to have intelligence significance; a technical intelligence source was also required. This meant if analysts couldn't back up their assessments with technical sources, it wasn't 'real' intelligence. With the guerrillas operating in a radio-free environment, these forces were of 'minor relevance.'[58] Is it any wonder then, that these forces were able to gather in such numbers before Tet and launch an offensive without being discovered by the military's technical intelligence systems?

There was, in MACV, almost a disdain for non-technical intelligence. This attitude was displayed by Air Force Colonel Edward Catton, who was the chief of the Joint Intelligence Branch in Saigon from June 1966 to June 1967. He was in charge of 'highly classified intelligence' of a technical nature. Colonel Catton rated the order of battle reports he produced based upon technical intelligence as accurate, current, and up to date. He described order of battle documents produced without technical intelligence as being of little value, nothing more than reference documents which 'shouldn't be confused with the military order of battle.'[59]

Another Colonel at MACV in 1967, who went on to become a Lieutenant General and head of the Defense Intelligence Agency, Daniel Graham, also belittled any order of battle that was produced without technical intelligence. When given a copy of an order of battle document produced without technical intelligence and asked if MACV called it an order of battle, he replied, 'Some did, some didn't, I for one.'[60] If you don't have technical intelligence, then it's not real intelligence.

Real intelligence, technical intelligence, was not available on guerrilla/militia forces; their intelligence was 'soft' and 'mushy.'[61] The same was not true of the main force units. These types of units were organized along the lines of conventional forces, and as part of their more extensive command and control capability, each battalion would typically have a signal platoon.[62] With a signal platoon operating radios, technical intelligence could then document the main force unit's presence and gather data on their numbers, plans, and intentions. Intelligence available on main forces was 'real,' technical intelligence. These were the units that counted, and could be counted.

The reliance of intelligence upon technical means reinforced the ethnocentric tendency to concentrate on the main force units. The combined effects of ethnocentrism and technocentrism fostered an increasingly biased picture of the enemy facing US and Government of South Vietnam forces. The focus was on enemy units of a conventional nature. The surprise of the Tet Offensive was to come from an enemy of an unconventional temperament.

Technocentrism and the Tet surprise

One of the ethnocentric sins to which General Davidson himself admitted was the 'scorn' in which he held the enemy's primitive communications system.[63] Yet it was the enemy's very lack of a sophisticated electronic communications system that allowed them to mass their forces unbeknownst to the US and Government of South Vietnam troops. The United States had the world's most sophisticated electronic signals intercept and radio direction finding capability. This technical intelligence aptitude, when used without the enemy's knowledge, produced highly accurate and reliable intelligence. It was not subject to emotions or foggy memories. The possibility of deception was an aspect to be considered, but if the collection ability and collection targets were closely held secrets, subject to release to only those individuals with the highest security clearances, then the risks of deception were greatly reduced.

Technical intelligence was also very timely and could be quickly analyzed and acted upon. This was in direct contrast to more primitive means of intelligence collection, such as human interrogations and defector debriefs, which took days, weeks, and even months before completed reports were forwarded to the field and to the analysts at MACV/J2. The same was true for captured enemy documents which first had to be transported to the translators, who then had to pore over the documents and sort out those needing immediate attention from those that could wait. Then the actual translation had to be made, before finally getting out a report days, weeks, or even months later. Technical intelligence was the preferred and most timely means of discerning the enemy forces and their movements which, when monitored over time, gave an indication as to intended targets.

Up to 80 percent of the intelligence collected in Vietnam has been attributed to technical intelligence.[64] At MACV, from June 1967 onward when General Phillip B. Davidson became the J2, the preferred collection resource was technical intelligence. To Davidson, intelligence derived from humans and documents was suspect and could seldom be trusted. This reliance upon technical intelligence proved to be an Achilles' heel for US intelligence in Vietnam, especially with regard to the guerrilla forces, because they simply did not use radios.[65] The more conventional-type units of the NVA main forces did use radios and therefore an abundant amount of information was collected and available on them. This reinforced the already present US tendency to concentrate on the main forces due to the ethnocentric biases of the US to relate to forces more akin to their own conventional units.

True to form, with the US already focused on the more conventional forces of the NVA, technical intelligence began to pick up increased radio activity along the border areas with North Vietnam and Laos, in particular in the vicinity of Khe Sanh.[66] Wirtz, in his book *The Tet Offensive: Intelligence Failure in War*, describes the technical infatuation and its effects during the time-frame leading up to the Tet Offensive:

> In early 1968, SIGINT [Signals Intelligence, a form of technical intelligence] revealed the movement of NVA units as they massed along the DMZ and the western border of South Vietnam, especially near Khe Sanh. In contrast, the VC units that were surrounding and infiltrating southern cities remained relatively quiet (they did not generate much radio traffic). As US intelligence agencies became increasingly mesmerized by the electronic image generated by the NVA, they tended to downplay captured documents and prisoner interrogation reports that indicated a VC attack against the cities of the south. Lacking SIGINT evidence, they dismissed other information that indicated that the communists intended to attack cities during the Tet holiday.[67]

'Mesmerized by the electronic image,' the US intelligence analysts relied upon their strong suit, technical intelligence. It confirmed for them what they had already intuitively deduced based upon their own predilection for the conclusion that the war was becoming more conventional in nature.[68] With the war estimated to be moving in the direction of conventional fighting, with technical intelligence providing an image of the NVA massing on the border areas, with recently completed wargames and intelligence all pointing to a conventional-style attack by the NVA forces in the border regions centered on Khe Sanh, little attention was paid to the primitive Viet Cong forces as they massed near the cities and towns of South Vietnam.

On intelligence and the measure of success

Vietnam was a war of numbers and statistics. Success was measured in body counts and weapons captured. The Americanization of the war had borne fruit in 1967 as the enemy's numbers began to decline. But as Sun Tzu warns, there is no advantage in numbers.

Hard numbers and Tet

Collaborating with the ethnocentric and technocentric views that focused attention on the enemy's conventional forces were the hard numbers that intelligence had on the main and local forces and the 'softness' of the estimates for the guerrilla and the banished militia forces. While the main and local force numbers were dropping, it was the guerrilla forces which had exhibited the greatest decline over the past year. Main and local forces had declined from a high of 127,200 in September 1966, to a low of 115,000 in the Order of Battle Summary for January 1968, a decline of 12,100. The guerrilla forces showed an even greater attrition rate, peaking at 126,200 in December 1966 and dropping to 72,600 in January 1968, a decline of over 50,000. An enemy suffering such losses seemed very unlikely to attempt a massive attack on the cities of South Vietnam.

Intelligence sources were also reportedly skeptical of the Viet Cong being able to mass any type of unit larger than a company. The chief of the pacification efforts in Vietnam for General Westmoreland, Robert Komer, reportedly stated just six weeks prior to the Tet Offensive that 'our information is that they can't put more than a company-sized unit into the field anywhere in South Vietnam.'[69]

Further, any analytical study on the Viet Cong forces, their capabilities and intentions was unlikely to find support in the intelligence environment of MACV in late 1967 and early 1968. Having just completed a long, drawn-out and vicious bureaucratic war with the CIA over who constituted the enemy and how many there were, it was unlikely that any investigation which might reopen the issue would have been initiated. This was especially true in light of the fact that it was MACV who insisted that the Viet Cong militia forces be dropped and it was based upon their data that the Viet Cong guerrilla forces had dropped by nearly 50,000.

James Wirtz noted this reluctance to reopen old bureaucratic wounds in his book *The Tet Offensive: Intelligence Failure in War*:

> Because information about the activity of VC guerrillas was viewed in the context of the order-of-battle dispute, a thorough study of VC activity before the Tet offensive would have threatened to turn again into a bureaucratic hot potato, threatening the tenuous compromise over estimates of enemy strength.[70]

General Bruce Palmer, Jr., writing in his book *The 25-Year War: America's Military Role in Vietnam*, also notes:

> Nevertheless, in hindsight I feel that the November 1967 agreed national estimate of enemy strength – generally lower than the CIA's estimate, which was later confirmed – probably helped reinforce the feeling in Vietnam prior to Tet 1968 that the enemy was not capable of conducting major, near-simultaneous, country-wide attacks. In turn, this may have contributed to the tactical surprise achieved by Hanoi.[71]

George C. Herring, in his book *America's Longest War*, also agreed with this viewpoint when he wrote, 'The North Vietnamese appeared so bloodied by the campaigns of 1967 that the Americans could not conceive that they could bounce back and deliver a blow of the magnitude of Tet.'[72] The numbers just did not support anything other that the cyclical campaigns that the enemy had been waging for years. If anything, the numbers indicated that the coming attacks could not match the scope and scale of earlier campaigns, except perhaps for the NVA forces, which had been becoming more and more dominant in the enemy's strategy.

The numbers for the NVA did not show the dramatic decline that had been eating away at the guerrilla forces. The NVA numbers had peaked at 55,400 in August 1966 and bottomed out at 47,900 in November 1966. The NVA had quickly recovered, however, as they reached a new high of 56,300 in April of 1967 and they stood only slightly down at 55,600 in January 1968. The numbers would definitely lead one to believe that any attacks would have to be spearheaded by the NVA who stood numerically far superior to the decimated Viet Cong forces. But as Lt. General Davidson so eloquently said, 'of such assumptions are surprises made.'[73]

It is the will

President Lyndon Baines Johnson lamented in his autobiography *The Vantage Point* that:

Never once was there a clear sign that Ho Chi Minh had a genuine interest in bargaining for peace. Never, through any channel or from any serious contact did we receive any message that differed signifi-cantly from the tough line that Hanoi repeated over and over again: Stop all the bombing, get out of Vietnam, and accept our terms for peace. The North Vietnamese never gave the slightest sign that they were ready to consider reducing the Communists' half of the war or to negotiate seriously the terms of a fair peace settlement.[74]

The communists were not going to compromise in the style that President Johnson had perfected in his years in Congress. Beyond President Johnson's simple naivety regarding the foe he faced, the passage speaks volumes regarding the enemy's resolve and determination to continue the war. And while General Westmoreland pounded away with his attrition strategy, nobody knew at what magical level the losses would become so painful that Ho Chi Minh and his minions would cease their aggression.[75] This was one of the true failings of intelligence according to General Phillip B. Davidson, the anticipation of a capitulation that never came.

When General Joseph A. McChristian arrived in Vietnam in 1965, he saw several tasks which had to be accomplished. 'Above all, we needed to know the quantity and quality of manpower the enemy could send to South Vietnam and *the will* of North Vietnamese leaders and soldiers *to persist*'[76] (author's emphasis). After nearly a year in country, McChristian had the opportunity to better understand his foe when the commanding officer of the 93rd Battalion, 2nd Viet Cong Regiment, Senior Captain Dang Doan, a North Vietnamese, was captured by the 1st Air Cavalry Division. McChristian personally interrogated the prisoner and was impressed by his military bearing and professionalism. McChristian later recalled of Senior Captain Dang Doan:

> He said he might not see it and his son may not see it, but they were going to persevere. This man was a regular army officer, extremely well disciplined, and I thought that here was the true example of the leadership of this country and their will to continue the war.[77]

General McChristian had a framed picture in his study of this North Vietnamese battalion commander, standing proud and upright, wearing a freshly laundered uniform, with feet firmly set in front of a rice paddy. McChristian had few doubts as to the enemy's will, he closed every briefing he gave on the enemy with 'The North Vietnamese and Viet Cong have *the will and capability* to conduct a protracted war of attrition at current levels of activity *indefinitely*.' Even General Davidson had to agree with this 'pat' assessment. He later admits,

We badly underestimated the resolve of Ho Chi Minh and his Politburo to unify Vietnam under communism. As we continued to increase United States forces and our pressure on the North, we kept waiting for Ho and company to cry 'uncle.' They never did, and we never grasped that while it was a limited war for the United States, it was a life-or-death struggle for the Vietnamese Communists.

Part III

The Tet Effect and intelligence principles in the twenty-first century

11 The Tet Effect in Iraq

Pre-empting credibility

Believe Him or Not:
Does Bush Have a Credibility Gap?

Cover *Time* magazine, 16 February 2004[1]

History never repeats itself; to replicate the circumstances, the themes, the patterns, the behaviors, *et al.* requires far too many variables to realign. History does not repeat; but certain circumstance, themes, patterns, behaviors do repeat, they repeat quite often, just not aligned in the same fashion and with the same relationships as before. History is replete with examples of mankind relearning the mistakes of their elders.

The variables of the Tet Effect – bad intelligence used by leaders to portray a disingenuous image to the public and then shown to be wrong with a resultant loss of credibility – have been repeated and probably will be repeated again. Such a pattern was played out during late 2002 and early 2003 as bad intelligence, bearing witness that Iraq still had weapons of mass destruction and links to al-Qaeda terrorists, was used by US and British leaders to convince the public that a pre-emptive attack was justified. The attack was successful, but no weapons of mass destruction were found and both the US leader, President George W. Bush and the British leader, Prime Minister Tony Blair, have suffered losses in credibility. The events did not play out exactly as they did in Vietnam, and the resultant loss of credibility has not been as severe, but the Tet Effect has repeated itself in Iraq.

Girding for war

America was forever changed on 11 September 2001 as terrorists violated the Islamic code for which they claimed to fight by killing over 3,000 innocents. The protective insulation the United States had clothed itself in was violently stripped away. America was now ready to gird itself for war, war against the terrorists who violated not only the codes of war, but the very foundation of civilization itself. The United States was forced to re-examine its defenses, its military, its very definition of war. The enemy was not an armed military force that wore the uniforms of a nation that had formally declared war against the US. The enemy was a shadowy, ill-defined, loose organization of individuals and groups with allegiance to no nation, sharing only one trait, hatred.

On 12 September 2001, President George W. Bush characterized the terrorist attacks as 'acts of war,' and called on the American public and the freedom-loving peoples of the world to remain strong in their resolve. He promised, 'The United States of America will use all our resources to conquer this enemy.'[2] The global war on terrorism was begun.

Three days later, in a radio address to the nation, President Bush laid out the American strategy. 'Victory against terrorism will not take place in a single battle, but in a series of decisive actions against terrorist organizations and those who harbor and support them. We are planning a broad and sustained campaign to secure our country and eradicate the evil of terrorism.' The first target was al-Qaeda leader Osama bin Laden and those who harbored him.

The September 11th links to Osama bin Laden and his al-Qaeda organization were strong and unmistakable, as were his ties and bonds to the Taliban government of Afghanistan. The United States brought together an innovative campaign against al-Qaeda and their Taliban allies. Through a skillful coalition of anti-Taliban forces with judicious use of embedded American soldiers on the ground, unchallenged American airpower, and close cooperation with neighboring countries, the US was able to deny al-Qaeda a safe haven, remove the rogue Taliban government, and begin the process of building a democracy for the people of Afghanistan. The global war on terrorism was successfully underway.

By January of 2002, President Bush was able to tell the nation in his 'State of the Union' address that in Afghanistan, 'The American flag flies again over our embassy in Kabul.' But, he cautioned, 'Our war against terror is only beginning.' He laid out two objectives. 'First, we will shut down terrorist camps, disrupt terrorist plans, and bring terrorists to justice. And, second, we must prevent the terrorists and regimes who seek chemical, biological or nuclear weapons from threatening the United States and the world.' He then identified the 'Axis of Evil:' the terrorists and the rogue states of North Korea, Iran, and Iraq.

Iraq was clearly identified as the most heinous, with an entire paragraph devoted to detailing the atrocities of Saddam Hussein and his regime. North Korea and Iran were allotted just one sentence each. Iraq, it was clear, would be the next target. President Bush laid down the gauntlet, letting the 'Axis of Evil' know that, 'America will do what is necessary to ensure our nation's security.' He then began to build the foundation for a pre-emptive attack. 'I will not wait for events, while dangers gather. I will not stand by, as peril draws closer and closer.'[3]

The strategies employed by America during the twentieth century have been based upon diplomacy first, then war when all else fails. This strategy worked well in World War I and II, and during the Cold War, including both military actions in Korea and Vietnam. Even in the post-Cold War world, diplomatic strategy and coalition-building were the precursors to war. But, as President Bush explained in a speech to the graduating cadets of West Point in June of 2002, the world had changed. 'For much of the last century, America's defense relied on the Cold War doctrines of deterrence and containment. In some cases, those strategies still apply. But new threats also require new thinking.'

The world was now a much more dangerous place, with rogue regimes producing weapons of mass destruction and terrorists willing to deliver such terrible weapons. 'If we wait for threats to fully materialize,' President Bush warned, 'we will have waited too long.' The war on terrorism, he continued, 'will not be won on the defensive. We must take the battle to the enemy, disrupt his plans, and confront the worst threats before they emerge.' If there was any doubt that the President was talking about taking pre-emptive action, he removed it when he declared that, 'our security will require all Americans to be forward-looking and resolute, to be ready for pre-emptive action when necessary to defend our liberty and to defend our lives.'[4]

The concept of pre-emption was made official US policy three months later when the Bush administration released the National Security Strategy. In his cover letter to the strategy, President Bush said,

> The gravest danger our Nation faces lies at the crossroads of radicalism and technology ... as a matter of common sense and self-defense, America will act against such emerging threats before they are fully formed. We cannot defend America and our friends by hoping for the best. ... History will judge harshly those who saw this coming danger but failed to act. In the new world we have entered, the only path to peace and security is the path of action.[5]

Pre-emptive attack was now official US policy. With such a doctrine, the role of intelligence became paramount. As President Bush's letter explained, 'So we must be prepared to defeat our enemies' plans, using the best intelligence and proceeding with deliberation.' To act pre-emptively requires foreknowledge of the enemy's capability and intent. Such foreknowledge is the realm of intelligence.

When leaders shape intelligence

The Bush administration had developed a policy of pre-emption based upon the threat of terrorists using weapons of mass destruction from a rogue nation against the United States or its allies. The rogue nations with weapons of mass destruction had been identified – North Korea, Iran, and Iraq. Of the three, Iraq was the most belligerent in displaying an aggressiveness and willingness to use such weapons. The case for a pre-emptive attack against

Iraq seemed straightforward and obvious. Iraq had used chemical weapons against Iran in their war in the 1980s and Saddam had used these same weapons against his own people. Saddam had a history of lying about and concealing his efforts to develop and produce weapons of mass destruction. There seemed no reason to doubt that Iraq did have weapons of mass destruction.

Open to debate, however, was the link between Iraq and terrorism. The Saddam regime had trained its own intelligence services in the techniques of terrorism, and some evidence showed various levels of support to regional terrorist organizations, but any 'established formal relationship' to al-Qaeda was tenuous and doubtful.[6]

The policy of pre-emptive attack as outlined by the Bush administration was directed at rogue nations with a weapons of mass destruction capability and the intent to use such weapons themselves or to give them to terrorists to use. The primary weapons of mass destruction are chemical, biological, radiological, and nuclear weapons. The US intelligence community was in agreement regarding Iraq having a biological and chemical weapons capability. Unfortunately, this knowledge was based on reliable information in most cases at least 15 years old and, in the best case, over five years old. In fact, no one in the US intelligence community had valid information confirming that Iraq possessed weapons of mass destruction. However, given the history of Saddam Hussein, it was not unreasonable to assume that he still possessed such weapons. There is a big difference between knowing and assuming, a difference that could mean war or no war.

While assessed as having a chemical and biological capability, there was a great deal of disagreement within the intelligence community regarding Iraq's intent to reconstitute its nuclear program. Debate centered primarily around interpreting the evidence, with the critical component being aluminum tubes, necessary for building a uranium enhancement centrifuge. Iraq was attempting to procure aluminum tubes in 2001 for use, it was claimed, in producing tubes for rocket launchers. The Central Intelligence Agency (CIA) assessed that the tubes were for a centrifuge and part of Iraq's attempt to reconstitute their nuclear program. Several within the intelligence community, including the Department of Energy, the experts in such matters, disagreed.[7]

The case for a pre-emptive attack based on Iraq's weapons of mass destruction capability was backed by the intelligence community. Except for the disagreement on reconstitution of Iraq's nuclear program, intelligence solidly backed the Bush administration when they began to argue for military action against Iraq. From the Bush administration's viewpoint, there was no doubt that Iraq had chemical and biological weapons, and they further believed that Iraq was attempting to revive their nuclear program.[8] The CIA, at least on this issue, was on the Bush team.

The issue of a link between Iraq and terrorism was more divisive, not within the intelligence community, but between the intelligence community and those in leadership positions. The declared enemy was al-Qaeda, and any link between this terrorist organization and Iraq would provide the most compelling justification for a pre-emptive attack against Iraq. Unfortunately for the Bush administration, there was no evidence upon which the intelligence community could assess that there was a formalized link between Iraq and al-Qaeda. There were reports of some meetings, and even of some individual training, but no evidence of an ongoing Iraqi/al-Qaeda connection.[9]

To complicate matters, however, there were reports, unsubstantiated and with no additional verification, that perhaps there was a stronger connection between Iraq and al-Qaeda. The most commonly referenced being meetings that allegedly occurred in 1999 between September 11th lead hijacker Muhammed Atta and the station chief of the Iraqi Intelligence Service in Prague, Ahmad Khalil Ibrahim Samir al Ari. The evidence of this meeting was inconclusive, and stronger evidence placed Atta elsewhere.[10] There was simply insufficient evidence and the intelligence community as a whole could not verify a continuing relationship between al-Qaeda and Iraq.

Such a link, however, was 'sensed' by certain leaders within the Bush administration. Responding 'to senior policymaker interest in a comprehensive assessment of Iraqi regime links to al-Qa'ida,' the CIA produced *Iraq and al-Qaida: Interpreting a Murky Relationship* in June 2002.[11] Taking a 'purposefully aggressive' approach, the bottom line of the report was:

> Some analysts concur with the assessment that intelligence reporting provides 'no conclusive evidence of cooperation on specific terrorist operations,' but believe that the available signs support a conclusion that Iraq has had sporadic, wary contacts with al-Qaida since the mid-1990s, rather than a relationship with al-Qaida that has developed over time.[12]

Not an established, formal relationship, but perhaps 'sporadic, wary' contacts. Evidently not good enough for the Under Secretary of Defense for Policy, Douglas Feith.[13] Not satisfied with the CIA assessment that no link existed, not satisfied with the Defense Intelligence Agency (DIA) assessment that no link existed, he kept searching until he found someone who did believe in such a link. The someone was a lone DIA analyst who had 'discovered intelligence reporting from the mid-1990s that had not been incorporated into more recent finished products.'[14] Rebuffed by elements within DIA, the analyst passed on the information to the Office of the Under Secretary of Defense for Policy, which then had the analyst detailed to its own Policy Support Staff.[15]

This DIA analyst, now working on Feith's Policy Support Staff, reviewed the CIA's *Iraq and al-Qaida: Interpreting a Murky Relationship*, and concluded:

The report provides evidence from numerous intelligence sources over a decade on the interactions between Iraq and al-Qaida. In this regard, the report is excellent. Then in its interpretation of this information, CIA attempts to discredit, dismiss, or downgrade much of this reporting, resulting in inconsistent conclusions in many instances. Therefore, the CIA report should be read for content only – and CIA interpretation ought to be ignored.[16]

'[T]the CIA report should be read for content only – and CIA interpretation ought to be ignored.' In other words, do not rely on the CIA's experience as intelligence analysts to determine the credibility, validity, and strength of a report, look at the raw, unevaluated intelligence and judge for yourself; you can find the answers you seek. Finally, a lone analyst who could find a link simply by ignoring the analysis of the rest of the intelligence community. Seizing upon this recommendation, Feith sent the critique to his bosses, Deputy Secretary of Defense Paul Wolfowitz and Secretary of Defense Donald Rumsfeld.

The DIA analyst detailed to Feith's Policy Support Staff became part of an 'intelligence cell' within the Feith's Office of the Under Secretary of Defense for Policy that also included the Policy Counterterrorism Evaluation Group (PCTEG).[17] The PCTEG, was set up by Feith to study 'the policy implications of relationships among terrorist groups and their sources of support.'[18] The PCTEG, however, conducted predominantly intelligence analysis looking at both raw and finished intelligence to find what they needed.[19] What was needed was a link between al-Qaeda and Saddam Hussein, and the PCTEG was at least 'partly' focused on finding intelligence that could support such a link.[20]

The policy 'intelligence cell' within Feith's office also worked with a special assistant to Paul Wolfowitz, the Deputy Secretary of Defense. The special assistant created a briefing that criticized the intelligence community's analysis of the relationship between Iraq and al-Qaeda which was then presented to the Secretary of Defense Rumsfeld by two members of the policy 'intelligence cell.'[21]

Rumsfeld was 'impressed.' A delegation including Feith and members of the 'intelligence cell' then briefed George Tenet, the Director of Central Intelligence (DCI) and head of the CIA. While the DCI 'didn't think much of it,' he arranged a meeting between CIA and other intelligence community analysts and some members of the policy 'intelligence cell' to discuss their findings on terrorist links to Iraq.[22] The CIA analysts were not impressed either, but invited one of the policy 'intelligence cell' representatives (the DIA analyst) to write a dissenting view which would be included in an intelligence estimate. The DIA analyst refused, explaining later to the Senate Select Committee on Intelligence that 'I was an employee of Policy, not wearing an intelligence hat.'[23]

Having convinced their bosses at Defense that there was a link, the policy 'intelligence cell' was unsuccessful at swaying the intelligence community. Refusing to be thwarted, and without the knowledge of the DCI, members of Feith's policy office 'intelligence cell' briefed White House staffers, including the Deputy National Security Advisor, Steve Hadley, and the Vice President's Chief of Staff, Lewis Libby on 16 September 2002.[24] The briefing went 'very well;' the Bush administration had found a link between al-Qaeda and Iraq.

The Senate Select Committee on Intelligence conducted a review of pre-Iraqi War intelligence and issued a report on 7 July 2004. As part of their review, the committee looked into allegations of 'pressure' applied by policymakers on intelligence analysts to change their assessments. The overall committee report stated in its conclusions that 'The Committee did not find any evidence that administration officials attempted to coerce, influence or pressure analysts to change their judgments related to Iraq's weapons of mass destruction capabilities.'[25] Regarding 'pressure' to find a terrorist link, 'The Committee found that none of the analysts or other people interviewed by the Committee said that they were pressured to change their conclusions related to Iraq's links to terrorism.'[26]

There was little disagreement between the intelligence community and the Bush administration regarding weapons of mass destruction. All were in agreement that Iraq possessed a biological and chemical weapons capability. There was some disagreement within the intelligence community regarding Iraq's nuclear program, but the CIA view was the accepted view within the Bush administration, so there was no disagreement, no need for 'pressure.' What the Bush administration believed was confirmed by the intelligence community. There was no intense questioning or 'pressure' to justify the analysis, even though the analysis was based upon, at best, information that was five years old, and in most cases over 15 years old – not the best foreknowledge on the basis of which to conduct a pre-emptive war.

The Iraq capability, although later shown to be wrong, was not questioned. The same cannot be said of Iraq's intent, an intent based upon using terrorists to attack the United States with weapons of mass destruction. This intent rested upon establishing a link between Iraq and al-Qaeda. The Bush administration 'sensed' there was a link, but the intelligence community could not confirm, or even produce a reasoned assessment of a probable link between the two. Not satisfied, the Bush administration, through the Department of Defense Under Secretary for Policy, found a link. The solution, the Policy employees recommended, was to ignore the CIA analysis of the reliability of the sources and just take the raw information at face value. In such a manner, bypassing the recommendations of experienced intelligence analysts, the Bush administration found a means of establishing the link.

The question of an al-Qaeda link with Iraq was also investigated by the 9/11 Commission. The Commission took the extra step of examining in detail the alleged meeting between Atta and an Iraqi intelligence agent in

Prague. The detailed accounting of Atta cast doubt upon this report and the Commission concluded, 'The available evidence does not support the original Czech report of an Atta–Ani meeting.'[27] But still, both the President and Vice President contend that the alleged meeting has never been refuted. President Bush persists, 'The reason I keep insisting that there was a relationship between Iraq and Saddam and Al Qaeda' is 'because there was a relationship between Iraq and Al Qaeda.'[28] The Bush administration approach to intelligence appears to follow the recommendations of the defense policy office 'intelligence cell': read intelligence for 'content only,' and the analysis 'ought to be ignored.'[29]

A former intelligence office director at the State Department's intelligence arm, INR, characterized the Bush administration's approach to intelligence as 'faith-based' with a 'top-down' use of intelligence: 'we know the answers; give us the intelligence to support the answers.'[30] The use of the defense policy office 'intelligence cell' would seem to confirm this approach.

Another Department of Defense analyst raised concerns about a source known as Curve Ball who was the basis for an assessment that the Iraqis were using a mobile biological weapons trailer. This analyst had been the only US intelligence official to interview Curve Ball and he had grave doubts as to the validity of Curve Ball's information. He sent an email to the Deputy Chief of the CIA's Iraqi Task Force raising his doubts. The Deputy Chief responded, 'let's keep in mind that this war's going to happen regardless of what Curve Ball said or didn't say, and that the Powers That Be probably aren't terribly interested in whether Curve Ball knows what he's talking about. However, in the interest of Truth, we owe somebody a sentence of [*sic*] two of warning, if you honestly have reservations.'[31]

Intelligence knew what they were assessing and the administration knew what they wanted to hear. As a senior DIA intelligence analyst put it, 'Generally it was understood how receptive OSD (Office of the Secretary of Defense) civilians were to our assessments and what kind of assessment they would not be receptive to.'[32] The assessments of the intelligence community were accepted if they supported the administration's views, and they were ignored if they didn't.

Many of the intelligence analysts interviewed by the Committee did refer to the intense questioning which they received from administration officials, questioning which they often welcomed, but which became repetitive to the point of distracting them from their duties. Questioning is necessary and any leader would be foolish to accept analysis at face-value only. But once the answers have been explained and the logic behind them detailed, any further questioning becomes an annoyance. Intelligence analysts, to their credit, did not change their assessments.

While the Senate Committee looked for evidence of 'pressure' on intelligence analysts to change their views and reported that they found none, the real question was what did the administration do when they couldn't find the answers they wanted? The answer being, find something that does support what they believe. In the case of the defense policy office 'intelligence cell' recommendation this boiled down to, just conduct your own analysis and ignore what the experts say.

Intelligence supporting a pre-emptive attack against Iraq was shaped, from the top down, by the leaders of the Bush administration. Where the intelligence analysis backed the administration view, it was accepted without question. The intelligence assessment was that Iraq had a weapons of mass destruction capability; this was unhesitatingly accepted, even though it was wrong. Where the intelligence analysis differed from the administration view, it was questioned unremittingly, and other sources were established to give the answer sought. The intelligence assessment that there were no formal ties between al-Qaeda and Iraq was correct, but was not accepted by the Bush administration. Lacking the answer they sought from the intelligence community, the administration turned to an ad hoc team in the Department of Defense. This team recommended looking only at the raw intelligence to find a tie, and disregarding the analysis of the experts as to the validity of the source. Following such advice, many ties between Iraq and al-Qaeda can be found. But as the intelligence community warned, and both the 9/11 Commission and the Senate Select Committee on Intelligence confirmed, there was no formal link between al-Qaeda and Iraq.

All the questions from the Bush administration were focused in the wrong direction – their questioning revolved around finding a link between al-Qaeda and Iraq, the real questioning should have been directed at the analysis supporting the assessment that Iraq still had weapons of mass destruction.

The Bush administration had several outstanding public servants who had served in various positions in the government and who knew a thing or two about intelligence. Vice President Richard Cheney had been the Chief of Staff for President Gerald Ford, the Secretary of Defense for George H.W. Bush, and an elected congressman who served on the House Intelligence Committee. He knew intelligence and one of the top assignments given to him by President George W. Bush was to 'do intelligence.'[33]

The Secretary of Defense, Donald Rumsfeld, was on his second tour of duty in that position, having served previously under President Ford. Before becoming Secretary of Defense, he had served as President Ford's Chief of Staff, being replaced in that position by Cheney. Before joining the Ford White House, Rumsfeld had been a Counselor in the Richard Nixon White House and a Congressman for Illinois from 1963 to 1968.

Both Cheney's and Rumsfeld's top administrators also had extensive government service. Paul Wolfowitz, Rumsfeld's Deputy Secretary of Defense, is on his third pentagon tour; his first during the Carter administration as a Deputy Assistant Secretary and his second serving Cheney as the Under Secretary of Defense for Policy. He also had two assignments under the Ronald Reagan Presidency's State Department, serving first as the Assistant Secretary of State for East Asian Affairs and then as the Ambassador to

Indonesia, the world's largest Muslim nation. Wolfowitz has a history of challenging the intelligence community. Early in his career he worked with the Arms Control and Disarmament Agency (1973–77) where he chastised the intelligence community for cloaking weak analysis in the language of compromise that supported current US policy. He had a chance to challenge the current intelligence methods when he participated in the 'Team B' experiment, an endeavor that the intelligence community conducted in an attempt to critically seek alternative views and analysis to the 1977 National Intelligence Estimate on Soviet Union strategic military objectives. (Perhaps it was this experience that led to the formation of the defense policy office 'intelligence cell'?) A Wolfowitz protégé at Defense and State was Lewis Libby who now served as Vice President Cheney's Chief of Staff. While at the Pentagon's policy office, Libby's expertise was Iraq's chemical and biological weapons capability.[34]

These four – Cheney, Rumsfeld, Wolfowitz, Libby – did not 'sense' that Iraq had weapons of mass destruction, as Westmoreland and his staff had 'sensed' the communists were moving to big unit warfare; these four 'knew it.' While the intelligence community couched all its assessments in caveats of probability, these four believed 'without a doubt' that Iraq had weapons of mass destruction and ties to al-Qaeda.

On 26 August 2002, Vice President Cheney told a convention of the Veterans of Foreign Wars that, 'There is no doubt that Saddam Hussein now has weapons of mass destruction.'[35] This statement was repeated as a fact over and over again, including by President Bush. Less than a month after Cheney's claim, Bush told the nation in a radio address that, 'The Iraqi regime possesses biological and chemical weapons.'[36]

Secretary Rumsfeld testified before the Senate Armed Services Committee on 19 September 2002, 'He [Saddam] has amassed large clandestine stockpiles of biological weapons, including anthrax, botulism toxin, and possibly smallpox. He has amassed large clandestine stockpiles of chemical weapons, including VX, sarin, and mustard gas. His regime has an active program to acquire nuclear weapons. . . . We do know that the Iraqi regime has chemical and biological weapons of mass destruction . . . Iraq has these weapons.'[37]

Deputy Secretary for Defense, Wolfowitz not only knew that the Iraqis possessed weapons of mass destruction, but was convinced of a terrorist link. He was '10 to 50 percent sure' that Saddam Hussein was involved in the 9/11 attacks.[38] On 23 January 2003, he stated, 'Iraq's weapons of mass terror and the terror networks to which the Iraqi regime are linked are not two separate themes – not two separate threats. They are part of the same threat.'[39]

As Cheney's Chief of Staff, Libby naturally shared the same views as the Vice President; he was sometimes referred to as 'Dick Cheney's Dick Cheney.'[40] When a briefing by intelligence meant to prepare the American public for a pre-emptive attack on Iraq proved less than convincing, Libby was called in to revamp the briefing. He took the defense policy office 'intelligence cell' approach (having been briefed by several members of the defense policy office 'intelligence cell' in September 2002): ignore the analysis of the intelligence community and their assessment of the validity, and go directly to the raw information. His brief was to the point, with no qualifiers or caveats – Saddam had chemical and biological weapons and his ties to al-Qaeda were undeniable.'[41]

The Bush administration, with intelligence shaped to their needs, now began a public relations campaign to prepare for a pre-emptive war against Iraq.

Intelligence and the public perception of war

With intelligence to back a pre-emptive attack, the Bush administration began a public relations campaign to gain the support of American and world opinion. Two primary venues were chosen: a public speech by Secretary of State Colin Powell to the United Nations and a White Paper summarizing a classified National Intelligence Estimate (NIE) on Iraq's weapons of mass destruction.

In December of 2002, George Tenet, the DCI, was asked to prepare a briefing that could be released to the public providing the justification for a war against Iraq. He instructed his deputy, John McLaughlin, who had built his reputation at the CIA as an analyst, to prepare and present the briefing which was given to President Bush four days before Christmas. As described by Bob Woodward in his definitive book *Plan of Attack*, there was a great 'expectation' that the CIA could make the 'case' that Saddam had weapons of mass destruction.

> When McLaughlin concluded, there was a look on the president's face of, What's this? And then a brief moment of silence. 'Nice try,' Bush said. 'I don't think this is quite – it's not something that Joe Public would understand or would gain a lot of confidence from.' . . . Bush turned to Tenet. 'I've been told all this intelligence about having WMD and this is the best we've got?' From the end of one of the couches in the Oval Office, Tenet rose up, threw his arms in the air. 'It's a slam dunk case!' the DCI said.[42]

Underwhelmed by the evidence provided by the intelligence community, the Bush administration turned to their own experts to make the 'case.' President Bush warned Tenet, however, 'Make sure no one stretches to make our case.'[43] Tenet had his analysts provide a 40-page analysis paper making the case, with all sources footnoted. The analysis was given to Lewis Libby, the Vice President's Chief of Staff and Steve Hadley, the Deputy National Security Advisor. Three months earlier, these same two had received a briefing from the defense policy office 'intelligence cell', a briefing that had been developed by a Special Assistant to the Deputy Secretary of Defense.[44] The recommendation from the defense policy office 'intelligence cell' was that the intelligence community was too cautious, the intelligence should be looked at for content only, ignore the caveats. Libby and Hadley took the advice.

Taking charge of the briefing, Libby dropped the caveats. On 25 January 2003, just over a month after McLaughlin's 'this is the best that we've got?' presentation, Libby gave his 'slam dunk' briefing to a gathering that included National Security Advisor Condoleezza Rice, her deputy Hadley, and Wolfowitz. Libby 'began each section with blunt conclusions – Saddam had chemical and biological weapons, was producing and concealing them; his ties to bin Laden's al-Qaeda network were numerous and strong.'[45] Libby's 'case' went over much better.

Dropping the caveats made for a much stronger 'case.' The intelligence community, in their National Intelligence Estimate (NIE) on *Iraq's Continuing Programs for Weapons of Mass Destruction*, released on 4 October 2002, was quite emphatic that Iraq had weapons of mass destruction, but always used caveats to qualify their statements. After all, the intelligence community had no direct evidence and most of their sources were fifteen years old, five years old at best. In the NIE, the intelligence community stated, 'We judge that Iraq has continued its weapons of mass destruction programs in defiance of United Nations resolutions and restrictions.'[46] A fairly strong statement, but evidently not strong enough.

An unclassified 'White Paper' entitled *Iraq's Weapons of Mass Destruction Programs*, which mirrored the NIE, was released just three days later on 7 October 2002. The White Paper made a similar, but unqualified and categorical assessment; 'Iraq has continued its weapons of mass destruction programs in defiance of UN resolutions and restrictions.'[47] This was something that 'Joe Public would understand or would gain a lot of confidence from,' to borrow the words of President Bush.[48]

The NIE had been prepared at the request of Illinois Senator Richard Durbin, a member of the Senate Select Committee on Intelligence, as Congress prepared in September and October of 2002 to authorize President Bush to use military force in Iraq as he deemed 'necessary and appropriate.' The NIE was classified and available to Congress, while the White Paper, being unclassified, was openly available to the public. Congress understood the caveats, but accepted the intelligence community's judgment. The public, having heard both the President and Vice President categorically state that Saddam possessed weapons of mass destruction, was not given any caveats in the White Paper; 'Iraq has continued its weapons of mass destruction program . . .'

In a National Intelligence Estimate, the agencies which make up the intelligence community can disagree with an assessment made by the whole. When such a disagreement occurs, the dissenting party can have their view represented in a footnote. There were several such footnotes in the NIE, one in particular dealing with Iraq's attempts to resurrect its nuclear program, with which the State Department's intelligence division, INR, disagreed. Sections on Iraq's nuclear program were also questioned by the Department of Energy, the experts in such matters. Both exceptions were noted in the NIE. Not so in the White Paper; the American public was told, 'All intelligence experts agree that Iraq is seeking nuclear weapons . . .'[49] – a blatant misstatement.

With the NIE for Congress and the White Paper for the American public, President Bush was given authority to use military force as he deemed necessary against Saddam and Iraq. The House of Representatives passed the resolution 296 to 133 on 10 October 2002. The next day, the Senate followed suit, with 77 for and 23 against the resolution. The President had authority to pre-emptively attack Iraq, authority that was based on the American public's and Congress' perception that had been shaped by intelligence. The only remaining obstacle was the United Nations.

While the United States always maintained the right to self-determination, the legitimacy offered by an alliance or coalition made for stronger resolve and a lessening of the economic burden. The United Nations Security Council had sanctioned the first Gulf War, passing a resolution, 12–2, with China abstaining, authorizing the US and coalition partners to use 'all necessary means' against Iraq. Over a decade later, backed with authority from Congress to use military force against Iraq, the United Nations again sought to force Iraq into compliance with its accords; if Iraq had weapons of mass destruction, they must be destroyed. On November 8, less than one month after Congress authorized the use of force, the United Nations Security Council, by a vote of 15–0, told Iraq they would face 'serious consequences' if Saddam did not destroy his weapons of mass destruction. The UN also authorized inspectors to return to Iraq to verify the lack of, or destruction of, weapons of mass destruction. The only remaining obstacle was proof that Saddam had weapons of mass destruction.

After three months, the UN inspectors failed to find proof that Saddam had weapons of mass destruction. The Bush administration again turned to intelligence to make the 'case' that the UN inspectors had failed to make, to prove that Iraq had weapons of mass destruction. Back in December, President Bush had been unimpressed with the CIA's representation and had turned to Cheney's Chief of Staff, Lewis Libby, to make the case. In January, Libby made his case, devoid of any caveats, to Rice, Hadley, and Wolfowitz, who were impressed. The question now was, who would make the case to the American public, to the UN, to the world, that Iraq had weapons of mass destruction and an intent to use them. To make the case, someone with unquestioned credibility was necessary; the President turned to his Secretary of State, Colin Powell. 'You have the credibility to do it,' the President told him.[50]

Powell, often characterized as the 'Reluctant Warrior,' was not considered a primary player on the Bush policy team where Cheney, Rice, Rumsfeld, and often even Wolfowitz had more say at the President's councils. Powell always let his views be known and had frequently sparred verbally with Cheney, particularly when it came to the UN. Powell saw the UN as a necessary diplomatic option, while Cheney viewed the UN as an obstacle, an institution that served no purpose.[51] Powell had little personal time with the President, while Rumsfeld had more, and Cheney, as Vice President, naturally had a great deal. Now, when the time came for the final public relations push, it was Powell and his credibility that were needed on Bush's team.

The briefing that intelligence had presented to Bush back in December was unimpressive and did not make the case. The revamped briefing from Libby lacked credibility, with sweeping categorical statements, but no hard evidence to back them up. Vice President Cheney did ask Powell to at least look closely at Libby's terrorism claims. Powell did and he found them unsubstantiated and ridiculous; he tossed them out of the brief.[52] Powell was skeptical of Libby and thought that Cheney often converted the uncertainty and ambiguity of intelligence into fact.[53] Libby had condensed his case into a 60-page paper with back-up folders from the NSC and Cheney's office, but nothing directly from intelligence.[54] Powell went back to the intelligence community to begin building his case.

While Powell was preparing for his UN speech, President Bush was starting the new public relations campaign to prepare America and the world for pre-emptive war against Iraq. On 28 January 2003, he gave his State of the Union Address. In his 2002 address, he had introduced the 'Axis of Evil,' terrorism and the rogue states of North Korea, Iran, and Iraq. In 2003 he gave an update on each rogue state. In 2002 he devoted one sentence to Iran, in 2003 he gave them one paragraph. North Korea also had only one sentence in 2002, but had three paragraphs in 2003. And, as in 2002 when Iraq had the major coverage of 5 sentences, in 2003 it was once again the predominant rogue state with 24 paragraphs, over a quarter of the entire address, devoted to its evil.

'Whatever action is required, whenever action is necessary, I will defend the freedom and security of the American people,' President Bush told the Union. He reminded the people that America had sought a diplomatic solution. 'Almost three months ago, the United Nations Security Council gave Saddam Hussein his final chance to disarm. He has shown instead utter contempt for the United Nations, and for the opinion of the world.' Diplomacy had failed. 'The dictator of Iraq is not disarming. To the contrary; he is deceiving.' He reminded the nation that the arms of Iraq were the weapons of mass destruction. 'Year after year, Saddam Hussein has gone to elaborate lengths, spent enormous sums, taken great risks to build and keep weapons of mass destruction.' Saddam had the capability. 'Evidence from intelligence sources, secret communications, and statements by people now in custody reveal that Saddam Hussein aids and protects terrorists, including members of al-Qaeda.' The threat from Iraq and the terrorists was clear. 'Before September the 11th, many in the world believed that Saddam Hussein could be contained. But chemical agents, lethal viruses and shadowy terrorist networks are not easily contained. Imagine those 19 hijackers with other weapons and other plans – this time armed by Saddam Hussein.'

The time for containment was past. The time for diplomacy was nearing the end. Saddam and his terrorist links and weapons of mass destruction were a threat, and America was not going to wait for a cataclysm to respond.

> The world has waited 12 years for Iraq to disarm. America will not accept a serious and mounting threat to our country, and our friends and our allies. The United States will ask the UN Security Council to convene on February the 5th to consider the facts of Iraq's ongoing defiance of the world. Secretary of State Powell will present information and intelligence about Iraq's legal [*sic*] – Iraq's illegal weapons programs, its attempt to hide those weapons from inspectors, and its links to terrorist groups.[55]

The charges had been made, now was the time for Secretary Powell to provide the evidence. With George Tenet sitting behind him, Secretary Powell addressed the United Nations Security Council on 5 February 2003. 'My colleagues, every statement I make today is backed up by sources, solid sources. These are not assertions. What we're giving you are facts and conclusions based on solid intelligence.'[56] Citing human sources, playing back intercepted telephone and radio conversations, and displaying satellite imagery, Powell laid out the evidence against the Saddam regime. 'The material I will present to you comes from a variety of sources. Some are US sources and some are those of other countries. Some of the sources are technical; such as intercepted telephone conversations and photos taken by satellites. Other sources are people who have risked their lives to let the world know what Saddam Hussein is really up to.'

Powell offered evidence enumerating the varied and continued deception employed by Iraq to stymie the UN inspections. 'This effort to hide things from the inspectors is not one or two isolated events. Quite the contrary, this is part and parcel of a policy of evasion and deception that goes back 12 years, a policy set at the highest levels of the Iraqi regime.'

Powell displayed to the UN and the world evidence of Iraqi weapons of mass destruction, including biological, chemical, and nuclear programs. 'There can be no doubt that Saddam Hussein has biological weapons and the capability to rapidly produce more, many more. . . . Saddam Hussein has chemical weapons. Saddam Hussein has used such weapons. And Saddam Hussein has no compunction about using them again – against his neighbors and against his own people. . . . We have no indication that Saddam Hussein has ever abandoned his nuclear weapons program. On the contrary, we have more than a decade of proof that he remains determined to acquire nuclear weapons.'

And Powell provided evidence of Iraq's links to terrorism. 'Our concern is not just about these illicit weapons; it's the way that these illicit weapons can be connected to terrorist and terrorist organizations that have no compunction about using such devices against innocent people around the world.' Powell had found a link between al-Qaeda and Iraq in the person of Abu Musab al-Zarqawi, 'an associate and collaborator of Usama bin Laden and his al-Qaeda lieutenants.' (Abu Musab al-Zarqawi was associated with the Kurdish area of Iraq over which Saddam Hussein had no control, and many consider him a rival, not an associate, of Osama bin Laden.)[57]

After over an hour of playing intercepts, explaining photographs, playing video tapes, citing human sources, elaborating on the evidence and making the case against Saddam, Powell concluded,

> We know that Saddam Hussein is determined to keep his weapons of mass destruction, is determined to make more. Given Saddam Hussein's history of aggression, given what we know of his grandiose plans, given what we know of his terrorist associations, and given his determination to exact revenge on those who oppose him, should we take the risk that he will not someday use these weapons at a time and place and in a manner of his choosing, at a time when the world is in a much weaker position to respond? The United States will not and cannot run that risk for the American people. Leaving Saddam Hussein in possession of weapons of mass destruction for a few more months or years is not an option, not in a post-September 11th world.[58]

The case had been made, the evidence presented. The United States was not going to wait for Saddam to act; pre-emption was coming and the American public was ready. America was going to hit first. The credibility of Powell, of the President, of the United States was on the line.

A matter of trust

The quality of the intelligence and the degree of certainty necessary before launching a pre-emptive attack were certainly discussed within the Bush administration. According to Bob Woodward in his book *Plan of Attack*, 'The underlying intelligence about the threat from another country, the power and quality of information, was a point worth discussing, Rumsfeld believed. What information would you require, and with what degree of certainty, before you launched a pre-emptive attack?'[59] With a unanimous judgment from the intelligence community that Iraq had biological and chemical weapons, and a known, effective terrorist operating in Iraq (albeit in an area controlled by Kurds, not Saddam), the case for a pre-emptive attack seemed to be a 'slam dunk.'

On 19 March 2003 at 10:16 pm Eastern Standard time, President Bush announced to the nation that the war against Iraq and Saddam's regime had begun. Less than one month later, on 9 April, US troops and Iraqi citizens together dragged down a statue of Saddam Hussein in downtown

Baghdad, bringing a symbolical end to the tyrant's bloody regime. On 1 May, President Bush declared an end to major combat operations in Iraq. In less than a month and a half, the US achieved its goal of regime change in Iraq. Saddam was gone and in all the combat operations, the feared use of weapons of mass destruction never occurred. Uncharacteristically, Saddam had shown restraint in the use of chemical and biological weapons. He had used them in his war against Iran, he had used them to suppress uprising within his own country. Backed into a corner with no way out, he did not use his weapons of vengeance.

Not to worry: on 13 April, three of the principals who had 'known' Saddam had weapons of mass destruction – Vice President Cheney, Under Secretary of Defense Wolfowitz, and Vice President Chief of Staff Libby – gathered for dinner at the Vice President's residence. When an acquaintance stated, 'I was just stunned that we have not found weapons of mass destruction' Wolfowitz and Cheney both responded, 'We'll find them.'[60]

Time to worry: on 2 October 2003, five months after the end of 'combat operations,' the Iraq Survey Group, tasked to find, document, and destroy Iraq's weapons of mass destruction, gave its initial report. David Kay, the leader of the team and special assistant to the DCI, revealed 'We have not yet found stocks of weapons.' He explained that 'our understanding of the status of Iraq's WMD program was always bounded by large uncertainties and had to be heavily caveated.' Kay was not ready to give up yet, 'we are not yet at the point where we can say definitely either that such weapon stocks do not exist or that they existed before the war.'[61]

Nearly three months later, on 28 January 2004, Kay was ready to give up the search for weapons of mass destruction. 'It turns out we were all wrong,' Kay testified to the Senate Armed Services Committee. Before the war started, Kay admitted that 'the best evidence that I had seen was that Iraq indeed had weapons of mass destruction.' He recommended that 'it is time to begin the fundamental analysis of how we got here, what led us here and what we need to do in order to ensure that we are equipped with the best possible intelligence as we face these issues in the future.'[62]

The Senate Select Committee on Intelligence took up the challenge to determine how intelligence had reached its erroneous conclusions long before Kay came to his revelation. In June of 2003, the Committee began a formal review of the pre-war intelligence on Iraq. Nearly a year later, the Committee released the first part of its findings on 7 July 2004. The bi-partisan Committee agreed to 117 conclusions, the first being: 'Most of the major key judgments in the Intelligence Community's October 2002 National Intelligence Estimate (NIE), *Iraq's Continuing Programs for Weapons of Mass Destruction*, either overstated, or were not supported by, the underlying intelligence reporting. A series of failures, particularly in analytic trade craft, led to the mischaracterization of the intelligence.'[63]

The Committee examined the intelligence supporting the NIE, the unclassified White Paper, and Colin Powell's presentation to the UN. In almost every instance, the intelligence was simply not supported by the evidence, or the evidence was overstated. One of the biggest problems was the lack of any sources with knowledge of weapons of mass destruction from within Iraq after 1998.[64] Not only did intelligence not have sources with knowledge of weapons, they had few sources, period. The head of the CIA Iraqi Operations Group said, 'I can count them on one hand and I can still pick my nose.'[65] These sources were outside Saddam's inner circle and had no direct knowledge of his weapons programs.

Where then did the evidence come from? If there was not enough intelligence to substantiate the conclusions of the NIE, the more categorical pronouncements of the unclassified White Paper, and the evidence provided by Colin Powell to the UN, then how did intelligence reach such a conclusion? One reason, the Committee found, was 'group think.' 'The Intelligence Community (IC) suffered from a collective presumption that Iraq had an active and growing weapons of mass destruction (WMD) program. This "group think" dynamic led Intelligence Community analysts, collectors, and managers to both interpret ambiguous evidence as conclusively indicative of a WMD program as well as ignore or minimize evidence that Iraq did not have active and expanding weapons of mass destruction programs.'[66]

The Committee limits 'group think' to the intelligence community only and stresses in its conclusions that there was no political pressure on analysts to change their assessments. Several members of the Committee disagree about the absence of political pressure.[67] When it came to weapons of mass destruction, there was little need for pressure, everyone from the President down believed that Saddam possessed weapons of mass destruction.

Within the Bush administration, 'group think' was also pervasive. Vice President Cheney was thought by some to be 'hell-bent' on Iraq, having a 'fever,' nothing else mattered.[68] While President Bush disagreed with the 'fever' characterization, he said he 'felt a conviction' in Cheney regarding Iraq.[69] No one within the administration questioned whether Iraq actually possessed weapons of mass destruction. The intelligence community at least qualified the assumption, writing 'We judge that Iraq has continued its weapons of mass destruction (WMD) programs' in the October 2002 NIE. From the highest levels of the administration, however, there were no qualifications. 'There is no doubt that Saddam Hussein now has weapons of mass destruction,' Vice President Cheney told the Veterans of Foreign Wars in August 2002.[70] At all levels, no one thought to question the most basic of assumptions.

Saddam had a history of possessing weapons of mass destruction, using them in war and in peace. He had a history of hiding and deceiving the international community regarding his compliance to rid his country of these weapons after the first Gulf War. Why would he now rid himself of such weapons, then continue to act as if he still had the weapons, denying his country the money which the international community was withholding because of his non-compliance? It did not make sense, but then that is the impossible job of intelligence, making the unknown, known.

When conducting a pre-emptive war, the evidence of imminent danger should be clear. Secretary of Defense Rumsfeld believed, according to Woodward's *Plan of Attack*[71] that the intelligence upon which a pre-emptive attack was based should be vetted. The Bush administration, however, was adamant that they did not need, nor could they afford, to wait for a 'smoking gun' in the form of a 'mushroom cloud.'[72] Certainly, the 'degree of certainty' need not be a 'mushroom cloud,' but should there not at least be a 'gun?'

There was no 'smoking gun,' not even a 'gun' to be found in Iraq. After over a year of searching, Saddam's weapons of mass destruction were no where to be found. The reason for pre-emption was a fallacy; a fallacy based on assumptions and intelligence over five years old. The intelligence community has again been investigated for dereliction of duty, with the verdict that they 'either overstated, or were not supported by, the underlying intelligence reporting,' and had succumbed to 'group think.'[73]

Despite the bad intelligence and the stretching of the available information by the Bush administration that 'without a doubt' Iraq had weapons of mass destruction, America was triumphant in Iraq. While it appears that Saddam did not have weapons of mass destruction, there is little doubt that the people of Iraq and the world are better off without him. But, the nagging question remains, was the intelligence examined closely enough to justify pre-emptive war or had 'the powers that be' already decided on war. Were the leaders being honest or disingenuous? Were the leaders 'hell-bent' on war and determined to find the intelligence to support pre-emption? Were the leaders being honest? Can they be trusted? These are questions of credibility.

Early in his tenure as Secretary of Defense, Donald Rumsfeld drafted a memo on 'Guidelines When Considering Committing U.S. Forces.' He wrote, 'U.S. leadership must be brutally honest with itself, the Congress, the public and coalition partners.'[74] And most prophetic, 'avoid arguments of convenience,' he warned, 'they will be deadly later.' With the war over and no weapons of mass destruction to be found, 'later' was now.

As it was with Tet, bad or skewed intelligence presented by leaders to shape the American perception has been shown to be wrong and, as then, the credibility of the leadership is questioned. The cover of the 16 February 2004 issue of *Time* magazine carried the headline 'Believe Him or Not, Does Bush Have A Credibility Gap?' and devoted eight pages to the question. *The Economist*, not forgetting its British roots, questioned both the credibility of President Bush and Britain's Prime Minister Tony Blair with its 15 July 2004 cover, 'Sincere Deceivers.'

President Bush, according to a *Time*/CNN poll conducted in February 2004, had suffered a loss of credibility. Only 44 percent of Americans believed that the President was a leader to be trusted while 55 percent had reservations and doubts as to the President's credibility.[75] In July, *The Economist* found that 61 percent of Americans believed they had been given false information regarding weapons of mass destruction. When asked who they felt was to blame for the false information, intelligence takes the brunt with 70 percent believing that they were responsible. The White House was blamed by 59 percent. 'In making the case for war, in effect, they [Bush and Blair] gambled,' *The Economist*'s editorial stated, 'that the facts found in Iraq would bear out their claims. They haven't. The result is not only damage to the personal credibility of America's president and Britain's prime minister. It is real damage to the ability of those countries, and probably others, to deal with future military and terrorist threats. . . . the next time politicians call for military action to deal with such threats, on the basis of intelligence warnings, even more people will refuse to believe them. Well-intentioned or not, such salesmanship has made us all less safe, and more vulnerable to terrorists.'[76]

The Tet Effect has struck again; the consequences are just as dire, if not more so. The credibility of the President has been shaken; the ability of the United States to take action compromised.

12 Intelligence principles in the twenty-first century
Still valid after all these years

Proper relationship between intelligence producers and consumers is one of utmost delicacy.

Sherman Kent[1]

What was the quality and power of the intelligence that provided the case for a pre-emptive war? Was the right information available with a degree of certainty to justify a pre-emptive war? Was it discussed? These are valid questions that demand answers. The answers reveal underlying tensions and drama within the intelligence community and between intelligence and those who use their products. As in Vietnam, the failings of intelligence in Iraq can be traced to the failure to adhere to the principles of intelligence.

In Vietnam, intelligence played out a drama that revealed four morals: intelligence must remain objective, must not succumb to ethnocentrism, cannot rely on technology alone, and must understand that the will of the opponent is the measure of victory. These four morals, or intelligence principles, are just as valid today as they were in Vietnam. The violation of these principles results in questionable intelligence and can ultimately lead to a loss of credibility of not only the intelligence community, but also those leaders who use the intelligence.

In Iraq, intelligence is again involved in a drama that highlights the importance of these same four principles. The objectivity of intelligence was hindered by a leadership that only questioned assumptions that were contrary to the administration 'group think.' Objectivity was further clouded by the dual responsibilities of the Director of Central Intelligence to implement policy through covert operations, while at the same time providing analysis that could potentially contradict that same policy. Ethnocentrism hindered, and continues to hinder, accurate analysis of terrorism and tyranny. One well-placed, reliable spy would have been worth more than all the technical collection capability of the United States. And again, as in Vietnam, the measure of success in Iraq was misplaced. The removal of Saddam Hussein was not the measure of victory, it was breaking the will of all those who resist.

On intelligence and objectivity

Sherman Kent, the patron father of US intelligence analysis, thought the relationship between the intelligence analyst and those in leadership positions was very delicate. 'Proper relationship between intelligence producers and consumers is one of utmost delicacy. Intelligence must be close enough to policy, plans, and operations to have the greatest amount of guidance, and must not be so close that it loses its objectivity and integrity of judgment.'[2]

The analyst cannot afford to buy in to current policy; to do so would bias the analysis. But, at the same time, Kent believed that the analyst could not afford to work in a vacuum; the analyst needed guidance. The raison d'être for intelligence is to be used in the making of decisions. Leaders make decisions. Intelligence must know and understand what issues are being wrestled with and what information is needed to help the leader make their decision. Intelligence, like a book that is never opened, has no purpose unless it is used.

Leaders make decisions and have an 'intense commitment to the success' of their policy, according to Deputy Secretary of Defense Paul Wolfowitz in an article on the relationship of intelligence and policymakers.[3] If intelligence challenges the assumptions of policy, Wolfowitz suggests that intelligence must emphasize the evidence, laying out the facts and their relationships. The analysts must also be prepared to defend their position.

Such a situation arose concerning the link between al-Qaeda and Saddam Hussein. However well laid out the evidence, Wolfowitz and Don Feith, the Under Secretary of Defense for Policy, would not let go of their 'hunch' that such a link existed. After extensive and continued questioning of the analysts, Feith established an 'intelligence cell' within his office.

This 'intelligence cell,' wearing a 'policy hat,' sifted the intelligence and conducted their own examination of the evidence to find support for their boss's policy. The defense policy office 'intelligence cell' solution of taking only evidence that supported their policy and ignoring the professional assessment of its validity, provided support to the policy preference of Feith and Wolfowitz. The assessments of the defense policy 'intelligence cell' was then shared with other like-minded policymakers (such as Lewis Libby, the Vice President's Chief of Staff), who were also frustrated with the failure of intelligence to find a link between al-Qaeda and Saddam Hussein.

The objectivity of intelligence appears to have remained intact under scrutiny from the 'intelligence cell' (not political pressure according the Senate Select Committee on Intelligence). The facts, as laid out by the intelligence community, were confirmed by the 9/11 Commission's bi-partisan examination of the evidence. Their conclusion – the weak evidence of a formalized link between Saddam Hussein and al-Qaeda was contradicted by too much good evidence to the contrary.[4]

The Senate Select Committee on Intelligence found that the scrutiny and questions by the administration to find a link were warranted; which they were, to a point. However, when the evidence was laid out and explained, just as Wolfowitz advised in the intelligence/policymaker relationship article, the scrutiny should have decreased, but it did not. The scrutiny and questions continued until the formation of a non-intelligence group that found the answers sought by Feith and Wolfowitz. Intelligence, thus far, has been proven correct in their assessments of Iraqi links to terrorism, yet they were questioned incessantly. Where the intelligence was wrong – in the assessment that Iraq had weapons of mass destruction – not one question was raised. The evidence here was just as weak, if not weaker (the information was, at best, over five years old). Why was this assessment not questioned by the policy and intelligence communities?

Why question something that had a clear history? Saddam had possessed weapons of mass destruction, had used weapons of mass destruction, and had hidden weapons of mass destruction from UN inspectors. With a pre-emptive war on the horizon, was it not the objective duty of intelligence to verify that Iraq still had such weapons. The very basis of the war was that Iraq's weapons of mass destruction were a threat to the United States, its allies, and the stability of the region. With such a threat, both President Bush and his National Security Advisor, Condoleezza Rice, warned that the US could not afford to wait for 'a smoking gun in the form of a mushroom cloud.'[5] But shouldn't intelligence at least have verified that there was a gun?

The intelligence analysis supporting the assessment that Iraq had weapons of mass destruction was found to be overstated and lacking convincing evidence.[6] The evidence was predominantly over fifteen years old, and, at best, five years old. There were some who questioned the intelligence on certain aspects of Iraq's weapons of mass destruction programs, but few (if any) who challenged the basic assumption that Saddam had such weapons. Everyone, from the President and those in his administration to the most junior analyst in the intelligence community, succumbed to 'group think.' The entire group – leaders, policymakers, and the intelligence community – lost their ability to think objectively. With such scrutiny to find a tenuous link between al-Qaeda and Hussein, what sort of pressure would have been brought to bear on an analyst who questioned the very foundation of the pre-emptive war policy against Iraq?

While the intelligence community apparently maintained its objectivity regarding the link between al-Qaeda and Saddam Hussein, and fell victim to a cumulative loss of objectivity and 'group think' regarding Iraq's weapons of mass destruction, there is little doubt there is a conflict of interest and loss of objectivity when intelligence crosses over into the realm of implementing policy through covert operations.

The Central Intelligence Agency consists of two primary organizations. One is an organization that conducts analysis based on all types of information collected through various sources. The second is an organization that conducts operations – secret operations. Often these secret, or covert, operations are for the purposes of collecting intelligence to be used by the first organization in their analysis. In the course of collecting information, these operatives, or spies, come into contact with various individuals. Such contacts become very valuable, not only for collecting information, but for conducting other types of secret missions. Missions such as those influencing the policy of another nation (for example, by supplying money to a political party that is friendly to the US), or perhaps hindering the actions of nations hostile to the US (such as helping the mujahidin to fight the Soviets in Afghanistan), or even bringing about regime change within a country hostile to the United States (such as bringing the Shah to power in Iran). Such covert operations clearly advance the policy of the United States and its leaders.

As the nominal head of all US intelligence organizations, the Director of Central Intelligence (DCI) is, first and foremost, the advisor to the President on intelligence matters and the head of the CIA and its two primary organizations. As the head of the analysis organization, the DCI must remain unbiased and provide objective intelligence to assist the administration policymakers. As the head of the secret operations organization, the DCI recommends and executes actions that carry out administration policy. The potential for a conflict of interest is definitely present.

In July of 2002, the CIA inserted agents into Iraq to develop sources to collect intelligence and begin resistance movements against Saddam Hussein.[7] The Iraqis were understandably reluctant, having previously been abandoned by the CIA after similar efforts. The sources wanted assurance that the US was serious and was going to attack. Buttressed by the administration's talk of pre-emptive war and the passage by Congress of a resolution authorizing the President to use whatever means were necessary, the CIA was able to build from scratch a remarkable spy network and establish the funding for anti-Saddam movements. President Bush's DCI, George Tenet, was an effective member in carrying out the administration's Iraq policy.

However, when Tenet arrived with his deputy to present the 'case' for launching a pre-emptive attack against Iraq he could hardly be considered objective. He had American agents, with their lives on the line, and an incredible spy network of Iraqis whose lives and the lives of whose families depended upon the US going to war against Iraq by February 2003.[8] When the deputy DCI presented the 'case,' the President was less than impressed – '. . . this is the best we've got?'[9] The DCI, with lives at stake, had a vested interest in carrying out the policy, and did not recommend a re-evaluation of the assumptions and the intelligence. The case, and the intelligence it was built upon, was obviously less than convincing; the President had said so himself. Yet Tenet instead assured the President that the case was a 'slam dunk.'

There were several documented instances when the 'case' appeared to be much weaker than a 'slam dunk,' which should have resulted in an objective person pausing to question the relative and basic assumptions of the assessments. The first was the brief given to the President by the deputy DCI, a man who had made his reputation as an analyst at the CIA. The case for a pre-emptive attack based on the available evidence was just not there. The evidence was too weak. Next was at a briefing given by General Tommy Franks in September 2002. The general told President Bush and the National Security Council, 'We've been looking for Scud missiles and other weapons of mass destruction for ten years and haven't found any yet, so I can't tell you that I know that there are any specific weapons anywhere. I haven't seen Scud one.'[10] And finally, when Secretary of State Colin Powell was preparing to give his briefing to the United Nations, he found much of the evidence inferential, and had to add his personal interpretation to make a case.[11] Powell made the case based more on his credibility than the validity of the intelligence, some of which was deemed questionable even by some in the intelligence community.[12]

George Tenet was present in all these instances, and undoubtedly more frequently. The paucity of the intelligence as demonstrated in these three instances should have alerted the DCI to the fact that the intelligence was not there to support the policy. However, the DCI was also carrying out policy through secret operations in Iraq, operations that would be endangered should there even be a delay in the attack.[13] Under such circumstances, even the most honest of men cannot truly be objective. The case for pre-emptive war based on weapons of mass destruction and a tie between al-Qaeda and Saddam was weak, but went unchallenged.

The position of the DCI will always be tenuous when it comes to questions of objectivity and policy bias. The CIA has always been a dual-personality; the scholarly analyst and the cowboy spy. Such a personality is bound to have problems. In the name of objectivity, the two need to be separated and led by two different directors. As a minimum requirement, the DCI should be first and foremost the leader of all intelligence organizations with a separate director for the CIA. Such a step will help with objectivity, but will never fully smooth the path of the 'delicate' relationship between intelligence and those who lead by making decisions.

On intelligence and ethnocentrism

How does one think like a terrorist, a person who is filled with hate and a fanatical religious frenzy, willing to kill on a massive scale while dying themselves and leaving behind family, friends, and loved ones? How does one think like a tyrant, willing to kill on a massive scale both external and internal enemies, to crush life from thousands with excruciating torture, brutal military might, and horrific weapons of mass destruction? How does one, brought up in a free and open society, educated in tolerant and broadminded colleges, where the closest brush with death is likely to be an accident on the freeway, possibly hope to understand and think like a terrorist and a tyrant?

The task at hand for intelligence requires a totally new way of thinking, one which is at odds with the traditional American values, even at odds with what would be considered rational.

In the old days of intelligence analysis, a scholar could study a country and come to understand its culture and its ways. The threats faced by America and its allies came from those nations who were industrialized and westernized. Such countries shared a common history and culture. Even the Soviet Union shared a common Eurocentric history. Today, a single person can possess all the lethal capability of a well-armed military. Weapons of mass destruction are not the sole province of nations. A single individual or a small cell can kill thousands. The old days when all an intelligence analyst had to do was study a country are gone. Nations, ethnic groups, tribes, clans, organizations, cells, individuals now all pose a potential threat to the civilized world.

Nations, ethnic groups, tribes, clans, organizations, cells, individuals that do not necessarily share a Eurocentric history. Terrorism has been around for a long time, but never before has the terrorist had such a powerful arsenal. September 11th was the terrorist act that broke the American threshold of acceptable collateral damage and brought terrorism into the realm of war. War has traditionally been defined in the Eurocentric vein of nation against nation. The official Department of Defense definition still carries this connotation, even with President Bush declaring a global war on terrorism.[14] Many, such as Martin van Creveld in his prescient book *The Transformation of War*, have been arguing for over a decade that war is not the sole domain of nation states. September 11th was the day on which the definition of war was transformed in America.

Such a transformation is also required of intelligence. Studies of countries do not reflect the world of terrorism. The world is not a neatly ordered and categorized collection of nations. Robert Kaplan has exposed this fallacy as the 'Lies of the Mapmakers' in his book *The Coming Anarchy*. The nicely categorized political outlines on a map are, Kaplan argues, 'an invention of modernism,' a modernism shared by only a small select few. The vast majority of the citizens of the world are not loyal to a nation; their loyalties lie with their families, their clan, their tribe, their ethnic group, their religion. These are the types of groupings that control and set the values for most of the world's population, not the governments of states.

How does an intelligence analyst, brought up in the luxury of the modern world and educated in western ideals, hope to comprehend and understand the priorities of a Somali clan lord, the strategy of a Serb military leader in Bosnia, the intent of an Iraqi tyrant, the mind of a jihad terrorist. Kaplan, again in *The Coming Anarchy*, warns, 'A person raised in a middle- or upper-middle-class suburban environment, a place ruled by rationalism in the service of material progress, has difficulty imaging the psychological state of affairs in a society where there is little or no memory of hard work achieving its just reward, and where life inside a gang or a drafty army barracks constitutes an improvement in material and emotional security.'[15] First-hand experience can help if the familiarity leads to a better understanding of different cultures. Kaplan, however, believes that such experience is far too often clouded by an impulse to try to find ways of making western ideals work, at the expense of understanding. Kaplan turns to literature to provide empathy, understanding, and imagination. He explains, 'in the guise of fiction a writer can more easily tell the truth.' He even recommends a book, *Nostromo* by Joseph Conrad, a book where the 'landscape ambience is a tightly controlled, strategic accompaniment to political realism.'[16]

The greatest aids that this author found in trying to understand the reality of Bosnia-Herzegovina and the Balkans was not the Department of Defense country handbook, but Ivo Andrić's Noble Prize winning novel *The Bridge on the Drina* and Rebecca West's amazing travelogue *Black Lamb and Grey Falcon, A Journey through Yugoslavia*. Kaplan's updated travelogue *Balkan Ghosts* was also of great benefit and his other books and those in similar vein serve to open vistas to the troubled world outside of western society.

Another indispensable source to understanding the world outside the west is the spy. Saddam Hussein and his Baathist Party did not share a Eurocentric culture, nor do the peoples who are scattered throughout the region called Iraq. Saddam and his minions wielded great power in a manner incomprehensible to most civilized peoples. He waged war with weapons of mass destruction against Iran and those who opposed him within Iraq. Why then, would such a ruthless regime secretly get rid of such a capability? Only Saddam and those with a need to know within his regime could have known. To have known such a thing would have required a spy. A spy helps to understand those concepts that are alien to the civilized and rational way of thinking. The spy is one tool that helps break the mold of ethnocentrism. Unfortunately, spying has become a lost art.

On intelligence and technocentrism

Despite a call by President Bush to focus on intelligence derived from human sources (HUMINT for HUMan INTelligence), which includes spies, the United States still has far to go to unshackle itself from its dependence on more technical methods of gathering intelligence. In a speech to the cadets of the Citadel on 11 December 2001, President Bush announced his intention to 'rebuild our network of human intelligence.'[17] Yet, as war loomed with Iraq, the United States had only four spies in the Iraqi government, and these with no information or access to critical information on Saddam's terrorist links or weapons of mass destruction. The Senate Select Committee on Intelligence criticized the Central Intelligence Agency for not having a single spy with knowledge of Iraq's weapons of mass destruction.[18]

All the technical capability of the United States intelligence community proved inadequate in providing information on Iraq's weapons of mass destruction and ties to al-Qaeda. A single, well-placed spy would have been worth more than all the billions spent on modern technological collection means. The spy is the means into the mind of the tyrant and the terrorist. Spying, however, is a very delicate and devious matter; an endeavor never really fully appreciated by the United States.

A spy goes against the very nature of American values. A spy is a traitor, a person willing to sell information detrimental to their nation or compatriots. The type of information needed is not typically possessed by the upstanding citizens of a nation, but is more often in the possession of very mean and despicable people. To deal with a spy is to often deal with the dregs of society, not with the people found on the society pages. Dealing with drug dealers and thugs, the people with access to information vital to our nation's security, is simply part of the CIA's job yet the CIA has been rebuked more than once for dealing with such people.

Once a spy, a traitor, or a thug, has been procured, how does one know this despicable source is telling the truth. Double agents abound, deceit runs rampant. Some sources will tell you anything, true or false, that you want to hear for a price, others carry hidden agendas that look to advance a certain cause. Many an Iraqi refugee wanted the United States to attack Saddam and were willing to tell tales that pushed the US in the direction of war. One such story was the non-existent mobile biological weapons vans that Secretary of State Colin Powell told the United Nations that Saddam was using to conceal his biological warfare program. Even as Powell prepared the night before the UN presentation, the only US intelligence agent to have talked to the source warned his superiors the information was dubious.[19] A delicate business, dealing with spies and lies.

Another unsavory aspect of human intelligence is torture. The question has often been raised, is torture justified? In modern civilized society the answer is typically 'no'. But since 11 September 2001, even civilized society is reassessing its answer. The 11 January 2004 cover of *The Economist*, asked the question, 'Is torture ever justified?' While torture is banned by international law, *The Economist* points out there are varying methods and degrees of subtle questioning techniques that border on torture. And outright torture may be a necessity in certain cases, 'It is tempting to argue that torture is justified in rare cases.' However, 'attempts to use torture sparingly have quickly led to widespread abuse.'[20] Such abuses have occurred in Israel and been reviewed by their Supreme Court. At Abu Ghraib, the specter of American abuse arose, morphing the image of America from that of a liberator to that of an oppressor.

The January 2002 issue of *The Atlantic Monthly* was entitled 'The Hard Questions,' and explored the issues that America faced in the aftermath of September 11th. 'Must We Torture?' was one of the five questions. Bruce Hoffman attempted to explore the issue he called 'A Nasty Business,' by pointing out that the endeavor to collect good intelligence against terrorists was 'an inherently brutish enterprise, involving methods a civics class might not condone.' Hoffman recommends all spies, soldiers, and students watch the film *The Battle of Algiers* which documented the French efforts to combat terrorism in their attempts to retain colonial control over Algiers in the late 1950s. The film's 'fundamental message that only information can effectively counter terrorism is timeless,' Hoffman writes. 'Equally disturbing and instructive, however, are the lengths to which security and military forces need often resort to get that information.'[21] Hoffman provides insight, but in the end he answers the question with a question, 'In the quest for timely, "actionable" intelligence will the United States, too, have to do bad things – by resorting to measures that we would never have contemplated in a less exigent situation?'[22]

Would the torture of one individual be justified if the information obtained resulted in the saving of 3,000 innocent lives, if it could prevent another September 11th? What if it could save only 1,000 or just 10? At what point does the torture inflicted pay for the lives of the innocent? What about a military situation? Is torture justified if it saves a platoon, a company, a battalion, a division? These are ugly questions that most civilized people don't like to consider. Yet, they are a part of the world of intelligence and one that must be clearly defined in the interest of national security and to avoid debacles such as Abu Ghraib.

There is no doubt that human intelligence efforts are difficult, yet it is only through such sources that the information which can guarantee the security of the civilized world can be obtained. The United States has the world's most advanced technical collection programs, but still has far to go in learning the delicate art of human intelligence.

On intelligence and the measure of success

There was a conscious effort to avoid numbers in the Iraq war.[23] The Bush administration did not want any degree of fixation on numbers as a gauge for success. Success, according to President Bush, was the removal of Saddam Hussein from power.[24] Not a difficult task for intelligence – to determine if Saddam has been removed from power. On 1 May 2003 President Bush ostensibly declared victory when he announced the cessation of hostile combat. It became even easier when Saddam was actually captured on 13 December 2003. But hostilities continue. Again, as in Vietnam, the will of the people has been ignored.

There will always be those who prefer the tyranny of a home-grown leader to the compassion of the conqueror. One of the biggest criticisms of the Bush administration's policy has been their lack of foresight in determining what Iraq would be like after the removal of Saddam Hussein. Intelligence did not foresee any formidable armed resistance; this despite their own reports of confirmed terrorist training of Saddam's security forces. Many understood the diversity of Iraq's ethnic make-up, but few foresaw any problems. The simple assumption that Iraq would embrace the liberators and take on the mantle of democracy seemed natural, but it carries implications of ethno-centrism. What was the intelligence supporting such an assumption?

There was an assumption throughout the Bush administration, including the military and intelligence, that support for the Saddam regime would crumble as the US commitment to remove Saddam increased. According to Bob Woodward in his book *Plan of Attack*, 'This important argument was based less on solid intelligence from inside Iraq than assumptions about how people should feel toward a ruthless dictator. The paucity of U.S. human intelligence sources inside Iraq meant evidence about Iraqi popular opinion or likely reaction to an American invading force was thin.'[25]

The *New York Times* headline from 20 October 2004 declared that 'Poor Intelligence Misled Troops About Risk of Drawn-Out War.' CIA agents even went so far as to smuggle in small US flags for liberated Iraqis to wave. But, '[j]ust as the intelligence about Iraq's presumed stockpiles of unconventional weapons proved wrong, so did much of the information provided to those prosecuting the war and planning the occupation.'[26] Intelligence misread the people and did not understand the 'will' of some Iraqis to resist.

More American soldiers have been killed after combat operations were declared at an end on 1 May 2003 than before. The will of Iraq's diverse population remains unclear. There is no doubt, however, that some Iraqis remain resolved to foil any US efforts in Iraq. The measure of success in Iraq remains uncertain, Saddam is gone, but US soldiers continue to die. The question of 'will' remains unanswered.

Intelligence principles endure

Tet and the Vietnam War belong to a bygone era of American history. The communist scourge has faded away like a specter in the full light of day. The threats that America, the western and civilized worlds now face are different. The requirements of intelligence have changed; the principles have not. Intelligence can never afford to champion a single policy option, it must remain forever aloof and objective in looking at an issue. Yet, intelligence can not reside in an ivory tower and make lofty assessments, it must deal and work with those who make decisions. Intelligence must know its customer and seek guidance if it is to provide a useful product. Intelligence unused is useless and might as well never have been produced. The very purpose of intelligence is to be used in the decision-making process. But just as worthless as unused intelligence is biased intelligence. Intelligence, to be truly useful, must be objective.

Being objective also means being forthright in what is known and what is not understood. When adjudicating the validity of various sources of untold veracity, the window of certainty is small. What is known must be clearly stated and the remaining assessment must be reasoned and logical. That which is reasoned and logical can take on many variations and the most likely explanations must be offered, even if they contradict. The decision maker's role is to make decisions, intelligence's is to help in making the decision. Offering differing explanations may not seem to be helpful to the decision maker, but to limit an explanation to only one option when more interpretations are possible is, in effect, making a decision, one that is not the responsibility of intelligence.

One sure method to eliminate obtuse arguments is to know the enemy. To know the enemy is to think like the enemy and that means thinking unlike an American. Ethnocentrism is the greatest hindrance to accurate intelligence assessment, the bane of the intelligence analyst. American values and American military strategy are alien to those who seek to harm the civilized world. The harsh realities of areas where the basic necessities of life are contested do not foster the ideals of democracy. Survival is often a matter of daily concern, not merely an accident of chance. Intelligence must forever look not to itself for the answer, but to the enemy.

The enemies of the civilized world are everywhere. The power of technology gives an individual the might of a nation. Technology can also assist in finding these individual threats, but technology cannot do it all. The individual who has the required information still remains the best source of intelligence. Technology is not the be-all and end-all, and the roles of the spy, of interrogation, of captured documents, still remain central to finding the information necessary to act and protect the nation.

To protect the nation is the ultimate goal, and to break the will of those with intentions to harm the nation is the ultimate measure of success. War remains a contest of wills, whether it be the will of one nation against the other, or the will of a single individual to harm the civilized world. The threat exists until the will to coerce is subdued.

The challenges of intelligence have always been demanding. In today's world where not only nations but individuals can wage war, the challenge is even more daunting. Adherence to the principles of intelligence remains the best assurance of success and a sure guard against the Tet Effect.

Notes

Introduction – Disturbing Vietnam memories

1 Sun Tzu, *The Art of War*, trans. Samuel B. Griffith (London: Oxford University Press, 1963), 62.
2 George C. Herring, *America's Longest War: The United States and Vietnam 1950–1975* (New York: Alfred A. Knopf, 1979), 183.
3 *Time*, 27 November 1967, 22.
4 Lt. General Phillip B. Davidson, USA (Ret.), *Secrets of the Vietnam War* (Novato, CA: Presidio, 1990), 43.
5 General William C. Westmoreland speech presented to the National Press Club on 21 November 1967 in *Vietnam: A History in Documents*, ed. Gareth Porter (New York: New American Library, 1979), 786–788.
6 'The reporters could hardly believe their ears. Westmoreland was standing in the ruins and saying everything was great.' In Don Oberdorfer, *Tet! The Turning Point in the Vietnam War*, Paperback edn. (New York: Da Capo Press, Inc., 1984), 33–34.
7 Art Buchwald, *The Washington Post*, 6 February 1968, quoted in Oberdorfer, *Tet!*, 157.
8 Peter McDonald, *Giap: The Victor in Vietnam* (New York: W.W. Norton and Company, 1993), 266.
9 Herbert Y. Schandler, *The Unmaking of a President: Lyndon Johnson and Vietnam* (Princeton, NJ: Princeton University Press, 1977), 75–76.
10 *Newsweek*, 9 February 2004, 27.
11 Lt. General Phillip B. Davidson, USA (Ret.), MACV/J2 from June 1967 to May 1969. Oral History Interview by Ted Gittinger on 30 June 1982. Maintained in the Lyndon Baines Johnson Library, Austin, TX. General Davidson refers to intelligence based upon human sources as 'low grade intelligence,' and implies that the best intelligence only comes from technical sources.

1 Tet – the surprise

1 Don Oberdorfer, *Tet! The Turning Point in the Vietnam War*, Paperback edn. (New York: Da Capo Press, Inc., 1984), 67–68.
2 Reference to Townsend Hoopes, *The Limits of Intervention* (New York: David McKay Company, Inc., 1969).
3 Oberdorfer, *Tet!*, 235.
4 *Time*, 22 December 1967, 15.
5 General William C. Westmoreland, USA (Ret.), *A Soldier Reports* (New York: Da Capo Press, Inc., 1980), 236–238.

6 Peter Bush, 'The Battle of Khe Sanh', 1968 in *The Tet Offensive*, eds. Marc Jason Gilbert and William Head (Westport, CT: Praeger Publishers, 1996), 195.
7 Westmoreland, *A Soldier Reports*, 316.
8 *Time*, 19 January 1968, 12.
9 *Time*, 19 January 1968, 20.
10 Lt. General Phillip B. Davidson, USA (Ret.), *Vietnam at War: The History 1946–1975* (New York: Oxford University Press, 1988), 474.
11 Lt. General Phillip B. Davidson, USA (Ret.), MACV/J2 from June 1967 to May 1969. Oral History Interview by Ted Gittinger on 30 March 1982. Maintained in the Lyndon Baines Johnson Library, Austin, TX.
12 Oberdorfer, *Tet!*, 124.
13 Oberdorfer, *Tet!*, 116.
14 Davidson, Oral History Interview by Ted Gittinger on 30 March 1982.
15 Davidson, *Vietnam at War*, 475.
16 Davidson, *Vietnam at War*, 475.
17 Lt. General Phillip B. Davidson, USA (Ret.), *Secrets of the Vietnam War* (Novato, CA: Presidio Press, 1990), 186.

2 After Tet – the reality

1 General William C. Westmoreland, USA (Ret.), *A Soldier Reports* (New York: Da Capo Press, Inc., 1980), 325.
2 All statistics in this section come from John E. Mueller, *War, Presidents and Public Opinion* (New York: John Wiley & Sons, Inc., 1973), 54–55.
3 Robert S. McNamara, *In Retrospect: The Tragedy and Lessons of Vietnam* (New York: Times Books, 1995), 313
4 McNamara, *In Retrospect*, 313.
5 McNamara, *In Retrospect*, 314–315.
6 McNamara, *In Retrospect*, 308.
7 Westmoreland, *A Soldier Reports*, 325.
8 Westmoreland, *A Soldier Reports*, 362.

3 Before Tet – the delusion

1 Sun Tzu, *The Art of War*, trans. Samuel B. Griffith (London: Oxford University Press, 1963), 100.
2 Admiral U.S.G. Sharp and General William C. Westmoreland, *Report on the War in Vietnam (As of 30 June 1968)* (Washington: GPO, 1968), 156.
3 General William C. Westmoreland, USA (Ret.), *A Soldier Reports* (New York: Da Capo Press, Inc., 1980), 153.
4 www.twainquotes.com web site compiled by Barbara Schmidt, <http://www.twainquotes.com/Statistics.html> accessed on 13 July 2004.
5 Don Oberdorfer, *Tet! The Turning Point in the Vietnam War*, Paperback edn. (New York: Da Capo Press, Inc., 1984), 196.
6 Lieutenant General Bernard William Rogers, USA, *Vietnam Studies: Cedar Falls–Junction City: A Turning Point* (Washington: GPO, 1974), 158.
7 General Bruce Palmer, Jr., USA (Ret.), *The 25-Year War: America's Military Role in Vietnam* (Lexington, KY: The University Press of Kentucky, 1984), 179.
8 Patrick J. McGarvey, *Visions of Victory: Selected Communist Military Writings, 1964–1968* (Stanford, CA: Hoover Institution on War, Revolution and Peace, 1969), 213.
9 McGarvey, *Visions of Victory*, 20.

10 Westmoreland, *A Soldier Reports*, 161.
11 Westmoreland, *A Soldier Reports*, 161.
12 Westmoreland, *A Soldier Reports*, 105.
13 Westmoreland, *A Soldier Reports*, 153.
14 Westmoreland, *A Soldier Reports*, 153.
15 *The Pentagon Papers*, Gravel Edition, Volume 4 (Boston: Beacon Press, 1971), 425.
16 *The Pentagon Papers*, 442.
17 *MACV Order of Battle Summary for May 1967* (Saigon: HQ MACV, 1967), I–12 through I–15.
18 Sun Tzu, *The Art of War*, 63, 64.
19 Sun Tzu, *The Art of War*, 122.
20 Carl von Clausewitz, *On War*, edited and trans. by Michael Howard and Peter Paret (Princeton, NJ: Princeton University Press, 1976), 75.
21 Clausewitz, *On War*, 77.
22 Clausewitz, *On War*, 87–88.
23 *The Pentagon Papers*, 442.
24 Westmoreland, *A Soldier Reports*, 102, 105, 121, 369, 409.
25 With all due respect to Russell F. Weigley, *The American Way of War: A History of United States Military Strategy and Policy* (Bloomington, Indiana: Indiana University Press, 1973).
26 Major General Joseph A. McChristian, USA (Ret.) interview with author on 17–18 January 1992.
27 McChristian, interview with author.
28 Lieutenant General Phillip B. Davidson, USA (Ret.), *Secrets of the Vietnam War* (Novato, CA: Presidio, 1990), 10.
29 *The Pentagon Papers*, 518.
30 Davidson, *Secrets of the Vietnam War*, 37. I prefer to use figures from General Davidson as he was the most skeptical regarding the self-defense forces. Here he states that the 'militia forces,' which he defines as including guerrillas and self-defense forces, were undercounted by 62,000. As the bulk of the increase was with the self-defense forces, I generously use the figure of 50,000.
31 McChristian, interview with author.
32 Davidson, *Secrets of the Vietnam War*, 104.
33 Harold P. Ford, *CIA and the Vietnam Policymakers: Three Episodes 1962– 1968* online edition in Episode 3 section at footnote 9. (Springfield, VA: National Technical Information Service, 1998), URL: <http://www.odci.gov/csi/books/vietnam/index.html> accessed 13 July 2004.
34 Richard Helms with William Hood, *A Look Over My Shoulder: A Life in the Central Intelligence Agency* (New York: Random House, 2003), 309.
35 Helms, *A Look Over My Shoulder*, 325.
36 *Report of the Conference to Standardize Methods for Developing and Presenting Statistics on Order of Battle Infiltration Trends and Estimates*, (Camp Smith, HI: HQ CINCPAC, 1967), 1.
37 Sam Adams, *War of Numbers: An Intelligence Memoir* (South Royalton, VT: Steerforth Press, 1994), 89.
38 *Report of the Conference to Standardize*, cover letter dated 21 February 1967.
39 *Report of the Conference to Standardize*, 29.
40 Adams, *War of Numbers*, 89–90.
41 *Report of the Conference to Standardize*, B-2.
42 General William Westmoreland (MACV/Commander) message to Chairman, Joint Chiefs of Staff, 20 August 1967. Maintained at Texas Tech University, Vietnam Archives, Lubbock TX in Pike Collection, Unit 8, Box 20, Folder 3.

43 Helms, *A Look Over My Shoulder*, 328.
44 Helms, *A Look Over My Shoulder*, 325–326.
45 Helms, *A Look Over My Shoulder*, 326.
46 Special National Intelligence Estimate (SNIE) 14.3–67, *Capabilities of the Vietnamese Communists for Fighting in South Vietnam* (Washington: CIA, 1967), 2–3.
47 Walter Isaacson and Evan Thomas, *The Wise Men: Six Friends and the World They Made* (New York: Simon and Schuster, Inc., 1986), 676–677.
48 Isaacson and Thomas, *The Wise Men*, 678.
49 Isaacson and Thomas, *The Wise Men*, 679.
50 Isaacson and Thomas, *The Wise Men*, 680.
51 Isaacson and Thomas, *The Wise Men*, 680.
52 Westmoreland, *A Soldier Reports*, 230–231.
53 Westmoreland, *A Soldier Reports*, 228.
54 Oberdorfer, *Tet!*, 103.
55 SNIE 14.3-67, 3.
56 Herbert Y. Schandler, *The Unmaking of a President: Lyndon Johnson and Vietnam* (Princeton, NJ: Princeton University Press, 1977), 62.
57 *Time*, 27 November 1967, 22.
58 Oberdorfer, *Tet!*, 105–106.
59 Oberdorfer, *Tet!*, 105.
60 W. W. Rostow, *The Diffusion of Power: An Essay in Recent History* (New York: The Macmillan Company, 1972), 480.
61 All statistics in this section come from John E. Mueller, *War, Presidents and Public Opinion* (New York: John Wiley & Sons, Inc., 1973), 54–55.
62 SNIE 14.3–67, 3.
63 Rostow, *Diffusion of Power*, 480.
64 Rostow, *Diffusion of Power*, 480.

4 The effect of Tet – a loss of trust

1 General William C. Westmoreland, USA (Ret.), *A Soldier Reports* (New York: Da Capo Press, Inc., 1980), 321.
2 Walter Isaacson and Evan Thomas, *The Wise Men: Six Friends and the World They Made* (New York: Simon and Schuster, Inc., 1986), 685.
3 Theodore H. White, *The Making of the President 1968* (New York: Atheneum Publishers, 1969), 5.
4 Don Oberdorfer, *Tet! The Turning Point in the Vietnam War*, Paperback edn. (New York: Da Capo Press, Inc., 1984), 251.
5 W. W. Rostow, *The Diffusion of Power: An Essay in Recent History* (New York: The Macmillan Company, 1972), 482–483.
6 Rostow, *The Diffusion of Power*, 482–483.
7 Rostow, *The Diffusion of Power*, 482.
8 Isaacson and Thomas, *The Wise Men*, 687.
9 Isaacson and Thomas, *The Wise Men*, 687.
10 Isaacson and Thomas, *The Wise Men*, 682–683.
11 Isaacson and Thomas, *The Wise Men*, 690.
12 Isaacson and Thomas, *The Wise Men*, 694.
13 Isaacson and Thomas, *The Wise Men*, 695.
14 Isaacson and Thomas, *The Wise Men*, 696.
15 Isaacson and Thomas, *The Wise Men*, 698.
16 Isaacson and Thomas, *The Wise Men*, 699.

17 Herbert Y. Schandler, *The Unmaking of a President: Lyndon Johnson and Vietnam* (Princeton, NJ: Princeton University Press, 1977), 262–263.
18 Isaacson and Thomas, *The Wise Men*, 702.
19 Isaacson and Thomas, *The Wise Men*, 702.
20 Lyndon Baines Johnson, *The Vantage Point: Perspectives of the Presidency 1963–1969* (New York: Holt, Rinehart and Winston, 1971), 417–418.
21 Schandler, *The Unmaking of a President*, 263.
22 Isaacson and Thomas, *The Wise Men*, 703.
23 Johnson, *The Vantage Point*, 422.
24 Johnson, *The Vantage Point*, 384.
25 Isaacson and Thomas, *The Wise Men*, 705.
26 *The Pentagon Papers*, Gravel Edition, Volume 4 (Boston: Beacon Press, 1971), 596–602.
27 Johnson, *The Vantage Point*, 436–437.
28 Oberdorfer, *Tet!*, 34.
29 Reference to Ernest B. Ferguson, *Westmoreland: The Inevitable General* (Boston: Little and Brown, 1968).
30 Westmoreland, *A Soldier Reports*, 358.
31 George C. Herring, *America's Longest War: The United States and Vietnam 1950–1975* (New York: Alfred A. Knopf, 1979), 191.
32 Schandler, *The Unmaking of a President*, 235.
33 Schandler, *The Unmaking of a President*, 83.
34 Phillip B. Davidson, *Secrets of the Vietnam War* (Novato, CA: Presidio, 1990), 103–104.
35 Davidson, *Secrets of the Vietnam War*, 107.
36 Westmoreland, *A Soldier Reports*, 318.
37 Johnson, *The Vantage Point*, 384.
38 Davidson, *Secrets of the Vietnam War*, 111.
39 James J. Wirtz, *The Tet Offensive: Intelligence Failure in War* (Ithaca, NY: Cornell University Press, 1991), 23.
40 Davidson, Oral History Interview by Ted Gittinger on 30 March 1982.
41 Westmoreland, *A Soldier Reports*, 330.
42 Westmoreland, *A Soldier Reports*, 321.
43 Schandler, *The Unmaking of a President*, 75.
44 Westmoreland, *A Soldier Reports*, 321.
45 Davidson, *Secrets of the Vietnam War*, 104.
46 Davidson, *Secrets of the Vietnam War*, 175.

5 The Tet effect – intelligence and the public perception of war

1 General Creighton Abrams (MACV/Deputy Commander) message to Chairman, Joint Chiefs of Staff, 20 August 1967. Maintained at Texas Tech University, Vietnam Archives, Lubbock, TX in *Westmoreland vs. CBS* Collection, Box 11, Folder 42.
2 Brig. General Davidson (MACV/J2) message to Brig. General Godding (MACV/Deputy J2 attending conference in Washington, DC), 19 August 1967. Maintained at Texas Tech University, Vietnam Archives, Lubbock, TX in Pike Collection, Unit 8, Box 20, Folder 3.
3 General Creighton Abrams (MACV/Deputy Commander) message to Chairman, Joint Chiefs of Staff, 20 August 1967. Maintained at Texas Tech University, Vietnam Archives, Lubbock, TX in *Westmoreland vs. CBS* Collection, Box 11, Folder 42.

4 General William Westmoreland (MACV/Commander on vacation in Philippines) message to Chairman, Joint Chiefs of Staff, 20 August 1967. Maintained at Texas Tech University, Vietnam Archives, Lubbock, TX in Pike Collection, Unit 8, Box 20, Folder 3.

5 Special National Intelligence Estimate (SNIE) 14.3–67, *Capabilities of the Vietnamese Communists for Fighting in South Vietnam* (Washington: CIA, 1967), 2.

6 Setting the stage – the enemy's war

1 Sun Tzu, *The Art of War*, trans. Samuel B. Griffith (London: Oxford University Press, 1963), 122.

2 Mao Tse-Tung, *On Guerrilla Warfare*, trans. Samuel B. Griffith (New York: Praeger Publishers, 1961), 89.

3 Mao Tse-Tung, *Quotations from Chairman Mao Tse-Tung* (Peking: Foreign Language Press, 1967), 88.

4 Mao, *Quotations*, 61.

5 Mao, *On Guerrilla Warfare*, 96.

6 Mao, *On Guerrilla Warfare*, 97.

7 Mao, *On Guerrilla Warfare*, 96.

8 General William C. Westmoreland, USA (Ret.), *A Soldier Reports* (New York: Da Capo Press, Inc., 1980), 54.

9 Lieutenant General Phillip B. Davidson, USA (Ret.), *Vietnam at War: The History 1946–1975* (New York: Oxford University Press, 1988), 8.

10 Douglas Pike, *PAVN: People's Army of Vietnam* (New York: De Capo Press, Inc., 1986), 39.

11 Pike, *PAVN*, 39.

12 Douglas Pike, *Viet Cong: The Organization and Technique of the National Liberation Front of South Vietnam* (Cambridge, MA: The M.I.T. Press, 1966), 85.

13 Pike, *PAVN*, 216.

14 Pike, *PAVN*, 216.

15 Pike, *PAVN*, 217.

16 Westmoreland, *A Soldier Reports*, 126.

17 Westmoreland, *A Soldier Reports*, 153.

18 Admiral U.S.G. Sharp and General William C. Westmoreland, *Report on the War in Vietnam (As of 30 June 1968)* (Washington: GPO, 1968), 110.

19 Hung P. Nguyen, 'Communist Offensive Strategy and the Defense of South Vietnam' in *Assessing the Vietnam War: A Collection from the Journal of the US Army War College (A Review of Recent Vietnam War Histories)* eds Lloyd J. Matthews and Dale E. Brown (Washington: Pergamon-Brassey's International Defense Publishers, 1987), 104.

20 Lieutenant General Phillip B. Davidson, USA (Ret.), *Secrets of the Vietnam War* (Novato, CA: Presidio, 1990), 20.

21 Davidson, *Secrets of the Vietnam War*, 21.

22 Vo Nguyen Giap and Van Tien Dung, *How We Won the War* (Philadelphia, PA: RECON Publications, 1976), 34.

23 *The Conference to Standardize Methods for Developing and Presenting Statistics on Order of Battle Infiltration Trends and Estimates* (Camp Smith, HI: HQ CINCPAC, 1967), B-1.

24 J.M. Carrier, *A Profile of Viet Cong Returnees: July 1965 to June 1967* RM-5577-ISA/ARPA, (Santa Monica, CA: The Rand Corp., 1968), 6.

25 *Area Handbook for Vietnam*, George L. Harris, *et al.* (Washington: GPO, 1962), 3.

26 Pike, *Viet Cong*, 234.
27 Pike, *Viet Cong*, 236.
28 Sam Adams, *War of Numbers: An Intelligence Memoir* (South Royalton, VT: Steerforth Press, 1994), 79.
29 Pike, *Viet Cong*, 234.
30 Carrier, *A Profile of Viet Cong Returnees*, 6.
31 Carrier, *A Profile of Viet Cong Returnees*, 7.
32 US Military Assistance Command, Vietnam, *Handbook for US forces in Vietnam* (Saigon: HQ MACV, 1968), 26–73.
33 Davidson, *Secrets of the Vietnam War*, 33.
34 Davidson, *Secrets of the Vietnam War*, 33.
35 Carrier, *A Profile of the Viet Cong Returnees*, 6.
36 Davidson, *Secrets of the Vietnam War*, 64.
37 Bob Brewin and Sydney Shaw, *Vietnam on Trial: Westmoreland vs. CBS* (New York: Antheneum, 1987), 302.
38 Mao Tse-Tung, *On Guerrilla Warfare*, trans. Samuel B. Griffith (New York: Praeger Publishers, 1961), 80–81.
39 Pike, *Viet Cong*, 234.
40 Pike, *Viet Cong*, 237.
41 Pike, *Viet Cong*, 237.
42 Pike, *Viet Cong*, 237.
43 M. Anderson, M. Arnsten and H. Avech, *Insurgent Organization and Operations: A Case Study of the Viet Cong in the Delta, 1964–1967* RM-5239-1-ISA/ARPA (Santa Monica, CA: The Rand Corp., 1967), 8.
44 Anderson, Arnsten and Avech, *Insurgent Organization and Operations*, 137–139.
45 Davidson, *Secrets of the Vietnam War*, 32.
46 Pike, *Viet Cong*, 237.
47 Anderson, Arnsten and Avech, *A Case Study*, 11.
48 Anderson, Arnsten and Avech, *A Case Study*, 139 and 143.
49 Anderson, Arnsten and Avech, *A Case Study*, 139, 140 and 144.
50 Sharp and Westmoreland, *Report on the War*, 88.
51 Sharp and Westmoreland, *Report on the War*, 95.
52 Westmoreland, *A Soldier Reports*, 154.
53 Pike, *Viet Cong*, 147.
54 Michael Lee Lanning and Dan Cragg, *Inside the VC and the NVA: the Real Story of North Vietnam's Armed Forces* (New York: Ivy Books, 1992), 96.
55 Sharp and Westmoreland, *Report on the War*, 183.
56 Sharp and Westmoreland, *Report on the War*, 194.
57 Sharp and Westmoreland, *Report on the War*, 195
58 Anderson, Arnsten and Avech, *A Case Study*, 151–152.
59 Anderson, Arnsten and Avech, *A Case Study*, 151–152.
60 Pike, *PAVN*, 47.
61 Pike, *Viet Cong*, 76.
62 Pike, *Viet Cong*, 109.
63 Pike, *Viet Cong*, 166.
64 Pike, *Viet Cong*, 154–155.
65 Pike, *Viet Cong*, 143.
66 Pike, *Viet Cong*, 136.
67 Pike, *Viet Cong*, 147.
68 Pike, *Viet Cong*, 147.
69 Pike, *Viet Cong*, 148.
70 Pike, *Viet Cong*, 148.

71 Malham M. Wakin, *The Viet Cong Infrastructure: Modus Operandi of Selected Political Cadre* (Saigon: Unknown, 1968), 5.

72 The Phoenix Program had its roots in the Combined Intelligence Staff, which was established in November 1966 by Brigadier General Joseph A. McChristian and the South Vietnamese Police Chief, Brig. General Nguyen Ngoc Loan (made infamous by the newspaper photograph of him killing a Viet Cong guerrilla, who had his hands tied behind his back, with a pistol on the streets of Saigon during the Tet Offensive), see Major General Joseph A. McChristian, *Vietnam Studies: The Role of Military Intelligence 1965–1967* (Washington: GPO, 1974), 71–78. The Combined Intelligence Staff was set up specifically to gather intelligence on the VCI in Military Region IV and pass the data to the South Vietnamese police and the US Army 199th Light Infantry Brigade which would then apprehend known VCI. This effort was taken over by Robert Komer upon McChristian's departure from Vietnam and evolved into what became known as the Phoenix program. Several books document this program, in particular see William Colby, *Lost Victory* (Chicago: Contemporary Books, 1989), 244–258, 331–334 and Dale Andrade, *Ashes to Ashes: The Phoenix Program and the Vietnam War* (Lexington, MA: Lexington Books, 1990).

7 Setting the stage – Vietnam intelligence in 1967

1 Lieutenant General Phillip B. Davidson, USA (Ret.), *Secrets of the Vietnam War* (Novato, CA: Presidio, 1990), 14.

2 General William C. Westmoreland, USA (Ret.), *A Soldier Reports* (New York: Da Capo Press, Inc., 1980), 180–182, 254, 272, 318.

3 With all due respect to Russell F. Weigley, *The American Way of War: A History of United States Military Strategy and Policy* (Bloomington, IN: Indiana University Press, 1973).

4 Major General Joseph A. McChristian, USA (Ret.) interview with author on 17–18 January 1992.

5 Davidson, *Secrets of the Vietnam War*, 67.

6 McChristian, interview with author.

7 Lieutenant General Phillip P. Davidson, USA (Ret.), MACV/J2 from June 1967 to May 1969. Oral History Interview by Ted Gittinger on 30 March 1982. Maintained in the Lyndon Baines Johnson Library, Austin, TX.

8 An intelligence drama – the protagonists

1 Sun Tzu, *The Art of War*, trans. Samuel B. Griffith (London: Oxford University Press, 1963), 145.

2 Major General Joseph A. McChristian, USA, *Vietnam Studies: The Role of Military Intelligence 1965–1967* (Washington: GPO, 1970), 19.

3 McChristian, *Vietnam Studies*, 3.

4 McChristian, *Vietnam Studies*, 15.

5 McChristian, *Vietnam Studies*, 16.

6 Major General Joseph A. McChristian, USA (Ret.) interview with author on 17–18 January 1992.

7 Lieutenant General Phillip B. Davidson, USA (Ret.), *Secrets of the Vietnam War* (Novato, CA: Presidio, 1990), 34.

8 McChristian interview with author on 17–18 January 1992.

9 McChristian, *Vietnam Studies*, 10–11.

10 McChristian interview with author on 17–18 January 1992 and shortened version in McChristian, *Vietnam Studies*, 10.

11 McChristian interview with author on 17–18 January 1992.
12 McChristian interview with author on 17–18 January 1992.
13 McChristian interview with author on 17–18 January 1992.
14 Lieutenant General Bernard William Rogers, USA, *Vietnam Studies: Cedar Falls–Junction City: A Turning Point* (Washington: GPO, 1974), 74.
15 McChristian, *Vietnam Studies*, 10.
16 McChristian, interview with author on 17–18 January 1992.
17 McChristian, interview with author on 17–18 January 1992.
18 McChristian, interview with author on 17–18 January 1992.
19 McChristian, *Vietnam Studies*, 110.
20 *MACV order of battle Summary August 1967* (Saigon: HQ MACV, 1967), I–24, I–25.
21 Davidson, *Secrets of the Vietnam War*, 43.
22 Davidson, *Secrets of the Vietnam War*, 42.
23 Davidson, *Secrets of the Vietnam War*, 12.
24 General William C. Westmoreland, USA (Ret.), *A Soldier Reports* (New York: Da Capo Press, Inc., 1980), 180–182, 254, 272, 318.
25 Westmoreland, *A Soldier Reports*, 428.
26 Westmoreland, *A Soldier Reports*, 323.
27 Westmoreland, *A Soldier Reports*, 180–182.
28 Davidson, *Secrets of the Vietnam War*, 10.
29 McChristian interview with author on 17–18 January 1992.
30 McChristian interview with author on 17–18 January 1992.
31 David M. Barrett (ed.) *Lyndon B. Johnson's Vietnam Papers: A Documentary Collection* (College Station, TX: Texas A&M University Press, 1997), 413.
32 McChristian interview with author on 17–18 January 1992.
33 McChristian, *Vietnam Studies*, 157.
34 McChristian interview with author on 17–18 January 1992.
35 McChristian interview with author on 17–18 January 1992.
36 Sam Adams, *War of Numbers: An Intelligence Memoir* (South Royalton, VT: Steerforth Press, 1994), 89.
37 Davidson, *Secrets of the Vietnam War*, 5–6.
38 Davidson, *Secrets of the Vietnam War*, 10.
39 Davidson, *Secrets of the Vietnam War*, 10.
40 Davidson, *Secrets of the Vietnam War*, 11.
41 Lieutenant General Phillip B. Davidson, USA (Ret.), MACV/J2 from June 1967 to May 1969. Oral History Interview by Ted Gittinger on 30 March 1982. Maintained in the Lyndon Baines Johnson Library, Austin, TX.
42 Davidson, *Secrets of the Vietnam War*, 13.
43 *The Pentagon Papers, Gravel Edition* (Boston: Beacon Press, 1971), 518.
44 Davidson, *Secrets of the Vietnam War*, 111.
45 Davidson, *Secrets of the Vietnam War*, 67.
46 Lieutenant General Phillip B. Davidson, USA (Ret.), *Vietnam at War: The History 1946–1975* (New York: Oxford University Press, 1988), 571.
47 Davidson, *Vietnam at War*, 595.
48 Gabriel Kolko, *Anatomy of a War: Vietnam, the United States, and the Modern Historical Experience* (New York: The New Press, 1985), 370.
49 Kolko, *Anatomy of a War*, 373.
50 Davidson, interview by Gittinger.
51 Davidson, interview by Gittinger.
52 Davidson, *Secrets of the Vietnam War*, 46.
53 Davidson, interview by Gittinger.
54 Davidson, *Secrets of the Vietnam War*, 46.

55 McChristian, *Vietnam Studies*, 10.
56 Davidson, interview by Gittinger.
57 Davidson, *Secrets of the Vietnam War*, 33.
58 Davidson, *Secrets of the Vietnam War*, 43.
59 Davidson, *Secrets of the Vietnam War*, 33.
60 Bob Brewin and Sydney Shaw, *Vietnam on Trial: Westmoreland vs. CBS* (New York: Atheneum, 1987), 254.
61 Davidson, *Secrets of the Vietnam War*, 64.
62 McChristian interview with author on 17–18 January 1992.
63 Davidson interview by Gittinger.
64 Davidson, *Vietnam at War*, 584 and Davidson, Interview by Gittinger, 30 March 1982.
65 Davidson, *Secrets of the Vietnam War*, 9.
66 *CBS Reports: The Uncounted Enemy, A Vietnam Deception* broadcast 23 January 1982, transcript of broadcast in Burton Benjamin, *The CBS Benjamin Report* (Washington: The Media Institute, 1984), 34577.
67 Adams, *War of Numbers*, 6.
68 Adams, *War of Numbers*, 24–25.
69 Adams, *War of Numbers*, 39.
70 Adams, *War of Numbers*, 55. (Adams writes 'just short of 90' and 'almost 90,' for simplicity, I used 88.)
71 Adams, *War of Numbers*, 56.
72 Adams, *War of Numbers*, 57.
73 Adams, *War of Numbers*, 63.
74 Adams, *War of Numbers*, 60.
75 Adams, *War of Numbers*, 69.
76 Adams, *War of Numbers*, 69.
77 Brewin and Shaw, *Vietnam on Trial*, 14.
78 Adams, *War of Numbers*, 115.
79 M. Patricia Roth, *The Juror and the General* (New York: William Morrow and Company, Inc., 1986), 64.
80 Davidson, *Secrets of the Vietnam War*, 56.

9 An intelligence drama – a three act tragedy

1 Sam Adams, *War of Numbers: An Intelligence Memoir* (South Royalton, VT: Steerforth Press, 1994), 89.
2 Adams, *War of Numbers*, 89.
3 *The Conference to Standardize Methods for Developing and Presenting Statistics on Order of Battle Infiltration Trends and Estimates*, (Camp Smith, HI: HQ CINCPAC, 1967), 2.
4 *The Conference to Standardize*, 10.
5 M. Anderson, M. Arnsten and H. Avech, *Insurgent Organization and Operations: A Case Study of the Viet Cong in the Delta, 1964–1967* RM-5239-1-ISA/ ARPA (Santa Monica, CA: The Rand Corp., 1967), 12.
6 *The Conference to Standardize*, 10.
7 *The Conference to Standardize*, 11.
8 *The Conference to Standardize*, 11.
9 Adams, *War of Numbers*, 89–90.
10 Adams, *War of Numbers*, 90.
11 Bob Brewin and Sydney Shaw, *Vietnam on Trial: Westmoreland vs. CBS* (New York: Atheneum, 1987), 8.
12 Adams, *War of Numbers*, 90.

13 Adams, *War of Numbers*, 90.
14 *CBS Reports: The Uncounted Enemy, A Vietnam Deception* broadcast 23 January 1982, transcript of broadcast in Burton Benjamin, *The CBS Benjamin Report* (Washington: The Media Institute, 1984), 34577.
15 General William C. Westmoreland, USA (Ret.), *A Soldier Reports* (New York: Da Capo Press, Inc., 1980), 275.
16 George Carver (CIA/SAVA attending meetings in Saigon) message to HQ CIA, 10 July 1967. Maintained at Texas Tech University, Vietnam Archives, Lubbock, TX in Pike Collection, Unit 8, Box 20, Folder 3.
17 Thomas Powers, *The Man Who Kept the Secrets: Richard Helms and the CIA* (New York: Alfred A. Knopf, 1979), 186–187.
18 Brigadier General Godding (MACV/Deputy J2 attending Conference in Washington, DC) message to Brigadier General Davidson (MACV/J2), 19 August 1967. Maintained at Texas Tech University, Vietnam Archives, Lubbock, TX in Pike Collection, Unit 8, Box 20, Folder 3.
19 Brigadier General Davidson (MACV/J2) message to Brigadier General Godding (MACV/Deputy J2 attending conference in Washington, DC), 19 August 1967. Maintained at Texas Tech University, Vietnam Archives, Lubbock, TX in Pike Collection, Unit 8, Box 20, Folder 3.
20 Robert Komer (MACV/Chief of Pacification) message to George Carver (CIA/ SAVA), 19 August 1967. Maintained at Texas Tech University, Vietnam Archives, Lubbock, TX in Pike Collection, Unit 8, Box 20, Folder 2.
21 General Creighton Abrams (MACV/Deputy Commander) message to Chairman, Joint Chiefs of Staff, 20 August 1967. Maintained at Texas Tech University, Vietnam Archives, Lubbock, TX in *Westmoreland vs. CBS* Collection, Box 11, Folder 42.
22 General William Westmoreland (MACV/Commander on vacation in Philippines) message to Chairman, Joint Chiefs of Staff, 20 August 1967. Maintained at Texas Tech University, Vietnam Archives, Lubbock, TX in Pike Collection, Unit 8, Box 20, Folder 3.
23 Ellsworth Bunker (US Ambassador to Vietnam) message to Walter W. Rostow (National Security Advisor), 29 August 1967. Maintained at Texas Tech University, Vietnam Archives, Lubbock, TX in Pike Collection, Unit 8, Box 20, Folder 3.
24 Lieutenant General Phillip B. Davidson, USA (Ret.), *Secrets of the Vietnam War* (Novato, CA: Presidio, 1990), 47.
25 Davidson, *Secrets of the Vietnam War*, 46.
26 George Carver (CIA/SAVA attending conference in Saigon) message to Richard Helms (Director of CIA), 11 September 1967. Maintained at Texas Tech University, Vietnam Archives, Lubbock, TX in Pike Collection, Unit 8, Box 20, Folder 3.
27 Carver to Helms, 11 September 1967.
28 Carver to Helms, 11 September 1967.
29 Carver to Helms, 11 September 1967.
30 George Carver (CIA/SAVA attending conference in Saigon) message to Richard Helms (Director of CIA), 12 September 1967. Maintained at Texas Tech University, Vietnam Archives, Lubbock, TX in Pike Collection, Unit 8, Box 20, Folder 4.
31 Carver to Helms, 12 September 1967.
32 Carver to Helms, 12 September 1967.
33 Carver to Helms, 12 September 1967.
34 Carver to Helms, 12 September 1967.
35 Davidson, *Secrets of the Vietnam War*, 48.
36 George Carver (CIA/SAVA attending conference in Saigon) message to Richard Helms (Director of CIA), 13 September 1967. Maintained at Texas Tech University, Vietnam Archives, Lubbock, TX in Pike Collection, Unit 8, Box 20, Folder 4.

37 General William Westmoreland (MACV/Commander) message to Chairman, Joint Chiefs of Staff, 14 September 1967. Maintained at Texas Tech University, Vietnam Archives, Lubbock, TX in *Westmoreland vs. CBS* Collection, Box 1, Folder 31.
38 Westmoreland to Chairman, JCS, 14 September 1967.
39 George Carver (CIA/SAVA attending conference in Saigon) message to Richard Helms (Director of CIA), 14 September 1967. Maintained at Texas Tech University, Vietnam Archives, Lubbock, TX in Pike Collection, Unit 8, Box 20, Folder 4.
40 Adams, *War of Numbers*, 117.
41 Adams, *War of Numbers*, 118.

10 From tragedy, four morals – intelligence principles

1 Sun Tzu, *The Art of War*, trans. Samuel B. Griffith (London: Oxford University Press, 1963), 144.
2 Lieutenant General Phillip B. Davidson, USA (Ret.), *Secrets of the Vietnam War* (Novato, CA: Presidio, 1990), 151.
3 General Creighton Abrams (MACV/Deputy Commander) message to Chairman, Joint Chiefs of Staff, 20 August 1967. Maintained at Texas Tech University, Vietnam Archives, Lubbock, TX in *Westmoreland vs. CBS* Collection, Box 11, Folder 42.
4 Press release dated 30 July 1964, *Background Material for the information of newsmen specializing in Southeast Asian affairs*. Maintained at Texas Tech University, Vietnam Archives, Lubbock, TX in Pike Collection, Unit 3, Box 43, Folder 4.
5 Davidson, *Secrets of the Vietnam War*, 109.
6 Davidson, *Secrets of the Vietnam War*, 20.
7 DIA Delegation (visiting MACV/J2, Saigon) message to Director, DIA, 1 April 1967. Maintained at Texas Tech University, Vietnam Archives, Lubbock, TX in Pike Collection, Unit 8, Box 20, Folder 3.
8 Mao Tse-Tung, *On Guerrilla Warfare*, trans. Samuel B. Griffith (New York: Praeger Publishers, 1961), 73.
9 Douglas Pike, *PAVN: People's Army of Vietnam* (New York: Da Capo, 1986), 20.
10 Viet-Nam Documents and Research Notes, Document 6, *The People's Revolutionary Party in Rural Areas* (Saigon: Joint United States Public Affairs Office, October 1967), 8–9.
11 Pike, *PAVN*, 58–59.
12 Pike, *PAVN*, 89–90.
13 Mao, *On Guerrilla Warfare*, 80–81.
14 Carrier, J.M., *A Profile of Viet Cong Returnees: July 1965 to June 1967*. RM-5577-ISA/ARPA, (Santa Monica, CA: The Rand Corp., 1968), 6.
15 Carrier, *Profile of Viet Cong Returnees*, 26.
16 Carrier, *Profile of Viet Cong Returnees*, 47.
17 Carrier, *Profile of Viet Cong Returnees*, 50.
18 Carrier, *Profile of Viet Cong Returnees*, 69.
19 Carrier, *Profile of Viet Cong Returnees*, 105.
20 Sam Adams, *War of Numbers: An Intelligence Memoir* (South Royalton, VT: Steerforth Press, 1994), 105.
21 Bob Brewin and Sydney Shaw, *Vietnam on Trial: Westmoreland vs. CBS* (New York: Atheneum, 1987), 300–301.
22 *Department of Defense US Casualties in Southeast Asia: Statistics as of April 30, 1985* (Washington: GPO, 1985), 5.

23 Michael Clodfelter, *Vietnam in Military Statistics: A History of the Indochina Wars, 1772–1991* (Jefferson, NC: McFarland & Co., Inc., 1995), 241–242.
24 Davidson, *Secrets of the Vietnam War*, 67.
25 Davidson, *Secrets of the Vietnam War*, 68.
26 Russell F. Weigley, *The American Way of War: A History of United States Military Strategy and Policy* (Bloomington, IN: Indiana University Press, 1973), 464–467.
27 Davidson, *Secrets of the Vietnam War*, 25.
28 General William C. Westmoreland, USA (Ret.), *A Soldier Reports* (New York: Da Capo Press, Inc., 1980), 165.
29 Admiral U.S.G. Sharp and General William C. Westmoreland, *Report on the War in Vietnam (As of 30 June 1968)* (Washington: GPO, 1968), 176–180, 195.
30 Sharp and Westmoreland, *Report on the War*, 199.
31 Westmoreland, *A Soldier Reports*, 336.
32 Westmoreland, *A Soldier Reports*, 313.
33 Westmoreland, *A Soldier Reports*, 315.
34 *Time*, 9 February 1968, 24.
35 Davidson, *Secrets of the Vietnam War*, 67.
36 Davidson, *Secrets of the Vietnam War*, 67.
37 Davidson, *Secrets of the Vietnam War*, 67.
38 Davidson, *Secrets of the Vietnam War*, 9.
39 Clodfelter, *Vietnam in Statistics*, 240.
40 Davidson, *Secrets of the Vietnam War*, 20.
41 Davidson, *Secrets of the Vietnam War*, 21–21.
42 Davidson, *Secrets of the Vietnam War*, 104–5.
43 Don Oberdorfer, *Tet! The Turning Point in the Vietnam War*, Paperback edn. (New York: Da Capo Press, Inc., 1984), 162 and George C. Herring, *America's Longest War: The United States and Vietnam 1950–1975* (New York: Alfred A. Knopf, 1979), 189.
44 James J. Wirtz, *The Tet Offensive: Intelligence Failure in War* (Ithaca, NY: Cornell University Press, 1991), 206.
45 Westmoreland, *A Soldier Reports*, 339.
46 Wirtz, *The Tet Offensive*, 197.
47 Davidson, *Secrets of the Vietnam War*, 109.
48 Davidson, *Secrets of the Vietnam War*, 104.
49 Brewin and Shaw, *Vietnam on Trial*, 147–150.
50 Wirtz, *The Tet Offensive*, 274.
51 Sun Tzu, *The Art of War*, 147.
52 Sun Tzu, *The Art of War*, 149.
53 W.W. Rostow, *The Diffusion of Power: An Essay in Recent History* (New York: The Macmillan Company, 1972), 462–463.
54 Westmoreland, *A Soldier Reports*, 318.
55 Lieutenant General Phillip B. Davidson, USA (Ret.), Transcript of Oral History Interview by Ted Gittinger on 30 June 1982, 10.
56 Davidson, *Secrets of the Vietnam War* , 46.
57 Davidson, *Secrets of the Vietnam War*, 46.
58 Davidson, *Secrets of the Vietnam War*, 67.
59 Brewin and Shaw, *Vietnam on Trial*, 239.
60 Brewin and Shaw, *Vietnam on Trial*, 256.
61 Davidson, *Secrets of the Vietnam War*, 33–34.
62 M. Anderson, M. Arnsten and H. Avech, *Insurgent Organization and Operations: A Case Study of the Viet Cong in the Delta, 1964–1966*. RM-5239-1-ISA/ARPA. Santa Monica, CA: The Rand Corp., 1967, 12.

63 Davidson, *Secrets of the Vietnam War*, 111.
64 General Bruce Palmer, USA (Ret.), *The 25-Year War: America's Military Role in Vietnam* (Lexington, KY: The University Press of Kentucky, 1984), 63.
65 Davidson, interview by Gittinger.
66 Westmoreland, *A Soldier Reports*, 315.
67 Wirtz, *The Tet Offensive*, 274.
68 Davidson, *Secrets of the Vietnam War*, 67.
69 John Ranelagh, *The Agency: The Rise and Decline of the CIA* (New York: Simon and Schuster, 1986), 462.
70 Wirtz, *The Tet Offensive*, 162.
71 Palmer, *The 25-Year War*, 78.
72 Herring, *America's Longest War*, 189.
73 Davidson, *Secrets of the Vietnam War*, 104.
74 Lyndon Baines Johnson, *The Vantage Point: Perspectives of the Presidency 1963–1969* (New York: Holt, Rinehart and Winston, 1971), 250.
75 Davidson, *Secrets of the Vietnam War*, 151.
76 Major General Joseph A. McChristian, USA, *Vietnam Studies: The Role of Military Intelligence 1965–1967* (Washington: GPO, 1970), 6.
77 Major General Joseph A. McChristian, USA (Ret.) interview with author on 17–18 January 1992.

11 The Tet effect in Iraq – pre-empting credibility

1 *Time*, 16 February 2004, cover.
2 www.whitehouse.gov, 'Remarks by the President in Photo Opportunity with the National Security Team,' 12 September 2001, <http://www.whitehouse.gov/news/releases/2001/09/20010912-4.html> accessed 9 August 2004.
3 www.whitehouse.gov, 'President Delivers State of the Union Address,' 29 January 2002, <http://www.whitehouse.gov/news/releases/2002/01/20020129-11.html> accessed 9 August 2004.
4 www.whitehouse.gov, 'President Bush Delivers Graduation Speech at West Point,' 1 June 2002, <http://www.whitehouse.gov/news/releases/2002/06/20020601-3.html> accessed 9 August 2004.
5 www.whitehouse.gov, 'The National Security Strategy of the United States of America, September 2002' <http://www.whitehouse.gov/nsc/nss.pdf> accessed 9 August 2004.
6 intelligence.senate.gov, United States Senate Select Committee on Intelligence (SSCI), 'Report on the U.S. Intelligence Community's Prewar Intelligence Assessments on Iraq,' 7 July 2004, 346 <http://intelligence.senate.gov/iraqreport2.pdf> accessed 9 August 2004.
7 SSCI Report on Iraq Prewar Intelligence, 127.
8 SSCI Report on Iraq Prewar Intelligence, 461.
9 SSCI Report on Iraq Prewar Intelligence, 345–348.
10 SSCI Report on Iraq Prewar Intelligence, 340.
11 SSCI Report on Iraq Prewar Intelligence, 305.
12 SSCI Report on Iraq Prewar Intelligence, 306.
13 '. . . the Under Secretary of Defense for Policy (Feith) and the Secretary of Defense (Rumsfeld) were dissatisfied with the intelligence products they were receiving from the Intelligence Community on terrorism . . . ,' 307.
14 SSCI Report on Iraq Prewar Intelligence, 308.
15 SSCI Report on Iraq Prewar Intelligence, 308.
16 SSCI Report on Iraq Prewar Intelligence, 308.
17 SSCI Report on Iraq Prewar Intelligence, 309.

18 SSCI Report on Iraq Prewar Intelligence, 307.
19 SSCI Report on Iraq Prewar Intelligence, 311.
20 SSCI Report on Iraq Prewar Intelligence, 307.
21 SSCI Report on Iraq Prewar Intelligence, 309.
22 SSCI Report on Iraq Prewar Intelligence, 310.
23 SSCI Report on Iraq Prewar Intelligence, 310–311.
24 SSCI Report on Iraq Prewar Intelligence, 311.
25 SSCI Report on Iraq Prewar Intelligence, 284.
26 SSCI Report on Iraq Prewar Intelligence, 363.
27 www.9-11commission.gov, 'The 9/11 Commission Report,' 228–229, <http://
    www.9-11commission.gov/report/911report.pdf> accessed 9 August 2004.
28 *New York Times*, 18 June 2004, A18.
29 SSCI Report on Iraq Prewar Intelligence, 308.
30 SSCI Report on Iraq Prewar Intelligence, 279.
31 SSCI Report on Iraq Prewar Intelligence, 249.
32 SSCI Report on Iraq Prewar Intelligence, 280.
33 Bob Woodward, *Plan of Attack* (New York; Simon and Schuster, 2004), 29.
34 Bob Woodward, *Plan of Attack*, 48.
35 Bob Woodward, *Plan of Attack*, 195.
36 SSCI Report on Iraq Prewar Intelligence, 505.
37 SSCI Report on Iraq Prewar Intelligence, 504.
38 Woodward, *Plan of Attack*, 26.
39 Woodward, *Plan of Attack*, 463.
40 www.washingtonpost.gov, 'Who's Who in the White House,' updated 28 July
    2004 <http://www.washingtonpost.com/wp-srv/politics/administration/whbrief-
    ing/whoswho.html> accessed 9 August 2004.
41 Woodward, *Plan of Attack*, 289.
42 Woodward, *Plan of Attack*, 249.
43 Woodward, *Plan of Attack*, 250.
44 SSCI Report on Iraq Prewar Intelligence, 311.
45 Woodward, *Plan of Attack*, 289.
46 SSCI Report on Iraq Prewar Intelligence, 294.
47 SSCI Report on Iraq Prewar Intelligence, 294.
48 Woodward, *Plan of Attack*, 249.
49 SSCI Report on Iraq Prewar Intelligence, 290.
50 Woodward, *Plan of Attack*, 291.
51 Woodward, *Plan of Attack*, 157.
52 Woodward, *Plan of Attack*, 292.
53 Woodward, *Plan of Attack*, 292.
54 Woodward, *Plan of Attack*, 297.
55 www.whitehouse.gov, 'President Delivers State of the Union Address,' 28 January
    2003   <http://www.whitehouse.gov/news/releases/2003/01/20030128-19.html>
    accessed 9 August 2004.
56 www.state.gov, 'Remarks to the United Nations Security Council,' 5 February
    2003 <http://www.state.govsecretary/rm/2003/17300.htm> accessed 9 August
    2004.
57 There is still debate about Zarqawi and his links to al-Qaeda, many say he is a
    challenger to bin Laden. Regardless of that fact, he was not sponsored by Saddam
    Hussein, instead operating in the Kurdish controlled areas of Iraq. See Jason
    Burke, 'Think Again: Al Qaeda,' *Foreign Policy*, May/June 2004.
58 www.state.gov, 'Remarks to the United Nations Security Council,' 5 February
    2003 <http://www.state.govsecretary/rm/2003/17300.htm> accessed 9 August
    2004.

59 Woodward, *Plan of Attack*, 133.
60 Woodward, *Plan of Attack*, 412.
61 www.cia.gov, 'Statement by David Kay on the Interim Progress Report on the Activities of the Iraq Survey Group (ISG),' 2 October 2003 <http://www.cia.gov/cia/public_affairs/speeches/2003/david_kay_10022003.html> accessed 9 August 2004.
62 CNN.com, 'Transcript: David Kay at Senate hearing,' <http://cnn.com/2004/US/01/28/kay.transcript> accessed 9 August 2004.
63 SSCI Report on Iraq Prewar Intelligence, 14.
64 SSCI Report on Iraq Prewar Intelligence, 24.
65 Woodward, *Plan of Attack*, 107.
66 SSCI Report on Iraq Prewar Intelligence, 18.
67 SSCI Report on Iraq Prewar Intelligence, 449, 457–459, 500–501.
68 Woodward, *Plan of Attack*, 175, 292.
69 Woodward, *Plan of Attack*, 292.
70 SSCI Report on Iraq Prewar Intelligence, 502.
71 Woodward, *Plan of Attack*, 133.
72 Woodward, *Plan of Attack*, 179, 202.
73 SSCI Report on Iraq Prewar Intelligence, 14, 18.
74 Woodward, *Plan of Attack*, 19.
75 *Time*, 16 February 2004, 30.
76 *The Economist*, 17 July 2004, 11.

12 Intelligence principles in the twenty-first century – still valid after all these years

1 Sherman Kent, *Strategic Intelligence for American World Policy* (Princeton, NJ; Princeton University Press, 1949), 180.
2 Kent, *Strategic Intelligence*, 180.
3 Jack Davis, 'The Challenge of Managing Uncertainty: Paul Wolfowitz on Intelligence Policy Relations,' *Studies in Intelligence*, Volume 39, Number 5, 1996 <http://www.cia.gov/csi/studies/96unclass/davis.htm> accessed August 2004.
4 www.9–11commission.gov, 'The 9/11 Commission Report,' 228–229, <http://www.9–11commission.gov/report/911report.pdf> accessed 9 August 2004.
5 Bob Woodward, *Plan of Attack* (New York; Simon and Schuster, 2004), 179.
6 intelligence.senate.gov, United States Senate Select Committee on Intelligence (SSCI), 'Report on the U.S. Intelligence Community's Prewar Intelligence Assessments on Iraq,' 7 July 2004, 14 <http://intelligence.senate.gov/iraqreport2.pdf> accessed 9 August 2004.
7 Woodward, *Plan of Attack*, 140.
8 Woodward, *Plan of Attack*, 241.
9 Woodward, *Plan of Attack*, 249.
10 Woodward, *Plan of Attack*, 175.
11 Woodward, *Plan of Attack*, 309–311.
12 SSCI Report on Iraq Prewar Intelligence, 249.
13 Woodward, *Plan of Attack*, 241.
14 www.dtic.mil, Joint Publication 1–02, 'Department of Defense Dictionary of Military and Associated Terms,' 12 April 2001 (as amended through 9 June 2004), 219, 305 <http://www.dtic.mil/doctrine/jel/new_pubs/jp1_02.pdf> accessed 13 August 2004.
15 Robert D. Kaplan, *The Coming Anarchy* (New York; Vintage Books, 2000), 157.
16 Kaplan, *The Coming Anarchy*, 160.

17 www.whitehouse.gov, 'President Speaks on War Effort to Citadel Cadets,' 11 December 2001 <http://www.whitehouse.gov/news/releases/2001/12/2001211-6.html> accessed 9 August 2004.
18 SSCI Report on Iraq Prewar Intelligence, 260.
19 SSCI Report on Iraq Prewar Intelligence, 249.
20 *The Economist*, 11 January 2003, 'Special Report: Torture; Ends, means and barbarity,' 19.
21 Bruce Hoffman, 'A Nasty Business,' *The Atlantic Monthly*, January 2002, 51.
22 Hoffman, 'A Nasty Business,' 52.
23 Woodward, *Plan of Attack*, 327.
24 Woodward, *Plan of Attack*, 138.
25 Woodward, *Plan of Attack*, 81.
26 *New York Times*, 20 October 2004, A1.

Bibliography

Abrams, Creighton, General, USA, (While MACV/Deputy Commander). Message to Chairman, Joint Chiefs of Staff, 20 August 1967. Maintained at Texas Tech University, Vietnam Archives, Lubbock, TX in *Westmoreland vs. CBS* Collection, Box 11, Folder 42.

Adams, Sam. *War of Numbers: An Intelligence Memoir.* South Royalton, VT: Steerforth Press, 1994.

—— 'Vietnam Cover-Up: Playing War With Numbers.' *Harper's Magazine,* May 1975, 41–73.

Adler, Renata. *Reckless Disregard: Westmoreland v. CBS et al. and Sharon v. Time.* New York: Alfred A. Knopf, 1986.

Allen, George W. *None So Blind: A Personal Account of the Intelligence Failure in Vietnam.* Chicago: Ivan R. Dee, Publisher, 2001.

Ameringer, Charles D. *US Foreign Intelligence: The Secret Side of American History.* Lexington, MA: Lexington Books, 1990.

Anderson, M., Arnsten M., and Avech, H. *Insurgent Organization and Operations: A Case Study of the Viet Cong in the Delta, 1964–1966.* RM-5239-1-ISA/ARPA. Santa Monica, CA: The Rand Corp., 1967.

Andrade, Dale. *Ashes to Ashes: The Phoenix Program and the Vietnam War.* Lexington, MA: Lexington Books, 1990.

Andric, Ivo. *The Bridge on the Drina.* Chicago: The University of Chicago Press, 1977.

Area Handbook for Vietnam. Co-authors: George L. Harris, Robert J. Catto, Frederic H. Chaffee, Frederica Muhlenberg, Freances Chadwich Rintz and Harvey H. Smith. Foreign Areas Studies Division, The American University, Washington, DC. Reprint 1964. Washington: Government Printing Office, 1962.

Assessing the Vietnam War: A Collection from the Journal of the US Army War College (A Review of Recent Vietnam War Histories). Eds Lloyd J. Matthews and Dale E. Brown. Washington: Pergamon-Brassey's International Defense Publishers, 1987.

Atkeson, Edward B., Maj. Gen. USA. 'Counting Enemy in Vietnam: A Difficult, Frustrating Task,' *ARMY,* April 1985, 1–2.

Barrett, David M., ed. *Lyndon B. Johnson's Vietnam Papers: A Documentary Collection.* College Station, TX: Texas A&M University Press, 1997.

BDM Corporation. *A Study of Strategic Lessons Learned in Vietnam.* McLean, VA: BDM Corp., 1980.

Benjamin, Burton. *The CBS Benjamin Report*. Washington: The Media Institute, 1984.

Berman, Larry. *Planning A Tragedy: The Americanization of the War in Vietnam.* New York: W.W. Norton and Company, 1982.

Brewin, Bob and Syndney Shaw. *Vietnam on Trial: Westmoreland vs. CBS*. New York: Atheneum, 1987.

Bunker, Ellsworth (while US Ambassador to Vietnam). Message to Walter W. Rostow (National Security Advisor), 29 August 1967. Maintained at Texas Tech University, Vietnam Archives, Lubbock, TX in Pike Collection, Unit 8, Box 20, Folder 3.

Carrier, J.M. *A Profile of Viet Cong Returnees: July 1965 to June 1967*. RM-5577-ISA/ARPA. Santa Monica, CA: The Rand Corp., 1968.

Carver, George (CIA/SAVA attending meetings in Saigon). Message to HQ CIA. 10 July 1967. Maintained at Texas Tech University, Vietnam Archives, Lubbock, TX in Pike Collection, Unit 8, Box 20, Folder 3.

—— (CIA/SAVA attending conference in Saigon). Message to Richard Helms (Director of CIA), 11 September 1967. Maintained at Texas Tech University, Vietnam Archives, Lubbock, TX in Pike Collection, Unit 8, Box 20, Folder 3.

—— (CIA/SAVA attending conference in Saigon). Message to Richard Helms (Director of CIA). 12 September 1967. Maintained at Texas Tech University, Vietnam Archives, Lubbock, TX in Pike Collection, Unit 8, Box 20, Folder 4.

—— (CIA/SAVA attending conference in Saigon). Message to Richard Helms (Director of CIA). 13 September 1967. Maintained at Texas Tech University, Vietnam Archives, Lubbock, TX in Pike Collection, Unit 8, Box 20, Folder 4.

—— (CIA/SAVA attending conference in Saigon). Message to Richard Helms (Director of CIA). 14 September 1967. Maintained at Texas Tech University, Vietnam Archives, Lubbock, TX in Pike Collection, Unit 8, Box 20, Folder 4.

Clausewitz, Carl von. *On War*. Eds and trans. Michael Howard and Peter Paret. Princeton, NJ: Princeton University Press, 1976.

Clodfelter, Michael. *Vietnam in Military Statistics: A History of the Indochina Wars, 1772–1991*. Jefferson, NC: McFarland & Co., Inc., 1995.

Colby, William with James McCargar. *Lost Victory*. Chicago: Contemporary Books, Inc., 1989.

Conrad, Joseph. *Nostromo*. New York: The Modern Library, 1996.

Corson, William R. *The Armies of Ignorance: The Rise of the American Intelligence Empire*. New York: The Dial Press/James Wade Books, 1977.

Country Study: Republic of Vietnam. Walter Frank Choinski, Col, AUS (Ret.). Washington: American Institute for Research, 1965.

Creveld, Martin van. *The Transformation of War*. New York: The Free Press, 1991.

Cubbage, T.L. 'Westmoreland vs. CBS: Was Intelligence Corrupted by Policy Demands?' *Leaders and Intelligence*. Michael Handel, ed. London: Frank Cass & Co., 1988.

Davidson, Phillip B., Lt. Gen. USA (Ret.). *Vietnam At War: The History 1946–1975*. New York: Oxford University Press, 1988.

—— *Secrets of the Vietnam War*. Novato, CA: Presidio, 1990.

—— MACV/J2 from June 1967 to May 1969. Oral History Interview by Ted Gittinger, on 30 March 1982. Maintained in the Lyndon Baines Johnson Library, Austin, TX.

—— MACV/J2 from June 1967 to May 1969. Oral History Interview by Ted Gittinger, on 30 June, 1982. Maintained in the Lyndon Baines Johnson Library, Austin, TX.

—— (MACV/J2). Message to Brig. General Godding (MACV/Deputy J2 attending conference in Washington, DC). 19 August 1967. Maintained at Texas Tech University, Vietnam Archives, Lubbock, TX in Pike Collection, Unit 8, Box 20, Folder 3.

Defense Intelligence Agency (Delegation visiting MACV/J2). Message to Director, DIA. 1 April 1967. Maintained at Texas Tech University, Vietnam Archives, Lubbock, TX in Pike Collection, Unit 8, Box 20, Folder 3.

Donnell, John C. *Viet Cong Recruitment: Why and How Men Join.* RM-5486-1-ISA/ARPA. Santa Monica, CA: The Rand Corp., 1967.

Enthoven, Alain C. and K. Wayne Smith. *How Much Is Enough? Shaping the Defense Program, 1961–1969.* New York: Harper & Row, Publishers, 1971.

Fergurson, Ernest B. *Westmoreland: The Inevitable General.* Boston: Little and Brown, 1968.

Finnegan, John Patrick. *Military Intelligence: A Picture History.* Arlington, VA: History Office, US Army Intelligence and Security Command, 1984.

Ford, Harold P. *CIA and the Vietnam Policymakers: Three Episodes 1962–1968* online edition. Springfield, VA: National Technical Information Service, 1998. URL: <http://www.odci.gov/csi> accessed 21 December 1998.

Ford, Ronnie E., Capt. USA. *Tet 1968: Understanding the Surprise.* London: Frank Cass, 1995.

Gelb, Leslie H. and Richard K. Betts. *The Irony of Vietnam: The System Worked.* Washington: The Brookings Institution, 1979.

Harris, George L. *et al. Area Handbook for Vietnam.* Washington: US Government Printing Office, 1962.

Helms, Richard with William Hood. *A Look over My Shoulder: A Life in the Central Intelligence Agency.* New York: Random House, 2003.

Herring, George C. *America's Longest War: The United States and Vietnam 1950–1975.* New York: Alfred A. Knopf, 1979.

—— *LBJ and Vietnam: A Different Kind of War.* Austin, TX: University of Texas Press, 1994.

Hoang Ngoc Lung. *Indochina Monographs: Intelligence.* Washington, DC: US Army Center of Military History, 1976.

Hoffman, Bruce. 'A Nasty Business,' *The Atlantic Monthly,* January 2002, 49–52.

Hoopes, Townsend. *The Limits of Intervention.* New York: David McKay Company, Inc., 1969.

Isaacson, Walter and Evan Thomas. *The Wise Men: Six Friends and the World They Made.* New York: Simon and Schuster, Inc., 1986.

Isserman, Maurice. *Witness to War Vietnam: Personal Narratives from the Conflict in Vietnam.* New York: The Berkley Publishing Group, 1995.

Johnson, Lyndon Baines. *The Vantage Point: Perspectives of the Presidency 1963–1969.* New York: Holt, Rinehart and Winston, 1971.

Jones, Bruce E. *War Without Windows.* New York: Berkley Books, 1987.

Kaplan, Robert D. *Balkan Ghosts: A Journey through History.* New York: St. Martin's Press, 1993.

—— *The Coming Anarchy.* New York: Vintage Books, 2000.

Kent, Sherman. *Strategic Intelligence for American World Policy*. Princeton, NJ: Princeton University Press, 1949.

Knoebl, Kuno. *Victor Charlie: The Face of War in Vietnam*. New York: Frederick A. Praeger, Publishers, 1967.

Kolko, Gabriel. *Anatomy of a War: Vietnam, the United States, and the Modern Historical Experience*. New York: The New Press, 1985.

Komar, Robert W. *Bureaucracy at War: US Performance in the Vietnam Conflict*. Boulder, CO: Westview Press, 1986.

—— (While MACV/Chief of Pacification). Message to George Carver (CIA/SAVA). 19 August 1967. Maintained at Texas Tech University, Vietnam Archives, Lubbock, TX in Pike Collection, Unit 8, Box 20, Folder 2.

Lanning, Michael Lee and Dan Cragg. *Inside the VC and the NVA: The Real Story of North Vietnam's Armed Forces*. Paperback edn. New York: Ivy Books, 1992.

Laqueur, Walter. *A World of Secrets: The Uses and Limits of Intelligence*. New York: Basic Books, Inc., Publishers, 1985.

Leites, Nathan. *The Viet Cong Style of Politics*. RM-5487-1-ISA/ARPA. Santa Monica, CA: The Rand Corp., 1969.

The Lessons of Vietnam. W. Scott Thompson and Donaldson D. Frizzell eds. New York: Crane, Russak and Company, 1977.

McChristian, Joseph A., Maj. General, USA. *Vietnam Studies: The Role of Military Intelligence 1965–1967*. Washington: US Government Printing Office, 1970.

—— Interview with the author on 17 and 18 January 1992.

McDonald, Peter. *Giap: The Victor in Vietnam*. New York: W.W. Norton & Company, 1993.

McGarvey, Patrick J. *Visions of Victory: Selected Communist Military Writings, 1964–1968*. Stanford, CA: Hoover Institution on War, Revolution and Peace, 1969.

Maclear, Michael. *The Ten Thousand Day War: Vietnam 1945–1975*. New York: Avon Books, 1981.

McNamara, Robert S. *In Retrospect: The Tragedy and Lessons of Vietnam*. New York: Times Books, 1995.

Major Problems in the History of the Vietnam War. Robert J. McMahon ed. Lexington, MA: D.C. Heath and Company, 1995.

Mao Tse-Tung. *Mao Tse-Tung on Guerrilla Warfare*. Trans. Samuel B. Griffith. New York: Praeger Publishers, 1961.

—— *Quotations from Chairman Mao Tse-Tung*. Peking: Foreign Language Press, 1967.

Marrin, Albert. *America and Vietnam: The Elephant and the Tiger*. New York: Viking, 1992.

Mueller, John E. *War, Presidents and Public Opinion*. New York: John Wiley & Sons, Inc., 1973.

Nguyen, Hung P. 'Communist Offensive Strategy and Defense of South Vietnam' in *Assessing the Vietnam War: A Collection from the Journal of the US Army War College (A Review of Recent Vietnam War Histories)*. Lloyed J. Matthews and Dale E. Brown eds. Washington: Pergamon-Brassey's International Defense Publishers, 1987.

Oberdorfer, Don. *Tet! The Turning Point in the Vietnam War*. Paperback edn. New York: Da Capo Press, Inc., 1984.

Palmer, Bruce Jr., General, USA (Ret.). *The 25-Year War: America's Military Role in Vietnam*. Lexington, KY: The University Press of Kentucky, 1984.

Pearce, Michael R. *The Insurgent Environment*. RM-5533–ARPA. Santa Monica, CA: The Rand Corp., 1969.

The Pentagon Papers, Gravel Edition, Volumes 1 through 4. Boston: Beacon Press, 1971.

Pike, Douglas. *PAVN: People's Army of Vietnam*. Paperback edn. New York: Da Capo Press, Inc., 1986.

—— *Viet Cong: The Organization and Technique of the National Liberation Front of South Vietnam*. Cambridge, MA: The M.I.T. Press, 1966.

—— *Viet Cong Strategy for Terror*. Saigon: Monograph for US Mission, Vietnam, 1970.

—— *War, Peace, and the Viet Cong*. Cambridge, MA: The M.I.T. Press, 1969.

Powers, Thomas. *The Man Who Kept the Secrets: Richard Helms and the CIA*. New York: Alfred A. Knopf, 1979.

Prados, John. *The Hidden History of the Vietnam War*. Chicago: Ivan R. Dee, Publisher, 1995.

Race, Jeffrey. *War Comes to Long An*. Paperback ed. Berkley, CA: University of California Press, 1973.

Ranelagh, John. *The Agency: The Rise and Decline of the CIA*. New York: Simon and Schuster, 1986.

Rogers, Bernard William, Lt. Gen. USA. *Vietnam Studies: Cedar Falls–Junction City: A Turning Point*. Washington: US Government Printing Office, 1974.

Rostow, W.W. *The Diffusion of Power: An Essay in Recent History*. New York: The Macmillan Company, 1972.

Roth, M. Patricia. *The Juror and the General*. New York: William Morrow and Company, Inc., 1986.

Schandler, Herbert Y. *The Unmaking of a President: Lyndon Johnson and Vietnam*. Princeton, NJ: Princeton University Press, 1977.

Shaplen, Robert. *The Lost Revolution*. New York: Harper and Row, Publishers, 1965.

Sharp, U.S.G., Admiral, USN and William C. Westmoreland, General, USA. *Report on the War in Vietnam (As of 30 June 1968)*. Washington: US Government Printing Office, 1968.

Smith, Eric McAllister. *Not By the Book: A Combat Intelligence Officer in Vietnam*. New York: Ivy Books, 1993.

Special National Intelligence Estimate (SNIE) 14.3-67. *Capabilities of the Vietnamese Communists for Fighting in South Vietnam*. Washington: CIA, 1967. Maintained at Texas Tech University, Vietnam Archives, Lubbock, TX in CIA Collection, Box 12, Folder 152.

Strategic Military Surprise: Incentives and Opportunities. Klaus Knorr and Patrick Morgan eds. New Brunswick, NJ: Transaction Books, 1983.

Strong, Kenneth Sir, Maj. Gen. (UK). *Men of Intelligence: A Study of the Roles and Decisions of Chiefs of Intelligence from World War I to the Present Day*. New York: A Giniger Book with St. Martin's Press, 1971.

Summers, Harry G., Jr. Col. USA (Ret.). *On Strategy: A Critical Analysis of the Vietnam War*. Novato, CA: Presidio Press, 1982.

—— *Vietnam War Almanac*. New York: Facts On File Publications, 1985.

Sun Tzu. *The Art of War*. Trans. Samuel B. Griffith. London: Oxford University Press, 1963.

Tanham, George K. *Communist Revolutionary Warfare: From the Vietminh to the Viet Cong*. Rev. edn. New York: Frederick A. Praeger, Publishers, 1967.

The Tet Offensive. Marc Jason Gilbert and William Head eds. Westport, CT: Praeger Publishers, 1996.

Trullinger, James W. *Village at War: An Account of Conflict in Vietnam*. Stanford, CA: Stanford University Press, 1994.

US Department of Defense. *Department of Defense US Casualties in Southeast Asia: Statistics as of April 30, 1985*. Washington: Government Printing Office, 1985.

US Military Assistance Command, Vietnam. *Handbook for US Forces in Vietnam*. Saigon: HQ MACV, 1968.

—— *Comprehensive Plan for South Vietnam*. Saigon: HQ MACV, 1963.

US Military Assistance Command, Vietnam/J2. *Order of Battle Summary for May 1967*. Saigon: HQ MACV, 1967.

—— *Order of Battle Summary for June 1967*. Saigon: HQ MACV, 1967.

—— *Order of Battle Summary for July 1967*. Saigon: HQ MACV, 1967.

—— *Order of Battle Summary for August 1967*. Saigon: HQ MACV, 1967.

—— *Order of Battle Summary for October 1967*. Saigon: HQ MACV, 1967.

—— *Order of Battle Summary for November and December 1967*. Saigon: HQ MACV, 1967.

—— *Order of Battle Summary for January 1968*. Saigon: HQ MACV, 1968.

—— *Order of Battle Summary for February 1968*. Saigon: HQ MACV, 1968.

—— *Order of Battle Summary for March 1968*. Saigon: HQ MACV, 1968.

—— *Order of Battle Summary for April 1968*. Saigon: HQ MACV, 1968.

—— *Order of Battle Summary for June 1968*. Saigon: HQ MACV, 1968.

—— *Order of Battle Summary for July 1968*. Saigon: HQ MACV, 1968.

—— *Order of Battle Summary for August 1968*. Saigon: HQ MACV, 1968.

—— *Order of Battle Summary for September 1972*. Saigon: HQ MACV, 1972.

US Military Assistance Command/Deputy J2 (Brig. General Godding attending Conference in Washington, DC). Message to Brig. General Davidson (MACV/J2). 19 August 1967. Maintained at Texas Tech University, Vietnam Archives, Lubbock, TX in Pike Collection, Unit 8, Box 20, Folder 3.

US Military Assistance Command, Vietnam/Joint US Public Affairs Office. Vietnam Documents and Research Notes, Document 6, *The People's Revolutionary Party in Rural Areas*. Saigon: Joint United States Public Affairs Office, October 1967.

US Military Assistance Command, Vietnam/Press Office. Press Release, *Background Material for the information of newsmen specializing in Southeast Asian affairs*. 30 July 1964. Maintained at Texas Tech University, Vietnam Archives, Lubbock, TX in Pike Collection, Unit 3, Box 43, Folder 4.

US Military Assistance Command, Vietnam and RVNAF, Joint General Staff. *Campaign Plan AB 141: Campaign Plan for Military Operations in the Republic of Vietnam – 1966*. Saigon: HQ MACV, 1965.

—— *AB 142: Combined Campaign Plan 1967*. Saigon: HQ MACV, 1966.

—— *AB 143: Combined Campaign Plan 1968*. Saigon: HQ MACV, 1967.

US Pacific Command. *The Conference to Standardize Methods for Developing and Presenting Statistics on Order of Battle Infiltration Trends and Estimates*. Camp Smith, HI: HQ CINCPAC, 1967.

Vietnam: A History in Documents. Gareth Porter ed. New York: New American Library, 1979.

Vietnam: The Definitive Documentation of Human Decisions. Vol. 1. Gareth Porter ed. Stanfordville, NY: Earl M. Coleman Enterprises, Inc., Publishers, 1979.

Vietnam: The Definitive Documentation of Human Decisions. Vol. 2. Gareth Porter ed. Stanfordville, NY: Earl M. Coleman Enterprises, Inc., Publishers, 1979.

The Viet-Nam Reader: Articles and Documents on American Foreign Policy and the Viet-Nam Crisis. Marcus G. Raskin and Bernard B. Fall eds. Rev. paperback edn. New York: Vantage Books, 1967.

The Vietnam War: The History of America's Conflict in Southeast Asia. Bernard C. Nalty ed. New York: Smithmark Publishers, 1996.

Vo Nguyen Giap. *People's War, People's Army: The Viet Cong Insurrection Manual for Underdeveloped Countries*. London: Frederick A. Praeger, Publishers, 1971.

Vo Nguyen Giap and Van Tien Dung. *How We Won the War*. Philadelphia, PA: RECON Publications, 1976.

Volkman, Ernest and Blaine Baggett. *Secret Intelligence: The Inside Story of America's Espionage Empire*. New York: Doubleday, 1989.

Wakin, Malham M. *The Viet Cong Infrastructure: Modus Operandi of Selected Political Cadre*. Saigon: Unknown, 1968. Part of the Air Force Academy Special Collection, Air Force Academy Library, CO. Call Number DS557.H6 W14.

Weigley, Russell F. *The American Way of War: A History of United States Military Strategy and Policy*. Bloomington, IN: Indiana University Press, 1973.

West, Rebecca. *Black Lamb and Grey Falcon: A Journey through Yugoslavia*. New York: Penguin Books, 1994.

Westmoreland, William C., General, USA (Ret). *A Soldier Reports*. Paperback edn. New York: Da Capo Press, 1980.

—— (MACV/Commander). Message to Commander in Chief, Pacific Command. 14 June 1967. Maintained at Texas Tech University, Vietnam Archives, Lubbock, TX in Pike Collection, Unit 8, Box 20, Folder 3.

—— (MACV/Commander). Message to Commander in Chief, Pacific Command. 29 June 1967. Maintained at Texas Tech University, Vietnam Archives, Lubbock, TX in Pike Collection, Unit 8, Box 20, Folder 3.

—— (MACV/Commander on vacation in Philippines). Message to Chairman, Joint Chiefs of Staff. 20 August 1967. Maintained at Texas Tech University, Vietnam Archives, Lubbock, TX in Pike Collection, Unit 8, Box 20, Folder 3.

—— (MACV/Commander). Message to Chairman, Joint Chiefs of Staff. 14 September 1967. Maintained at Texas Tech University, Vietnam Archives, Lubbock, TX in *Westmoreland vs. CBS* Collection, Box 1, Folder 31.

White, Theodore H. *The Making of the President 1968*. New York: Anthenaeum Publishers, 1969.

Wirtz, James J. *The Tet Offensive: Intelligence Failure in War*. Ithaca, NY: Cornell University Press, 1991.

Woodward, Bob. *Plan of Attack*. New York: Simon and Schuster, 2004.

Index

Figures are shown in italics